AF885430

Release Your Obsession with Money

Heal from the Inside Out

Dr. Lisa M. Ortigara Crego

Release Your Obsession With MONEY: Heal from the Inside Out
Copyright © 2021 Dr. Lisa Ortigara Crego
E-Book ISBN: 978-0-9993025-9-0
Paperback ISBN: 978-0-9993025-8-3
Library of Congress Control Number: 2021946342

All rights reserved. No part of this book may be reproduced, stored in a retrieval system, or transmitted in any form or by any means without the prior written permission of the publishers, except by a reviewer who may quote brief passages in a review in a newspaper, magazine, or journal.

The author of this book does not dispense medical advice or prescribe the use of any technique as a form of treatment for physical, emotional, or medical problems without the advice of a physician, either directly or indirectly. The intent of the author is only to offer information of a general nature to help you in your quest for emotional, spiritual, and physical well-being. In the event you use any of the information in this book for yourself, which is your constitutional right, the author and the publisher assume no responsibility for your actions.

Madeira Publishing

Madeira Publishing
Hollywood, Florida
Madeirapublising.com

More Obsession-Helping
Release Your Obsession Books

Release Your Obsession with Food:
Heal from the Inside Out

Release Your Obsession with Diet Chatter:
Heal from the Inside Out

Release Your Obsession with Cheat DAZE:
Heal from the Inside Out

Release Your Obsession with AGING:
Heal from the Inside Out

Release Your Obsession:
Collection One

"Dr. Ortigara Crego is a clinical psychotherapist, helping patients overcome their obsessions. The latest in her series in books is titled, ***Release Your Obsession with MONEY: Heal from the Inside Out***. People's obsessions seriously screw up their lives, whether it's eating, drinking, clothes, body surgery, or addictions like gambling, drinking and drugs.

If you're looking for a cure, ***from the inside out***, this book must be top of your list.

My favorite thought relating to this book is that you are not your car or your house. You are not your job or your profession. You are not your debts or your six-figure bank account. You are not your clothes or your friends, or your membership at the golf club. You're not who you think you are, and you are so much more.

Metacognition is thinking about your thinking. So what are you thinking about? You can become your obsession, or you can live alongside life's issues and enjoy every single moment while managing your behaviors in exemplary fashion. The choices lie within us, and Dr. Lisa leads us to beneficial outcomes."

–Vince Stevenson, author of ***Fear Doctor and Anxiety Quick Wins*** herself, and in a highly readable fashion, shares intimate knowledge that worked miracles for her."

–author G. Miki Hayden, ***The Naked Writer***

"Direct, informative, and insightful advice from THE obsession and addiction expert. Dr. Lisa shares easy-to-understand counsel targeting those struggling with understanding their relationship with money.

Providing revealing insights from her own experience, she focuses on the pitfalls of incorrectly interacting with the almighty dollar on personal and professional levels.

Over time, Dr. Lisa has taught her readers to overcome obsessions with food, diets, and aging. Her recent subject matter makes a profound impact on all who need to understand the psychology behind their actions.

Whether you wish to invest, make your money work for you, or accept a lack of it - cash in on Dr. Lisa's guidance. I'm glad I did!"

–author Jerri Lee George, ***CATER$AVVY "Secrets of the Trade Revealed"***

"Money is not the key to true wealth in life. Rather, appreciating the most out of the world around us and people in our lives is where true riches are made. Through her lived experiences and instructive anecdotes in ***Release Your Obsession with MONEY: Heal from the Inside Out***, Dr. Lisa gives readers a roadmap for how to work towards being content with what we have. Her words work to make us twice as rich."

–podcast host David Drucker, ***Host of the Panther Personalities Podcast***

"Dr. Lisa has done it again with her latest book in the series, Release Your Obsession…this time with money.

She outlines a specific approach and methods to heal yourself from the inside out with our obsession with money. Interestingly, it comes in three ways: obsessing over the lack of money, obsessing over making more money, or obsessing over how to keep the money you have.

In addition to the references from her clinical expertise and research-based psychological methods, Dr. Lisa also includes numerous personal and practical examples from her own patient files. These include experiences from families, from business associates, even from her own life.

This book is not for someone looking for a quick self-help fix. Rather, it is a comprehensive journey through the stages required to truly release your obsession with money. This includes exercises and questions for reflection Dr. Lisa adds at the close of each chapter.

No doubt this recent volume in Dr. Lisa's series adds to her leadership on the subject of overcoming our obsession — truly showing us a bridge from where we are to where we want to be. I think she presents us with an important key to unlocking a new world of possibilities."
–author Mark Stinson, ***Unlocking Your World of Creativity***

"Dr. Lisa gives straightforward advice for those in a money quandary—nearly everyone we know. She tells readers about individuals she has worked with, bringing them to their senses regarding how to have enough to live on. As in all her books, Dr. Lisa tells the truth about how she did it for

MEDICAL DISCLAIMER

The information presented in this book is the result of twenty-five-plus years of practice experience and observational research by the author. The author of this book does not dispense medical advice or prescribe the use of any technique as a form of treatment for physical, emotional, or medical problems without the advice of a physician, either directly or indirectly. The information in this book, by necessity, is of a general nature and not a substitute for an evaluation or treatment by a competent medical and/or psychological specialist. If you believe you are in need of medical or psychological intervention, please see a medical and/or psychological practitioner as soon as possible. Furthermore, the publication is sold with the understanding that neither the author nor the publisher is engaged in rendering legal, investment, accounting, or other professional services. If legal advice, or other expert assistance is required, the services of a competent professional person should be sought. The stories in this book are true. The names and circumstances of the stories have been changed to protect the anonymity of patients. The intent of the author is only to offer information of a general nature to help you in your quest for emotional, spiritual, and physical wellbeing. In the event you use any of the information in this book for self-improvement, which is your constitutional right, the author and the publisher assume no responsibility for your actions.

DEDICATION

I dedicate this book to my father,
Benjamin Ortigara,
who reminded me how important it is
to earn, save, and pray.
I miss you since you've been gone,
November 16, 2017,
but I still hear and live your wise words.
I love you, Dad.

Table of Contents

Foreword

by Dr. Howard Rankin

Lisa Ortigara Crego is an expert on obsession. She writes about a range of obsessions based on her knowledge, extensive clinical practice, and personal experience, a fantastic combination. This, her most recent offering, a book on the personal and cultural obsession with money, may just be her most important.

Several years ago, I had a client who lived in a beautiful house in a spectacular neighborhood in my glamorous hometown of Hilton Head Island, South Carolina. However, after her husband became heavily involved in drugs, she divorced. About a year later, I ran into her, and she told me she was now living in a mobile home in the middle of nowhere.

"I have never been happier." She beamed at me with an authentic smile.

Research on happiness suggests that after over about seventy-thousand dollars a year in this country, money does not add to our measure of happiness. The biggest obstacles to meaning and purpose around the world, which is how happiness is really defined, are anxiety and depression. Unfortunately, we all hear many stories of people who acquire money, and their lives go rapidly downhill. They become addicts, perhaps criminals, and often they go broke–even after winning tens of millions of dollars. Of course, financial stress is very real, but the relief of stress results in relief, not happiness.

Life—and happiness—are about purpose and meaningfulness, not possessions. Interestingly, Harvard researchers questioned the finding mentioned above, that happiness doesn't increase with more money. They actually compared the happiness of people with two-million dollars to those with more than ten-million dollars. The richer group appeared to be happier due to one cause: They were able to donate their money to philanthropies they believed in, thus boosting their sense of purpose.

We do have a major money problem in the U.S. for two key reasons.

First, the culture worships money and possessions, and escaping that mindset is difficult.

Second, most people are very poor at numbers and don't understand the fundamentals of compounding. This makes them extremely vulnerable when dealing with money and comprehending the costs and payoffs of spending and saving. My favorite example…

I will give you three-million dollars now, or I will give you a penny today and double the amount I give you every day for the next 30 days. Which will you choose?

Take the three mil, right!

If so, you'd lose more than two million, because the other scenario generates more than five-million dollars.

Or if you save ten dollars a week and invest it at a return of five percent per year, how much will you have in ten years? About seventy-five hundred dollars.

Changing any habitual mindset and the thinking that is seared into your brain as a result is difficult, but certainly not impossible. And Dr. Ortigara Crego is the expert to help you release probably your—and many other people's—worst obsession—the one with the not-so-almighty and horribly overrated dollar.

In this book, Dr. Lisa will give you the tools you need to reassess your relationship with money, and with your most important asset—yourself.

–Dr. Howard Rankin, author of *I Think Therefore I Am Wrong* & Podcast Host: *How Not to Think*

Introduction

There is no point at which you can say,
"Well, I'm successful now.
I might as well take a nap."
~Carrie Fisher

Imagine you could have all the riches you need. That nobody, or nothing could stand in your way as you move toward self-reliance. It's possible. How? Remove your obsession with money and watch it flow in your direction.

Why are so many people obsessed with money? Is it the quest for happiness—the belief that money will fix all ills? Money, many believe, is power. With it, you can go anywhere, do anything, and be anything your heart desires.

Money affects so many aspects of our lives that it can become an obsession for some to the point at which it's always on their minds.

Some of us obsess because we're struggling for more, while others focus on seeing their bank accounts grow larger, and still others cling to what they already have.

For those suffering from money aversion, on the other hand, their obsession can cause severe depression and/or anxiety. The goal is to stop the worry, the scrutinizing of every aspect of our finances, and watch our capital and investments flourish.

This doesn't mean either spend willy-nilly or be so tight we can have no joy…but we can seek balance. In everything we do, we need balance. Take the food we eat. What we take into our bodies needs to be whole and real and balanced to lead us to a healthier life.

Or take aging, not only will healthful foods support the process, but will contribute to good health, including a sound mentality—a healthy mind in a healthy body.

Life would be much simpler if we were all born with a golden spoon to eat with. Or would it? Some would argue inherited money differs from earned money. Throughout the following pages, I will challenge the differences.

Is money the root of *all* evil, or is it a cushion to start life comfortably? And when is a certain amount of money enough? Can we *take a nap* once successful? Or are we taking a nap before we're truly successful? What a conundrum.

That we all need money to survive is obvious, but we can embrace the journey—or not. *Well, I'm successful now; I might as well take a nap,* says it all. Life is a continuous expedition to a better self, a self with intention. This gift of embarking on such a search is within each of us—the money is not what speaks to our souls—our inner beings, but the riches within.

I started life in a household considered well-to-do. My father owned a chain of music stores and played his own tunes in very swanky nightclubs and for prominent politicians, and even movie stars. In my formative years, our family was financially comfortable. But life took many twists and turns for me. I knew what being around money was like and later what the experience was of being flat broke.

As a clinician, I see many patients chasing the almighty dollar, hoping it will buy them happiness. It won't. Happiness is an internal affair—money is only icing on the cake. This book, *Release Your Obsession With MONEY*, examines the psychology of money, along with the power of embracing a frugal lifestyle.

Shortly after graduating high school in a small town, Wautoma, Wisconsin, in 1974, I worked in a vitamin plant known as Shara Labs. My job was to paste the labels on the bottles. Taking bottle after bottle in hand, I slapped on the glue and the label, then placed each bottle in a slotted cardboard box. Eventually, I filled enough boxes in the day to make a fort all around my working station.

Hour after hour alone in my makeshift fortress, I became immersed in thoughts of wondering what would become of me. I had no formal education except for high school, and I knew I didn't want to paste labels on bottles all my life.

So, in hope of opportunity beyond that current job, I made my way back to Chicago where I had lived my first twelve years of life. With no car, no money, and now no employment, I crashed with my oldest sister for a few months, sleeping on her couch. I twice tried my hand as a secretary, starting off with a host of insecurities built on top of low self-worth. I couldn't turn out a page without a mistake. This was back in the days of the old-fashioned typewriter, the one with the white ribbon to wipe out mistakes. Each time the typist hammered on the keys making a mistake and then whitewashed the error, the white was not so white—especially in my case.

They fired me. Both times.

I set off to try my luck as a hostess at a restaurant, a job I knew well after bussing tables for years at the famous Silvercryst, tucked in the small town of Wautoma. I had more money then, after working lots of jobs as a kid, than in my early twenties in Chicago when I had no car, no home, and no stable employment.

In time, I wore out my welcome at my sister's. I was then at one of the lowest points in my life. I moved in with J., a bartender in her mid-fifties known to drink her pain away. I scraped together enough money to buy a car, a very rusty olive-green vehicle with so much rust you could see the pavement of the street. I was broke. And I had a full-blown undiagnosed binge eating disorder, which consumed every spare penny I could find.

Life didn't stay that way, of course; I webbed and weaved from having no education to being the proud possessor of a doctorate in addiction. Sometimes we require the road of hard knocks to wake the spark within and break through to the many wonders waiting to spring forth, as the reader will see in the pages ahead.

Body, Mind, And Spirit

Like many psychotherapists, I had built walls around myself as protection from the emotional pain I was feeling myself and seeing in patients as well. My training was on how to treat mental illness as it related to many psychological issues, particularly eating disorders, mood disorders, and addictions. I really wanted to take this work a step further and treat the complete self of body, mind, and spirit.

My goal then has always been to treat the *whole* person—starting with me. I began this quest when I realized I was partially there but had so much to learn about enjoying financial security without chasing the dollar.

Back in those early days, after leaving my sister's couch, I continued to accrue more debt than I could easily deal with. Consequently, I read every book on money I could get my hands on. But with every degree I added to my resume, I also fell further and further into a financial hole, as I was not only paying for my education with student loans, I was living on the borrowed money.

Deep in my core, I understood I'd take care of all the debt when I secured a degree, (and then another degree, etc.). I believed this positive outcome would be so. And it was, but not because of the degree(s) but because I came to understand how to release the obsession. And such a result can be so for you as well.

This is not a money book telling readers how to become rich, but a book on how not to chase the almighty dollar to solve depression, weight issues, fear of aging, eating disorders, etc. but to learn how we may live within our means and build security.

My mother-in-law was born and raised in Puerto Rico with barely a third-grade education. I'm uncertain if she could read and write more than the bare basics. Yet, she worked hard and saved, and accumulated quite a personal stash of capital. She was the one many family members went to for money. She always had a hoard of cash salted away.

Teaching readers to save for that "rainy day" and to become secure and content with the journey is, in part, the goal of this book. Sharing the understanding it's never too late to heal from the inside out and live life with intention—*and* that we're not our money—is the other part.

We spend thousands upon thousands of dollars on makeup and the newest, updated high-tech gadgets such as smart phones, iPads, and laptops, paying with credit cards, and creating more debt. But the psychology behind our choices produces this "I've arrived" sense of ourselves because of this new thing or that new thing. And this is not so.

Why A Book On Money?

Why a book on money when my background is psychology? Because I'm a teacher at heart and sharing what I've learned and passing it on to you is my most cherished gift. The great Dr. Bernie Siegel wrote, "I know now that we teach what we need to learn." I heard this message over and over as well from others who had walked before me in the helping industry. And so, now I'm teaching about releasing the obsession with money, something I once powered my way through.

During more than twenty-five years working in psychology as a clinical therapist and many years as a professor and author, I have been privileged to make my living teaching thousands of people—men and women, young and old—how to live their best lives through self-love, self-care, and spiritual awareness so they can heal from the inside out. And this transmission of knowledge includes how to gain financial peace, a prime area of individual concern that rocks the mental status of so many with depression and anxiety.

I wrote my first three books on obsession with food, mind chatter, and cheat days respectively. I thought I'd covered what I needed to say, but, once again, my work had only just begun. Day in and day out, I watched patients chasing youth and money and who were obsessed with their phones. It was then I crafted the next chunk of my advice on obsessions with *Release Your Obsession With Aging: Heal from the Inside Out*, which led to *Release Your Obsession with Money,* this very book you are reading now, to the next book on my agenda, *Release Your Obsession with Your Phone*. Obsessions have a way of jumping from one grip to another, yet all connecting.

I discovered a vast number of patients with eating disorders, if not all, had body image challenges lurking in the background. And with body image often come weight obsessions and body-part obsessions—and eventually with age obsession, trailing close behind. And somewhere weaving through all of this was the idea that money could fix everything, which it doesn't. Sure, we all need money to make ends meet, but is money going to buy you happy? I think not.

My goal here is to lead you to a healthy relationship with yourself, the richest commodity you could ever own. And webbed in and out are the other obsessions from the first four books, touching on weight and eating disorders as I thread through fear of aging, money obsessions, and that darn phone grip.

By the time you finish this book, you'll feel confident regarding what is right and what is not right for you. I promise.

I've helped patients and readers alike with weight issues, body image, diet obsessions, food addiction, and fear of aging, and now I'd like to help you live free from an obsession with money, always with the emphasis on healing from the inside out.

I recall all those years back worrying how I would pay my avalanche of debt, only accumulating more and more debt with each student loan, car loan, credit card build-up that was continuously growing. And funny, as broke as I was, I wasn't thinking about how I'd pay off this debt. I thought borrowing was a way of life for me—*for now*. I believed I'd find my way out of debt…

Today, I'm living debt free and in recovery from food addiction and binge eating disorder. The road was a long one, but the journey was certainly worth the while. And your journey will be worth the while too.

So, your money doesn't define you. Your social status does not define you, either. Nor does your body define you. Your business doesn't define you. No—only your authentic you defines you.

Release The Obsession

Stop and envision what you would feel like being at peace and not plagued by the obsession with money—knowing that for once that money is not all it's cracked up to be.

What would you feel like to master and work through what you're afraid of as you allow yourself to move through life with dignity and honor? Perhaps you have fears of not having enough money to carry you through life, or fears of not paying your bills, or perhaps you've put money in a position of power, or worse still, as being greater than God.

Perhaps the belief is that money will provide all you need. And it might—but chances are it won't, and certainly not in the same way as you imagine. So, spending precious moments focusing on the almighty dollar is a distraction from the plentiful riches within and without. The goal is to release squandering unrecoverable time and tap into the importance of life—*your most precious asset.*

As we move through life, we're entering the unknown—all of us. We don't know what to expect on any day, and perhaps others' misfortunes create obsessions and fears concerning our own forecasts.

When we embed another's misfortunes as a possibility that they could be ours, we fester with the worry—the obsession. If we stay in the now and embrace our good fortune, take care of ourselves with healthful nutrition, moderate exercise, and daily grooming and hygiene—particularly while living within our means—we are on our way to knowing when we have enough.

Perhaps you're chasing money and wanting to become rich and famous, believing that will bring back youth and postpone the inevitable—death. And maybe it will provide some relief to you psychologically. I'm not saying don't live your best life. But what I am saying is stop the chase for money, believing it's going to bring you everything you ever wanted. It won't.

One woman I saw years back, Penny, a now very savvy businesswoman, bought into the belief system that if she drove the BMW and lived in the million-dollar house wearing eight-hundred-dollar stilettos, she'd become somebody—that she'd reach this status she had longed for.

Now you might think, *What's wrong with that?* Heck Penny was living good, drinking the best wine, wearing designer clothes, and was the envy of all the women in her high-society group. She had an executive position in a high-end corporation. And she believed with this status she'd be happy. She wasn't. She was broke, yet looked rich.

Nothing is wrong with bettering the self, even if that means working toward your best self. But when you live the lie, it only brings misery. And to keep up the front becomes near impossible.

To want to live comfortably and have pleasant things in your life is fine. What's not okay is when the quest for money becomes obsessive and the belief systems say, *then I'll be happy*.

Free From The Money Grip

What would you feel like going anywhere with anyone, harboring no worries about money—or better yet, being satisfied with exactly who you are, as you are, *in your current money status*? To no longer use money as your go-to for happiness. To recognize expensive items won't fill your heart and soul with what you're really looking for. Living like a millionaire is not all that it's cracked up to be. It is not your fast track (back) to youth or as a means of achieving whatever you want—or whatever deals you've made with yourself.

Again, I'm not saying money for the basics, such as a roof over your head, food to eat, a car to carry you to and from work, isn't essential, because it is. We must have money for the basics to care for our needs. It's the *over*indulgence and dreaming to be rich to give you the perfect life that I'm addressing. It's making money your deity that will trip you up.

The rich and famous lifestyle, the movie star life are what suck you in with promises of happiness founded in glitz and glamour.

We don't know for a fact that a free flow of money will bring happiness and all the glitter and gold taunting us are what we need. The idea, though, is pulling people like you, and me, in—making a promise—perhaps that we can enjoy life like the handsome rich men and lovely rich women we've seen on television, in movies and magazines and on billboards.

It never occurs to us these seemingly carefree people might be in debt.

Money wants that are programmed in most of us might give the life we dream of—and for sure it does for some. To live in poverty is terrifying, and so many people do. But so many of those same individuals, who possess little, have so much more. They have spiritual enlightenment, love of self and family, rich community associations and connections to an earthly existence that rewards.

Rather than encouraging the belief that money will bring you fulfillment, this book will give you a sense of how to live in the *now*, how to use your time here on planet earth wisely. You don't have to live broke, but you also don't have to obsess over every product promise that pops up. Start with the basics and let that lead you…

The Promise

No book, psychologist, psychotherapist, spiritualist, or life coach can guarantee that your out-of-control obsession with money will ease for the rest of your life, or that you will always feel fantastic without stress or depressed moments, just as no one can guarantee you will live fruitfully without a hitch—or that you will live a life in perfect harmony every single minute of the coming time without a hiccup—even if you live in the best of situations.

But I can promise to show you ways to maneuver through life's difficulties, no matter the transition, through stages we all will greet as we move on through our years, and lead you to practice the suggestions laid out in this book. As you power through these pages, you will master your changes without fear or obsession. You will live your best life from the inside out.

By the time you finish reading ***Release Your Obsession With MONEY: Heal from the Inside Out***, you will understand how to skillfully arrest inner or outer turmoil focused on the almighty dollar—which can morph into terrific anxiety as you try to live a certain lifestyle beyond your means. For once, you will live free from the burdens and fears of what ifs, no longer white knuckling and forcing a financial change unnaturally.

You will no longer live for obtaining money but embrace the moment at each level as it unveils. You will have collected an arsenal of strategies to engage in measurable money intentions to set forth and silence the fear of not having enough, and once and for all free yourself from the burdens you have entrapped in your unreasonable *must-be-rich* mentality.

Explorations

I have set up this book, as I do all of my books, to take you through a series of investigations, just the way I would if you came to me weekly as a private patient for psychotherapy, sharing positive and negative experiences from my own life and the lives of others who walked this path prior to, during, and after recovery. The book opens with *my story*, followed by a discussion and understanding of ***Money—The Obsession***, unpacking the *what* and *why* as they're wrapped around a *money-is-in and broke-is-out* mentality.

My goal is to show you how to release obsessive, negative, self-destructive self-and-money-image connections and build a confident you on all fronts, financial and otherwise. My goal is to remove the money-as-the-center-of-your-universe attitude and replace it with positive self-reflection as your lifeline, no matter your current wealth status, whether you're poor or uber-rich and everything in between.

Along with an attempt to reveal how I have come to grips with the incessant *gotta-get-rich* mentality, I also endeavor to help readers meet this difficult challenge through practical, structured, step-by-step, synthesized information and advice, including anecdotes to show how individuals may find relief and resolution of never-ending issues arising from destructive thinking and behavior as it relates to winding down or winding up in life concerning money.

As you make your way through the chapters, you will encounter discussions about why money-wants can grip us and how intending to fight the financial situation tooth and nail, become a primary focus rather than the journey itself. I'll discuss how obsessive thinking leads to a frantic goal of fighting the life process—unnaturally. And I'll lead you to examine how questions of obtaining things you may neither need nor enjoy, an unreal image of yourself, and a false money-happy ideology take up residence in your life, as you navigate through your days.

A book on *money* obsessions would miss the mark if the topics of certain deteriorations such as worries over not having enough, being left destitute, that it's too late, or the onslaught of new bills, or the unexpected are ignored. Further, then we have to consider lifestyle, including necessities such as food, home, safety, living frugally, with the expectation of many that rich means happy. But does it?

Maybe you wonder what the body and body image, food, mood, and weight has to do with releasing your obsession with money or wealth or aging, this inner yearning for more, or maybe how psychology fits into the mix — these areas seem to contribute to the march toward the belief system money fixes all, while debt continues to add up.

But not to worry, realignment sorts through the process, making sense of it all as you move through and away from the obsession—to heal from the inside out.

From ***Money—The Obsession*** we continue into ***Realignment,*** which is the positive development of one's being, the advancement through the upheaval—the shift and renewal of your best you as you transition away from the obsession to a productive, happy, free-spirited self.

What can you do to alter the money quest? Should you sit idle and let time pass with no contribution toward an optimal life no matter the debt? NO, absolutely not. This is about *realigning* your thinking and behavior, moving away from the fear-grip of money-wants to the grace-grip, so you can embrace life, to remove the magical thinking about money.

And yes, you want to live exactly where you exist within yourself but as your *best self* because money does not define you. The goal is to reach your pinnacle of self-realization.

Working through and realigning using a bag of tools such as authenticity, spending less and earning more, along with SMART, a well-established tool to plan and achieve goals, are excellent starting places. Mixed in with the ***realigning*** phase, a major imperative is to have a new relationship with money, understanding how to save and live more frugally so that you can live more richly in the future. I encourage readers toward a whole-being approach: body, mind, and spirit.

How, you ask? First you must start from where you are and love you, recognizing the beautiful blessings conferred on you. Give thanks for your eyes to see, ears to hear, arms to hug, and legs to stand strong on, and then, as you venture out, you will embrace all situations money related. Being stacked with wisdom beyond that possessed by finances alone lends an opportunity for you to reset, but with greater vigor.

As you become more at ease, you'll handle twists and turns during scary times such as impending bills, lack of currency, or finding your happy. You'll be armed and ready to embrace life as it unfolds.

The chapters also unpack the importance of understanding and employing each tool on the journey of recovery from obsessive, inner, negative conversations such as, "but money will fix everything" or an "I will miss out if I don't join the rich club or have dollar abundance" kind of thought (and action) process.

As the ***realignment*** unfolds, the chapters explore food addiction and aging along with nutrition, mood, energy, and wrinkles. Eating quality, non-processed foods is the perfect start to healing the body—*inside and out.* Actual food is the key to ignite optimism and lessen anxiety, enhance energy, and provide an overall sense of wellbeing, not to mention slow the obsession with money as a cure-all. These explorations work together—*you'll see.* But we can discover a way out. I promise.

From ***Realignment*** you'll ***Turn The Corner*** where change takes hold, the change that you embrace with pride wherever you are in your life's journey. In this phase, you'll recognize that minor efforts go a long way. As you turn the corner with money, you will find that it's not defining you but now appears as an added asset. You'll discover it's never too late to live frugally, and thus you don't have to worry about not having enough. You will *feel* something happening.

The age-old saying, "The more you save, the more you have" is true. Start living on less so you'll live with more. Dream big without obsessing. This process is about living with less, connecting with your spiritual self, embracing nature, opening up your "God" connection, and becoming reacquainted with your spiritual self.

Turning the corner is about looking at what you have through a new lens. It's about *imagining* your prosperity into reality. We all need something to look forward to, no matter the age or chapter in our lives. The advice is not to give up, not now, never—but to take that last breath with a smile on your lips, knowing your trip through life was good—you did well.

The most important message as you turn the corner is to recognize and rehearse one reality in your thoughts over and over: *Money does not define you.*

As you turn the corner, you'll find the chapters speckled with words of self-care, self-love, and spiritual fueling, as these are the foundation of your wellbeing and the gateway to your highest hierarchy of need.

And of course, we will examine working through the emotional component that comes with the promise of *releasing your obsession with money* as we spend wisely and save with measurable intention, live debt free, and reroute the fretting to gratitude for breath and appreciation for our lives. We will look at how every day can be a good day, from start to finish. I incorporate all pathways to releasing your obsessions with money into this book.

If you will examine your personal inventory as questions appear following each chapter and practice the golden nuggets scattered throughout the pages, by the time you reach the end of this material, you will have changed your life.

My immediate goal is to help you release your obsession with negative money ideation and connect to a better you in twenty-one days or fewer, thanks to:

✓ The book's groundbreaking identification of the *what* and the *why* of believing *money* is the culprit—that riches will *complete* you.

- ✓ Incorporating easy, step-by-step customizable day-to-day "outpatient" actions to help you navigate through the jungle of old belief systems from childhood or cultural connections that living on less is NOT a good thing.
- ✓ Personal Inventory Questions throughout, designed to identify and reprogram your money quest mentality and open your unique natural/spiritual path to recovery.

My suggestion is that you first read through the book once to orient yourself to this approach. Then you can slowly read the book again—only this time working through the questions following the end of each chapter.

As you read, you'll also note that every chapter opens with an inspirational quote from a spiritual leader, author, or the Bible. Don't skip these valuable morsels of wisdom, as they're real treasures, designed to start you thinking at a deeper level.

Release The Obsession

We become attached to ideas and never let them go, creating a reference system that turns into our way of thinking, behaving, and acting out. My beloved mother-in-law, mentioned earlier, understood the simple basics of money with no formal education, let alone hoity-toity college degrees. She knew the basics of saving money led to freedom from financial worries. She realized that by living within her means she could afford a beautiful home and a nice car without the worry of debt.

My mother-in-law understood that debt was not good. She worked hard and long hours most of her life—but without drudgery. She knew that if you didn't have the money; you didn't buy. She lived in a simple way. She understood that if you saved you could buy when you wanted or needed to. She embraced everything she did—and always gave thanks to the God of her understanding.

Or take Penny referenced above, who lived way beyond her means to look and fit in with high society. She was broke. She wasn't living her truth, which led her to a deep depression and a life in which she was overwhelmed with anxiety. She was miserable, trying to pretend she was wealthy when she was in significant debt to the point where she filed for bankruptcy.

But Penny learned and turned her life around. She now lives within her means. She no longer struggles with money being the route to happiness or fitting in with the well-to-do crowd. She now believes she can be her authentic self and live within her income.

And now, Penny really has money, but it no longer owns her. When she let go, changed her relationship with money, lived within her earnings, she became wealthy. What an amazing transformation! She no longer had to "look" rich, because she *was* rich.

Penny once believed she wouldn't have the *right look* if she didn't buy the fancy clothes and shoes—making *looking* rich the center of her being rather than *feeling* secure within her income. She missed the here and now as she lived in her head, obsessing over whether she looked rich enough.

Penny missed seeing her inner beauty and her outer beauty as she was. Such a pattern could only cloud any opportunity to bathe in the love of self and connections with others.

That said, Penny also suffered from binge-eating disorder with a long, long history of dieting and bingeing, followed by more dieting and more bingeing. On any day, she might carry an additional twenty pounds due to binge fests—not to mention that binges are costly.

In time, Penny learned to break the negative pattern and move in a positive direction. She experienced her finances and body image with love and openness, while eating the healthy versions of food, discarding all self-degradation, replacing that with self-acceptance.

Please note that eating disorders, mental illnesses, mood disorders, and addictions are serious and often require a village to conquer. You owe it to yourself to tap into a pool of help, such as through psychotherapy, group therapy, individual sessions with a psychiatrist, and/or time spent in places of worship in further building your spiritual connection. I recommend twelve-step meetings, books on these topics, and any other mode of help that fits your needs and preferences.

Penny chose psychotherapy, hypnotherapy, and meditation, along with all spiritual practices, to work on her addiction to looking wealthy, binge eating, and addictive obsessions with sugar, flour, and wheat. She now continues to reach for self-actualization—the fulfillment and recognition of her talents and potential.

Where To Begin…

To heal your thoughts and behaviors, begin with self-love and self-care. The essence of what frees us from obsessive self-scrutiny is love. You can learn to love your situation, face it as it is now and move away from a *keeping up with the Joneses* mentality while you move into a natural life journey—to heal your body and heal your mind—*from the inside out.*

Glitz and glitter attract us, so we run after any means of defying aging, death denial, dieting to look young, accessing products that make false promises. We can't stop chasing the fads, the get-rich schemes, hoping that THIS TIME we'll break free from out-of-control thinking while body obsessing and longing for a false rich-life existence.

And yet, the money quest is consuming our thoughts: what to buy next to look like we made it.

News flash, more than not, the rich don't look rich at all, instead they live in simplicity.

A conditioning from the past hints that money is power, an end-all, be-all quest. I learned as a small child watching my father and his siblings live in a simple way, as if they had no money. They didn't flash fancy cars, jewelry, or money to *prove* something to someone. They worked hard and saved well. Simple.

The patients and people discussed in ***Release Your Obsession With MONEY*** range from individuals in their later teens and mid-twenties into adulthood, all the way to ninety and above—transitioning to the end of life. Those I mention in this book were acquaintances, people associated with twelve-step groups, and/or those in psychotherapy. Many passed away years back.

Under twelve-step protocol and patient confidentiality, I changed names and genders, nationalities, hair, and switched looks to keep each person, including acquaintances, anonymous. Often, a person mentioned is a combination of several persons, all harboring similar issues and backgrounds.

This is a book about getting out of your own way with money questing in order to become your true spiritual self without going into a swirl of obsessions over how much you have, or how you need to look or be a certain way.

If you're seeking something easy or fast, though, you have the wrong book. If you're looking for a book to help you become rich in a nanosecond without effort, you have the wrong book. If you're looking for a financial guru to explain in depth the ins and outs of money and investments, you have the wrong book.

But if you're looking for a book to lead you out of the self-degrading hunt for the almighty dollar, no matter your age—freedom beyond your wildest expectations, *long term*—this is the book for you. If you're looking to reach self-actualization—your highest spiritual self, you've found it.

Dave Ramsey, in his *The Total Money Makeover,* says, "IF YOU LIVE LIKE NO ONE ELSE, LATER YOU CAN LIVE LIKE NO ONE ELSE." I love this quote because it applies to so many areas besides your becoming debt free. Though this book is not a total money makeover, it is a total release of your obsession with money from a psychological and real-life perspective—*in the natural way,* of course.

No gimmicks, bells or whistles here. Understanding your relationship with money will set you free in ways you can't imagine. Money is not the route to all happy.

For you, here is the roadmap to learn *your* personal plan that works for you with living your authentic life, within your means and not letting other's ideas of money define you. You will learn to reset your ideal life, without pressing "gotta get rich, can't live without" buttons..

Release Your Obsession With MONEY: Heal from the Inside Out is for anyone trying to end the obsession with money worshipping. The goal is to end the pursuit after every get-rich scheme out there and lead you to heal from the inside out as I practice with the first four books.

I learned firsthand and now I'm passing it along to you…

Part I

Money—The Obsession

Chapter 1

My Story

Keep your face always toward the sunshine,
And shadows will fall behind you.
~
~ Walt Whitman

Though I was born to an upper-middle-class family, I learned by age twelve to fend for myself. I understood early in life what it was like to have, and then not.

My first paying job outside of babysitting, shortly before turning thirteen, was picking cucumbers in a field with Mexican migrant workers coming from Texas. I don't recall how I got that job, but I remember I was on a quest to earn money to buy a horse.

Sporting striped pedal pushers of lavender, powder blue, and yellow, a flowing Sunkist yellow top and white tennis shoes, bolting out of Mom's vehicle I skipped off to my first day on the job, filling the air with eau de toilette — toilet water, a lightly scented cologne. Catching a whiff of sweet lavender and neroli (orange-flower oil) disrupted the workers' mechanical pick-and-pack mode. In what seemed like slow motion, the workers looked up, mouths agape, witnessing the gringo…albino, that is, joining the work team.

The money I earned was based on how much I picked, eliciting fast picking and earnings that seemed like a lot in my teen mind. The more I picked, the more I made. I filled the black bucket to the brim, carrying it to my burlap bag, dumping it in, then started over, filling the black bucket again. This went on hour after hour under the scorching summer sun in the small town of Wautoma, Wisconsin.

And at some point these cucumbers made their way to become pickles in the town of Red Granite, Wisconsin. It never occurred to me at that age the pickles I loved so started off as cucumbers—the very ones that were in my salads. I gained a newfound appreciation for the vegetable—and for the work needed for it to get from the ground to the salad and even to the jar.

The migrants were poor, really poor, working to survive. Arriving in the thousands, mostly migrating from Texas during the summer months, a time long before the mechanical pickers, many lived in housing provided by the farmers and slept in bunk beds, while others slept in their camper trucks.

I worked to buy a horse.

Snickering, clucking of the tongue, whispering began about the gringo while they shook their heads. Once again, I felt like a misfit as I worked alongside the others. Rejected and resented, I provided for their amusement, while they knew what was in store for me.

Fingers blistered, lips swollen from the direct sun, aching in every part of my being, I received my first lesson that you have to work hard, really hard, *and smart* to make it.

The Chicano migrant workers scoffed at me when I arrived on the scene because they had little to no money, were deficient in the basic needs I took for granted. I was to them a poor, little rich girl, *pobre chica y chica rica.* This became a title I heard more than once growing up in my teen years in a small town in Wisconsin after leaving a very comfortable life in Chicago—a life where the world was right-side up and parental couples were intact, and money wasn't even a thought.

A Dirty Little Secret

This soon changed, and my life turned, with me often having to work two to three jobs to purchase clothes and school requirements—and my horse, Pasha. I had a dirty little secret. I couldn't stop eating candy, cakes, and doughnuts. At first, the eating of sweets was actually a non-issue because I was skinny. But when the weight piled on, fear gripped me—along with diet after diet after diet.

I was hungry for security, but I didn't know it. I grew up fast, with a split family—a brother and sister staying in Chicago with our dad and the remaining four of us with our mom in a small, non-winterized cottage made for summer retreats only.

This was the first of my hard lessons in life about money, body image, and the lack of love, including self-love.

Knowing what I know now, I wouldn't change a thing. My learning about survival and the quest to save money began early in life side by side with the Mexican workers I grew to love and respect. I wouldn't know the reality of being poor—really poor—from their perspective had I not spent an entire summer working with the beloved Chicano immigrants.

Soon, I blended in, even though I was the *pobre chica y chica rica.* I know I'm who I am today because of the trials and tribulations of my early life. I understand money from no worries, to stark fear, to living debt free, and within my means.

Love Thy Self

Self-care and self-love are paramount in all the books I pen because without these two complementary practices living a full, healthy life isn't possible. I didn't get that until my mid-adult life but get it I did—and so will you.

Maybe you learned at a young age that if you cared for yourself, you were being selfish—a message that can confuse, often creating guilt within. But living a full and healthy life requires attention to your self-needs, by you or someone who loves you if you can't care for yourself.

Living a full and healthy life doesn't mean you'll live a rich life, but it means you'll up your chances significantly of living your best life while here. And that is the goal, to live our best life in appreciation and gratitude.

The theme behind my message is not only to live a quality life as the goal, but to think about increasing *wealth* without obsession, with your complete self intact as your more important quest.

Rather than striving for a wealthy life, how about trying to increase your number of quality years filled with abundance? What is an abundant life? It's an existence of completeness, free of dysfunction, and free of believing money is going to fulfill your every wish. It's living as a whole you, body, mind, and spirit.

Self-actualization is what we strive for to become our authentic selves. As a college professor, I taught the concept of psychologist Abraham Maslow's hierarchy of needs, which points to individuals reaching their full potential. Students always thought that meant having enough money, but actually it means reaching your authentic self at a spiritual level—a want-for-nothing stage. It means reaching one's potential and one's self-fulfillment.

Maslow's pyramid starts with basic physiological needs such as food, water, warmth, and rest. Moving up a rung of the ladder, we come to safety and security, then followed by love and belonging, where intimate relationships and friendships develop. The next rung finds us at esteem needs, such as prestige and feelings of accomplishment. Last comes self-actualization, which means achieving one's full potential, including in creative activities. This last self-fulfillment is the place you want to reach, as it's the pinnacle of life, the situation where you can exhale and say, "It was good."

According to experts, Maslow's time-tested pyramid, first proposed in his 1943 paper "A Theory of Human Motivation" and his subsequent book *Motivation and Personality* needed to be updated to reflect our current times. Within these changes, the most controversial modification is that self-actualization no longer appears on the pyramid at all. I leave it in.

Some argue Maslow overlooked mate acquisition, mate retention, and parenting. I find those can merge into love and belonging, where intimate relationships and friendships develop in whatever definition fits your life.

My Life

My own independent life began very early. I had the basic needs fulfilled, such as food, water, warmth, and rest. And in those formative years I had safety and security. But as time marched on, the meeting of those basic needs became murky.

Moving up a rung of the ladder when the family moved to our summer cottage, the food and warmth were not always plentiful, and the safety and security were not in place as suddenly I was footloose and fancy free. I didn't receive the guidance I had in my earlier years.

And with that, I was lonely, missing love and belonging, at a time when intimate relationships and friendships progress. The phase of moving up the hierarchical rung to reach esteem needs such as prestige and feelings of accomplishment was missing, and of course I was too inexperienced in life to reach self-actualization—achieving my full potential, including in creative activities.

By the age of twelve, I was fending for myself for most of my needs. I barely had the food, water, warmth, and rest marking the early rungs of the ladder because I had to reach to fulfill my needs quite early on. Mom was showing German shepherds all around the country while Dad traveled between houses, and all my siblings left home young, leaving me to care for myself. Most times, I didn't feel secure, and I didn't feel safe. I was alone; hence, my eating disorders began.

I'm not saying my parents abused me, or that I had this horrible childhood, for I did not. Rather, I had a permissive, negligent mom and an absent father, which meant I had to figure out how to handle the basics early in life. I know Mom and Dad did the best they could from where they were. I love them both with my heart and soul—may they rest in peace.

The Millionaire Next Door

As noted in a previous book, my oldest sister, Christy, gifted me with *The Millionaire Next Door: The Surprising Secrets of American Health* way back in 1996. She handed the book out like candy to several of her siblings, as she was so impressed with the lessons it taught. I clung to my book, hoping one day I could be that person living free from money worries. I wanted to learn from that example firsthand and escape from the poor situation I found myself in.

The lesson, or secret I should say, is that the millionaire often is not who you think he is. He's the person living in the less-than-best house in the neighborhood, driving a car that's simple or aged, and not wearing the fancy clothes.

By the time this book landed in my hands, I had divorced my first husband, was raising a toddler single handedly, and was in debt up to my eyeballs, as noted in the introduction. But so much happened to me in the forefront of those years, the most important thing being that I was not well. I had an undiagnosed eating disorder, which nearly crippled me for a good chunk of my earlier life. I'm grateful for that too.

Hardships strengthen us—they give us courage—or they can pummel us in life when we adopt the poor-me attitude. I lived in the poor-me mindset for a long time in fact. I lived with a dusting of depression and anxiety and a hunger for something better.

My insecurities led to bad behaviors, all in the quest of trying to fit in. All in the quest of trying to be noticed—by someone—anyone. I was lonely and scared, and for sure not living my healthy, best life. So, in my teeny little mind I believed if I could just become thin enough, I could be noticed, and then I might be validated in all my seeking of self-love, belonging, excelling in life—and of course tucked in with this belief—financial independence. And so, in my distressed condition of being afraid, aroused by continuous impending worry and fear—sometimes real and sometimes imagined, I ate.

The Weight Struggle

When I was in my early teens, my weight climbed as my body was naturally growing into that of a woman. It terrified me. I believed I was fat. My weight was 142. I saw it as my curse. I felt unloved, ugly, and mostly insecure. If I only knew back then what I know now, I could have spared myself years of pain and uncertainty. I wasn't fat, as my thoughts had convinced my young self I was, I was simply growing.

My diets began.

I didn't see the weight as a natural process of a transformation from having a child's body to being in an adult's body, but as an affliction. In my mind, I was fat. I felt fat and thought I looked fat when I was just a kid body growing into a woman body which led to binge eating to comfort me yet shame me too.

I was out of control with food. I didn't love myself, or my body. I didn't see my weight as a gift or embrace my natural growing pains, but I took the change as a message that, well, I was worthless, dumb, ugly, and of course, fat.

And so my pursuit of being thin began. My fear was of not being pretty enough, thin enough, or smart enough. My weight jumped up and down from two-hundred-and-thirty-four pounds to one-hundred-and-twenty-nine pounds, and everything in between. But one-hundred-and-forty-two pounds seemed to stick as my set point. No, I didn't see it as a right weight for me at all, but as a curse—a curse that turned into self-hate of my body—and hate of the natural progression from girl to woman.

Taking care of ourselves is the one way to show self-love, and it starts with the basics as noted in Maslow's Hierarchy of Need. If the bottom rung isn't in place, the entire pyramid collapses. Perhaps, for me, trying to obtain the basic needs manifested as obsession with body and with weight.

Life is a good thing. Life means energy. Perhaps the magic elixir is to live a fulfilling life—not just for us, but also for others. Perhaps the magic is to wake up with a goal, to rise in the morning with intention—pursuing a life filled with purpose rather than focused on dread of self and body and our negatively perceived physical appearance.

The everyday problems of life defeat many of us—and when the pain is too great, the obsessions kick in to distract. We struggle with the distraction of not young enough, not skinny enough, or this food will make me feel better—just this once and continue on to *if I were only rich, then....*

Well, guess what? If you let these thoughts in, you will always find something to obsess about—distracters to the actual issues in life. Is the reality that you want money to make life better, or is your hunt for something deeper and more spiritual?

You can always lean into obsessing about something else that prevented you from living in the moment. Now, here you are still looking back and wishing. Stop. Step into exactly where you are with love and respect for yourself, and watch the magic begin.

You can permit obstacles to control your mind to the point at which they're uppermost and thus become the dominating factors in your thought pattern. Or, you can learn how to toss them from the mind by refusing to become mentally submissive to them, and by channeling spiritual thoughts to rise above obstacles that might have been defeating you. No more.

For sure, we face real challenges. I've dealt with many, including a failed first marriage, poverty, skin cancer, obesity, an eating disorder, obsessions and addictions, chronic fatigue, arthritis, being flat broke, and much more.

Every human being has a story, and I'm no different. Parts of **My Story** here are adapted from my first four books, as my story hasn't changed—though each book represents a different side of the wants and unresolved needs and how they can morph into other manifestations of self-obsession, such as, in this book, a fixation on the dollar.

My Start

Very often, the work we choose in order to make a living stems from deep-seated personal experiences. When I was just a small child, I lived the simple life of playing with the kids in the neighborhood from dawn to dusk. Running, laughing, and playing were the ingredients of my life when I wasn't in school—which I dreaded.

I loved my freedom and felt imprisoned in school where I would sit staring out the window, dreaming of running and playing and eating delightful treats. Drinking water from the hose, hanging from a tree branch, eating warm tomatoes from the garden should be my real way of life—or so I thought. Living that way I didn't have a care in the world. It provided all that I needed until it didn't.

My life of poverty began when Mom whisked us away from Chicago to the cottage in Wisconsin. The small town was cold, biting cold in the winter. The lake I only previously knew as thawed was now frozen in the winter, when no swimming, fishing, or frog catching were to be had. The weather was cold—simply freezing.

I don't like to be cold, which is why I moved to Florida as soon as I could after my first introduction when I was twelve, assisting my Grandmother Ruth and Grandfather Hale in their significant move to a sunny paradise. Mickey, who is one of my older sisters, and I traveled with them to what became my life later on.

So living with comfort, and then not, became my journey early in life. The experience molded me into who I am today. I learned to overcome a gripping eating disorder, facing every facet that lay within that disturbance, from the eating issue itself, to embracing aging gracefully, to understanding money and how it works.

Early in life, I heard my parents arguing over money. Mom spent and Dad saved. Dad started working very young, beginning with studying the accordion. He had no time to frolic with the neighbor kids as he was practicing what became his lifelong love and career—music. Music and building his financial empire gripped him from early on.

I was *that kid* who listened and assessed and processed in my mind what to avoid and what to accept. I was a thinker. I had my own issues going on with foods I used to console myself against my fears of the unknown in life. A big, imperfect, scary world lurked out there.

In our house, my parents argued over my mom's weight, money, politics, and a host of other concerns, all of which left me to comfort myself with food. I knew also that *an end to life awaits us all.* And that what you think you know, you don't. Innocence and youth prevent us from knowing the harsh realities of life and survival. My young mind wasn't ready for such a specific.

I preferred to put my emphasis on sweet, sticky foods, as they were exhilarating, felt good, not to mention tasted good to my newly awakening taste buds. These treats blocked anything negative—like the possibility of becoming poor or absolutely destitute, or any other such information my immature mind absorbed while most likely understanding the dilemmas out of context, with little logic to sort through these questions.

I developed as a sneaking, lying, stealing, food-hiding kid afraid of the harsh world out there. This was the 60s, a time filled with violence, riots, wars, and killings. *Let the fears begin…*

My full-blown eating disorder appeared at the tail end of my twelfth year, as I was budding on thirteen. Fortunately, in my late teenage years, I found my way to Weight Watchers and lost weight and built confidence, and my mood swings became less volatile.

The original Weight Watchers program back in the mid-1970s, under the guidance of Jean Nidetch, the founder of the organization, followed a "natural" food path adopted from diets used for diabetics in a hospital setting. *I instantly felt relief.* Little did I know at the time that I was sensitive to "processed" foods, which led to binge eating and crazy inner monologues.

With my false sense of success, I went to work for Weight Watchers, thinking I had finally found my ideal solution. But once the novelty of shedding weight lost its punch, periodic binges, mood swings, terrible fatigue, low self-worth, and low-grade depression again surfaced, not to mention that the negative inner diet chatter went from a whisper to a roar.

Out-of-control eating gradually allowed my weight to creep back on.

Eventually, I became conscious of a change in my behavior and moods with certain foods, as well as constant fatigue with other or the same specific foods. Some foods were so powerful they compelled me to eat enormous amounts, leaving me high, while others simply knocked me out. In either case, I lacked control.

These foods induced anger; anxiety, low self-esteem, and negative inner diet chatter not controlled, not to mention terrifying. This discovery was a tremendous breakthrough. My predicament wasn't my fault. I wasn't weak. I had a definite reaction to certain foods.

Still working for Weight Watchers while studying for my master's degree in mental health, I noticed I wasn't the only one going up and down the rollercoaster of how I ate—so were many Weight Watchers members and even members of the staff. I knew they were trying to "diet" the weight off, and like me, were running through the revolving door of Weight Watchers to find the resolution to a weight-loss impasse.

I knew intuitively the answer wasn't in just following the plan, because as wonderful as the program was (and still is), it didn't provide an educated, licensed psychotherapist. A psychotherapist could have walked the members through the *why* they were eating, as well as *what* they were eating, though most therapists wouldn't actually understand the situation if the member had a food sensitivity.

I knew I had to do something about this terrible problem for both me and for others, so with great trepidation, I left the fold that had initially showed me the way. I was frightened! I felt as if I were leaving the mother's womb as I stumbled off alone into the dark. I took with me little guidance, except knowing that certain foods were causing me to react with extreme highs and lows, and that my spirituality, which I grew up to respect, was stagnant because I couldn't see past the next, inevitable, binge.

My weight and my relationship with food were a constant struggle for me until I understood my chemical reaction to certain foods. After years of trial and error, research, clinical knowledge, weight loss, and stability of weight, I became calm.

These days, as I've moved into my later years of life, I continue to follow a simple formula, breaking down each meal in terms of structure and commitment rather than eating randomly. I also include daily exercise such as walking or biking along the ocean and try to live my best and fullest life as a prayer.

And this book, ***Release Your Obsession With MONEY: Heal from the Inside Out,*** which you hold in your hands (or on your digital reader), brings forth a combination of ways for you to live your best and fullest life without jumping from this quick get-rich kick to the next. It's a down-home book of spiritual awakening to lead you to your best self.

Once again I could walk others through the *why*, but this time why they were obsessing over money, as well as *what* behaviors were contributing to compulsive spending.

Now, of course, we want to look and feel our best, and if you spend money for self-improvement, that's great, but this is a book on escaping the mad chase to look rich, or merely are obsessed with money and what you think it might do for you. Only when the obsession is so gripping that you can't live in the now and enjoy the body, mind, and spiritual self, do these processes become life-sappers.

Start With Self-Care

Keep your face always toward the sunshine, and shadows will fall behind you (Walt Wittman). Create a fresh way of looking at yourself—less critical and less jonsing for riches, but accepting your life as you are right now, as you seek to become your best—within your financial means. And then watch the shadows fall behind you.

Self-care isn't selfish, but a loving, kind gesture to yourself. Self-care is not obsessing about this or that, but about feeding the self, whole and natural foods and taking time out for a walk, in nature or a swim in the sea and basking in what's free.

Self-love is treating yourself with kindness at exactly where you are right now. Yes, right now, not tomorrow or yesterday when you were younger and full of sass and vigor. Whatever future you would connect up with is what current you will do. Don't wait. And as you embody your future self, your brain will literally pave new pathways toward the new you.

Let's break free from obsessive thinking and greet life as it comes, armed and ready because you're practicing self-care and self-love, and employing help from others as you need to, so you can achieve self-actualization—reaching your personal fulfillment.

Don't fret that the conditions have to be perfect. No such thing as perfect may ever appear. You are *still* going to take that first step, but not obsessed. If you move in that direction now instead of later, when you have more financial stability, you will still be that many steps closer to your ability to handle any aspects of your life's progression this time next year by making healthy, self-love choices now.

Congratulations, you've already moved in the self-care direction, investing in yourself by purchasing this book! You're now well on your way. I hope that what I've written helps you to recognize, deal with, and resolve obsessive gotta-have-money thoughts to arrive mentally, understanding where the obsession stems from and how to transition to living in a more spiritually oriented realm. Keep your intention simple, and keep it real, and all the money will flow your way—I'm sure.

If the story of my own journey lifts and releases you from the pure hell of obsession, I will have accomplished my goal. Now is the time to dial down the obsessive money-defying thinking, and power up your best self. In Chapter 2, we take a peek into why money doesn't buy happy.

Personal Inventory Questions

1. We all have a story, so what's yours? You picked up this book because something resonated within you. Are you obsessed with money?
2. Self-care and self-love are paramount to living gracefully so that you can live a full, healthy life. Do you struggle with one or the other, or both?
3. My first paying job outside of babysitting, shortly before turning thirteen, was picking cucumbers in a field with Mexican migrant workers coming from Texas. I quickly

learned what working hard for the money meant. I also learned what poor really looks like. What about you? What did you learn from your first job? Did it set the tone for future jobs?

4. Self-actualization is what we strive for to become our authentic selves. Have you reached your authentic self at a spiritual level—a want-for-nothing stage? Have you reached your potential, your self-fulfillment? What is your idea of self-fulfillment? Is it a pocket full of money? No? Then what?
5. My own independent life began very early. At first, I had the basic needs such as food, water, warmth, and rest, and in those very formative years, safety and security. But as time marched on, those basic needs seemed to become my own responsibility. Did you have a cozy first start to life or did you have struggles?
6. I was *that kid* who listened and assessed and processed in my mind what to avoid and what to accept. I was a thinker. What kind of kid were you?
7. In our house, my parents argued over my mom's weight, money, politics, and a host of other concerns, all of which left me to comfort myself with food. External events, local and national politics, and world events often mark or define our relationship with money, food, body, self-image and aging, hence confusing the actual, personal situation with the *feel-good feeling* or *feel bad feeling* of what is going on outside ourselves. Can you recall situations outside yourself that frightened you? Did/does foods pacify you, or was money what you hungered for?
8. My start with obsessions was with food, which led to body weight that dominated my thoughts. Do you have persistent ideas, images, or desires that take you hostage in your thoughts? What are they, and what happens when

you obsess over them? How did/do they factor into your relationship with maturing into adulthood and beyond?

9. You can permit obstacles to control your mind to the point at which they are uppermost and thus dominate your thought. Or, you can learn how to toss them from the mind by refusing to become mentally submissive to them—and by practicing channeling spiritual thoughts so you can rise above the obstacles supposedly defeating you. What obstacles seem to stand in your way? What positive ideas can replace the obstacles?
10. Life is a good thing. Life means energy. Perhaps the magic elixir is to live for the fulfillment of life—not just for us, but also for others. Perhaps the magic is to wake up with a goal, to rise in the morning with intention—pursuing a life filled with purpose rather than dread of self and body and obsession with acquiring riches as we journey through life. What are your intentions?

Chapter 2

Money Doesn't Buy Happy

The thing always happens that you really believe in; and the belief in the thing makes it happen.
~Frank Lloyd Wright

The mind is incredibly powerful. What we think often becomes so. If you think the only way to happy is by having loads of money, and you don't, you most likely won't be happy. As the American architect Frank Lloyd Wright pens, "*The thing always happens that you really believe in; and the belief in a thing makes it happen.*"

So, if you believe the only way to be happy is to have money—and lots of it—then you create that outcome to, occur Yep, you will not be happy if you don't have lots of cash, because you believe without lots of money you won't be happy.

The good news is that we can always change our minds. We can always change our thoughts. Believe you will have all that you need, and you will. If you believe you'll be comfortable financially, and you act as if this is a truth, that *belief in a thing* makes it happen.

Now not that if you believe you will inherit money, then that belief in inheriting money makes it happen. That is out of your control. You can't make another's actions happen, only yours. So if you're banking on Uncle Mark's money coming to you, that's not quite what we're talking about here. And if you do inherit Uncle Mark's money, who's saying it won't slip through your fingers, leaving you once again without. And who's to say Uncle Mark's money is going to bring you joy?

Is Uncle Mark's money going to make you happy? Many believe this to be true. I hear it all the time, "If I had money I'd buy a new house and then I'd be happy." "If I had money, I'd pay off all my bills and then I'd be happy." "Oh, if I had money, everything would be different. I could do whatever I want." Really!! I don't think so. Yes, money provides opportunities that perhaps you didn't have before, but it is no guarantee of the giggle train. Really.

I remember a lovely girl waiting for her father-in-law's passing, because she was looking forward to inheriting the motherload of money—and oh how happy she would be then. Well, she inherited a large sum of money and spent it just as quickly as it came. Here today, gone tomorrow. And sadly all those years she waited for the father-in-law to pass, banking on happy to arrive as soon as he transitioned, didn't manifest.

The riches aren't what will make you happy, but the quality of your life. This was a hard lesson for my patient to learn, and I'm not sure if she learned it as she continued to chase the money in one form or another, wasting valuable time trying one get-rich scheme after another.

And this type of obsessive thinking happens not only with money, it happens when the domination of one's thoughts or feelings are orchestrated by a persistent idea, image, desire, or feeling. Yes, you can think your way into obtaining something, but it can be a negative directive or an urgency so gripping it becomes unhealthy. Truly, as popular belief sketches, if you see it and believe it in your mind, you can make the desired object come to fruition, but what urgency do you put behind it, and is holding the goal impeding your quality of life? Or worse, is it taking over your life, preventing you from living in the moment—in the now.

Just like when I was younger, I obsessed over becoming thin. I thought about the object of my longing with every waking breath and even dreamt of it when in a deep sleep. During twenty-four hours a day, seven days a week, I obsessed over this for a good thirty years. Over a period of thirty years I believed thin meant happy and then later learned this was not so.

Skinny does not make you happy. Defying aging does not make you happy. It's the quality of your life and living in the spiritual moment that makes you happy. Quality of life is not about our bodies, age, or the amount of money we have, no this affair of life we're involved in is actually much richer and much fuller than that. The happy part comes about through our connection to the surrounding real—the earth, ocean, people, animals; that's what makes us happy. We miss out on so much if we stay stuck in the obsession.

Without beating a dead horse here (sorry for such a visual!), money does not buy you happy. I know plenty of rich people (and so do you) who are quite miserable. What we do with our time is what counts. How we accumulate our funds is what matters. Living in a simpler realm and being in the moment is what produces contentment.

Now contentment doesn't mean you sit back and do nothing. It doesn't mean to accept you have not, and just be okay with it. No, it means living within your means and saving for that rainy day. When you live within your means and save, you can do great things that you thought only the rich could do. Keep it simple and watch the money grow.

And Then There Was Burt

Burt is a nice enough guy who worked for a company franchise chain, moving up the ladder, and nicely earning a handsome income. But he wasn't content with his life and was always searching for something. He looked high and low to find an antidote to relieve his discomforts of anxiety and fear.

Burt's first obsession was with food. He loved food beyond a normal enjoyment of nourishment. Food became his entertainment. He ate whatever his heart desired, whenever he wanted, in enormous amounts. Not uncommonly Burt would eat an entire pizza with all the fixings, washed down with gallons of beer, followed by a decadent mound of ice cream.

Burt gained weight. At first the gain was slow and steady, but soon the excess turned to obesity. Then the quest to diet took hold. He obsessed over every fad diet that came his way. And then Burt stumbled on cocaine and soon his appetite for food diminished, and a voracious hunger for the drug ensued to the point he inflicted nasal damage on himself, requiring plastic surgery.

Burt stayed addicted to cocaine for many years, spending his hard-earned money on white, puffy lines of powder. The drug made him feel euphoric, at least initially, until the need for it became so controlling; he had to go into rehab several times before he got it right.

And then, somewhere in all of this hardship, he experienced a series of unexpected deaths in his family: first his father, then his mother, and then his sister, and then his brother. Dark days for sure were present in Burt's life. But also an inheritance came down, a rather large one at that, all of which went to Burt—all of it, because the siblings had passed away, leaving Burt the sole heir. He was ecstatic with his newfound wealth.

Burt visited the local strip joints, spent money on girls, and smoked expensive cigars, along with driving fast sports cars. Donning his sunglasses day and night, he looked pretty darn important, and like a guy who had it all. He didn't. Burt was sad and lonely. He didn't have a wife, kids, or family. All he had was a pile of money that he soon blew through, which was about when I met Burt.

Burt realized the money was not bringing him the happy he so wanted, but it was bringing him a responsibility and a fear. He dabbled once again in cocaine, slipping back to an old familiar habit. He became paranoid, looking over his shoulder. He didn't know who was requesting his friendship, whether because of who he was or because of the goodies he could provide for them. He became distrustful of most and distant from all.

Night after night, Burt smoked his cigars, snorted a line while his hot-rod car sat idle in his driveway—lights off, sitting on his recliner, all alone in feeling lost and lonely. He couldn't understand how he was that unhappy when he was so rich and could have just about whatever he wanted. Why, he wondered, night after night, did he have such an empty spot in his heart?

Our work started with questioning this life he was living, looking at the parts he could change and the parts that were bringing him joy. The joy was in a deficit for sure, but a few things made him smile, like the bird feeder outside his window that attracted parrots of all sizes and colors. And the immense palm trees that swayed back and forth in his yard, waving as if to say, "Come out here with us. We'll show you happy—and it's free."

In time, we explored steps he could take to turn his life around. The first area of concern was his neglect of self. He was overweight, flushed red from high blood pressure, and had constant headaches. He also developed a habit of picking at his chin where he was sporting a beard, which now had empty patches showing red blotchy skin.

As Burt discussed his lifestyle and his understanding of what was going on with him, he had a glimpse of hope. He realized he wasn't appreciating nor respecting the money that had fallen so easily into his lap. He was out of control in every area and creating rifts between co-workers and the few friends he had.

We worked on what self-care would look like for him, and with gusto he dug into what needed to be done. He needed to groom himself, exercise, and change his foods as a first start in the healing process. He discovered a love for cooking he didn't even know he had. Soon, he was making himself fresh fish with loads of exotic vegetables roasted to perfection.

The weight came off, the itching ceased, his hair grew back where patches had taken over, and most important, he soon realized money was not the route to happiness, and in some way it was the root of all evil—his evil obsessions. After a few steps forward and several back, improvements took hold.

Burt began to live a simpler life, riding his bicycle to work instead of his eye-catching red Porsche. He awakened to an awareness of the life outside, hearing the sounds of nature for the first time in as far back as he could remember. He wanted to connect to the earth, to embrace the outdoors and feel the wind against his face, soaking in the natural warmth of the golden sun.

The earth is a healer. And as these pages unfold, you will find the connection of nature to become a theme as you tap into your understanding of your spiritual self. The healing powers of nature are a gift from Mother Nature that many of us often ignore. Stop and smell the flowers, and hear the birds sing, and see the butterflies in the sunshine dance by.

Outside my window, where I do most of my writing from home, is a ginormous palm tree that sprouted out of nowhere. We suspect a bird flew by, took a drink from a bowl held by a small statue of St. Francis of Assisi that stands in the yard, and most likely dropped the little seed to the ground right outside my window.

In a stretch of time, unbeknownst to me, the tree popped out of the earth and slowly grew to the point at which it was reaching to the height of the two-foot statue of St. Francis of Assisi (born in 1181 or 1182, passing October 3rd, 1226). He was the Roman Catholic Church's patron saint of animals, merchants, and ecology.

When I was a small child, this saint always mesmerized me when I worshipped in my church of St. Anthony's in Chicago—a church patterned after St. Anthony's of Padua in Italy. Interestingly, St. Francis abandoned a life of luxury after reportedly hearing the voice of God, who commanded him to rebuild the Christian church and to live in poverty. St. Francis is a saint I hold near to my heart.

To live in poverty and abandon his riches, a task most of us could or would never do, Francis turned to a life of helping the poor. And here, this magnificent palm tree and St. Francis sit right outside my window, reminding me of the magic of animals, saints, trees, and nature as I write a book on releasing the obsession with money so that you can heal from the inside out. There are no coincidences.

And the small seed that dropped from somewhere grew into a tall, majestic royal palm tree, now taller than my home with a round bottom the size of a large tractor tire, with ring markings and long branches reaching up to the sky, and waving its palm fronds that arch out creating a wide canopy for all to see. Palm trees and St. Francis both hold a special place in my heart, as do the powerful woods and ocean, along with birds and butterflies.

Earthing

I learned long ago that a power radiated from planet earth and that it brought me a sense of calm and ease, particularly in the woods. And today, people involved in the healing world actually advocate a practice known as Earthing. Earthing is a fast-growing movement based on the discovery that connecting to the earth's natural energy is essential for vibrant health. Most of us know this on a deep level, especially as children, but somehow the concept has been mostly forgotten. Connecting to the earth, however, is easy when outdoors by walking barefoot on the earth's natural soil or sand or grass. Something about the earth centers us and those who do this over time celebrate the benefits.

Burt's weight slimmed down, and his appreciation for the earth and life itself accelerated. He felt the earth speaking to him. At first, he thought his imagination was getting the best of him, but he soon realized the soil, grass, and trees radiated a natural energy. That energy embraced him—hugged him. It was Mother Earth to him.

Burt soon realized money didn't bring him love, or friendship, or most of all, the happy that he thought it would. Having the cushion and not fearing being destitute was great, but if he kept spending at the rate he was going, he wouldn't have his nest egg in a few short years. And he recognized the *stuff* he bought wasn't feeding his soul or healing his broken heart from all the losses he'd endured.

We worked on his pushing through the grief from all the losses that he masked with food, drugs, money, fast cars, and strip joints. He felt his sad. Really grieved the losses. The sobs that came from this large-framed man were the wailing he buried so deep within. Then the sound went from loud cries to the weeping of a small child.

Tears ran down Burt's face, spilling onto his shirt, soaking him in his sadness. I sat quietly for what seemed like an eternity, allowing him the space and distance he needed to feel his pain at a deep core level. When the room became still, silent, I waited for Burt to look up—our eyes met. His deep-blue eyes became really apparent for the first time. They had always seemed gray and muted, but now they were as bright as the blue of the sky on a crisp, clear day in the fall.

Soon, we talked and talked and talked some more, until clarity took hold. Burt is in a wonderful space now. He has saved money, just enough to feel secure. He lives a simpler life. He could afford to go to the finest restaurants, drive the fancy car once again, and date the hot chicks, but something shifted within him. He no longer needs that image to sustain him. He no longer has to prove anything to anyone. He grounded in the realness of life.

Life then took a totally different turn. Burt met the love of his life, and now he has two little girls and lives a quality, happy life within his means. He's enjoying a life he never thought possible for him. No pretending to be someone he wasn't. He no longer needs to have the fancy stuff around him because he sustains himself with love, real love.

And Burt has connected with nature, which he grew to love and appreciate. He couldn't believe that he never saw, really saw, the beauty laid before him, just outside his window.

I can still hear Burt saying, "I see the trees. I *really* see the trees with the blue sky in the background, like a painting. I never saw that before—my eyes were closed—and now they're open." The realization seems such a basic one, but many of us don't see the way we did as small children. Watch the child. Everything is awesome to them. Children look intensely at everything they see with great wonder. And then somewhere along the way that sense of the world is blurred, as other *stuff* comes front and center.

Sure, money is good. It gives you some room for security, but it doesn't make you giggly with joy twenty-four hours a day, seven days a week, and into eternity. In fact, you can't take it with you when you leave planet earth; you only take yourself just the way you came in. You go with you, nothing more. Your money and your fancy clothes, your gems of glitter and gold all stay behind. So enjoy them now with thanks and gratitude.

A Boatload Of Money

In fact, Devin and his wife, Martha, are quite wealthy. He's an airplane pilot, and Martha worked in real estate until she inherited a boatload of money from her father, a well-known entrepreneur. They have no children except for their brood of kitty cats that wander freely about their home.

Throughout their marriage, the couple ate a lot, smoked a lot, drank a lot, and shopped a lot. They overloaded their household with food, alcohol, and all the luxuries money could buy. They wanted for nothing. They could buy anything and everything without a moment of worry.

The two lived in a spacious six-bedroom home overlooking the Atlantic Ocean, but rarely looked out at the beautiful waters or walked the beaches. In fact, I recall one time Martha telling me the environment was too hot and too sticky with "all that salt in the air."

Devin and Martha held large, glamorous, lavish parties with the who's who in the community and made the local newspaper and magazine gossip columns frequently. In fact, they were the envy of many. They were rich, they lived by the ocean, and they wanted for nothing; nothing that money could buy was out of their reach.

And yet, the two were miserable and quite unhealthy. Both Devin and Martha were overweight by at least one hundred pounds each. Martha had the start of emphysema and at one time had resorted to a walker. She'd learned her poor behavior from her dad. Martha's father had died young from overconsumption of high-fat foods and alcohol, which led to obesity and alcoholism. He partied hearty and joked that you only live once—and that he wouldn't take it with him, so he might as well go down "eating, drinking, and being merry." Only problem was that he was not so merry. And nor was Martha, which led her to my couch many years ago.

So if money won't make us happy, what will? This was the start of our conversation when Martha began her self-discovery through psychotherapy. We explored where she might put her energy from now on. We explored what the next steps needed to be to revive her health first and then find her love of something to fill her life well.

Martha was kind, very kind. She loved to give and to help others. She was always baking lavish deserts and lovely meals to bring to those who had not. She did this regularly and bringing food to the less fortunate made her feel good. She had no problem loving and being generous to others, but had a terrible time giving love to herself.

With the extra weight on, Martha had trouble walking, so she began a very healthy, clean way of eating—and Devin went along for the ride. They both shed weight. Soon, the couple became more mobile, starting a walking exploration of the beach right out their door. Picking lovely seashells and feeling the warm, squishy sand between their toes as the salty water leaped up to their ankles made them laugh like children—something they hadn't done in quite a long while.

Martha and Devin realized they could do so much more to fill their lives besides ingesting rich foods and alcohol. They gave their time. Devin, being a pilot, could fly them all over the world to do something productive. They went to different parts of Africa and helped the poor. They built schools and homes for the needy. Their organization filled them with tremendous joy, far greater than any accumulation of money ever could.

Take Your Foot Off The Money Pedal

If you are searching for happy through money, you may find, like Burt, Martha, and Devin, that money is not all that it's cracked up to be. Money does not buy happiness. Personal, simple things in life can bring you greater joy if you stop and allow yourself to see and embrace them. The beauty is right in front of you. It always was and always will be, no matter where you live.

Go to the park, or the lake if it's near. Take a walk in the woods and pick wild berries and flowers. Or set up a bird feeder and watch what feather friends come to visit. Nature is free and quite entertaining and it's out there for all of us to enjoy. Go see.

As Frank Lloyd Wright has written, *"The thing always happens that you really believe in; and the belief in a thing makes it happen."* So really believe in your thing, and with this belief you will make it happen, I'm sure.

In the pages that follow you will read many stories from rags to riches and from riches to rags—from miserable to happy in the simplicity of life. You will read about the very wealthy—even famous wealthy people who are not so happy, and you will read about the person who has little but really has so much more than money.

If you take your foot off the pedal of obtaining money and learn to spend less, save, and maybe earn more, you will see your wealth grow. Hard work and smart work doing something you love and loving something you do, you'll never work a day in your life. And you'll find happy—that you earned. As we move on to Chapter 3, you'll see how far frugal can go.

Personal Inventory Questions

1. The mind is incredibly powerful. What we think often becomes so. If you think the only way to happy is by having loads of money, and you don't, you most likely won't be happy. As Frank Lloyd Wright writes, *The thing always happens that you really believe in; and the belief in a thing makes it happen.* What do you believe in?
2. So often we have a mistaken belief that if a financial inheritance comes, life will be bliss from then on. Do you have an experience to prove this to be wrong? Often, we learn from others that inherited money and the heir's life became worse than before the inheritance. Or perhaps you know of the opposite and the money was a true blessing. So what did these inheritors (or the lucky lottery winners) do differently?
3. The outdoor world heals us naturally. In what ways has it been a healer for you? Do you have a favorite place outside that brings you joy?
4. Burt was living in the fast lane, ignoring his health and living on his wealth. He was miserable and very unhealthy in his mind, body, and spirit. What parts of his story could you relate to?
5. Not uncommonly the quest for money allows health to go by the wayside. Why do you think that is so? Do you find this to be true in your own experience or what you've heard from others?
6. I learned long ago that a power resides in the earth that brings me a sense of calm and ease, particularly in the

woods. And today, many healers advocate a concept known as Earthing. Have you ever heard about earthing? Do you believe the idea holds some truth in it?

7. Sure money is good, it gives you room for security, but it doesn't make you giggly with joy twenty-four hours a day, seven days a week, and into eternity. In fact, you can't take it when you leave this planet; you only take yourself, just the way you came in. How does this thought resonate with you? Do you find truth in it?
8. Throughout Devin and Martha's marriage, they ate a lot, smoked a lot, drank a lot, and shopped a lot. They overloaded their household with food, alcohol, and all the luxuries money could buy. They wanted for nothing. Do you wonder what wanting for nothing might be like? What would change in your life?
9. So if money won't make us happy, what will? This was the start of our conversation when Martha began her self-discovery through psychotherapy. What will make you happy? And how can you take hold of it?
10. Martha and Devin realized they could do so much more to fill their lives besides imbibing rich foods and alcohol. They gave their time. Devin was a pilot who could fly all over the world and do something productive. What could you do to give of your time? And what would this give to you personally? How would it fill up your self-care tank?

Chapter 3

Living the Frugal Life

Once you make a decision,
the universe conspires to make it happen.
~Ralph Waldo Emerson

What is your decision? Do you want to obsess over money, or do you want to live in the land of plentiful? Decide and let the universe conspire to make it happen. Of course you can't sit on your laurels while you wish upon a star and then voila, there's the money falling from the heavens. No, the formula doesn't quite work like that. Release the grip and live frugally. Live simple. And then, great things happen.

You don't have to have that *thing*, at least not right now. Wait. You have plenty of time to get those things that you want, but not if you don't have the means. The process is very simple, really. When you live beyond your means, you might *look* as if you're wealthy but in fact, you're not and you never will be with that mindset. You will live in debt.

I know this firsthand because I didn't have the funds to go to college, let alone graduate school, and certainly not the doctoral schooling I took up. So what did I do? I borrowed student loan after student loan after student loan. And they gave these to me, even though I didn't have an actual job, and I was in debt with credit cards, mortgage, and car payments, and living way beyond my means.

By the time it all was said and done with the mortgage, student loans, credit cards and car loans, my husband and I were well over half-a-million dollars in debt. Oh, and did I mention I sent my youngest to a private school from pre-K all the way through high school, compliments of MasterCard? Now I wasn't buying fancy stuff or living a highfalutin life but living off of the credit cards and student loans and what little money I earned.

That I was *so* much in debt never occurred to me. I just didn't think about it, at least on a conscious level. No, I tucked the realization way back into the subconscious compartment in my brain to be looked at later—much later. I had the complete intention of paying off every penny I owed, not once thinking I'd fail to do so. And I did once I finished all my education.

For the time being, I paid the least amount toward my bills each month and just got by. I was on one mission: to earn my degrees. And to be honest, I don't regret one thing I did because I love my work and wouldn't be in my profession if I hadn't extended myself the way I did.

But had I known then what I know now, I might have gone about it a little differently. Perhaps attending a state school rather than a private school might have been a better option. And maybe finding a job that paid for part of my education could have been another option.

But, when we know better, we do better. Once I graduated with my last degree, I realized I really needed to dig my way out of debt. I wasn't exactly sure how I would do that, but I knew I would. And we did. I read and listened to everything I could regarding getting out of debt. The mission of squashing thousands and thousands of dollars of liability never frightened me. I may have been numb to it or maybe even in denial, but at the core of my being, I always knew I would pay my debt.

Money Books Galore

So I buried myself in one money book after another, looking for the answers. The first book I read, way back in 1996, *The Millionaire Next Door* by Thomas J. Stanley and William D. Danko got me thinking, planting the seed of the possibility of *me* being the millionaire next door, and how I was going to move past this debt.

And the second comprehensive book that led me out of debt was Dave Ramsey's *The Total Money Makeover*, back in 2003. I listened to his radio show at the time known as, "The Dave Ramsey Show," on the AM channel, which was crackly, depending on how my antenna received the wavelengths.

Today "The Ramsey Show," a three-hour, self-syndicated radio program and podcast broadcast out of Franklin, Tennessee, is one of the top ten most-listened-to radio shows since 2008. I still listen often, even though now I'm debt free, just to remind myself where I was and where I am. Of course the sound no longer crackles, as I'm hearing it from Sirius Radio, which is always clear as a bell unless I lose signal, which is very rare as it's a fully integrated satellite radio experience capable of giving a seamless delivery.

For sure I read tons of money books, which I will mention throughout my own pages, but the two core money books were *The Millionaire Next Door* and Dave Ramsey's *The Total Money Makeover*, hands down. I owe so much to these authors as I'm sure many debt-free millionaire next-door people do. And the interesting point with both books is that living on less brings you more.

Both books emphasize getting out of debt and living within your means. Of course then you can live in an *improved* fashion if you want to, but you don't. You'll find something sweet about knowing you can, so that then you don't want to. You'll see a psychological twist to it. Think about it, if you tell the little child they can't touch the television they want to touch the television—and then they become obsessed with the television.

This is a book about not being obsessed with spending less but about moving away from the money grip that is getting in the way of the quality of your life.

For the record, the millionaire next door is not who you think he/she is. The millionaire is NOT the person(s) with the glitz and glitter. She's not the ostentatious girl carrying the twenty-thousand-dollars and up Hermes Birkin handbag. He's not the guy wearing the Louis Vuitton Manhattan Richelieu men's shoes, priced at ten-thousand dollars and up.

No, the millionaire is the person with the simple car, modest home, who is living within or maybe even below his means. He's not the guy with the fancy car and fancy home with all the bells and whistles—though he could be. He doesn't have to be. He can be simple, knowing he can have all the fancy, but chooses not to. That caught my eye. I wanted to be the millionaire next door, the simple one, by choice.

And of course Dave Ramsey is the champion of leading people out of debt so they can scream, "I'M DEBT FREE!!!!!" I so wanted to do that, to the point I even practiced the scream a few times—but I'm really a behind the scenes kinda gal so I never did scream, but I could. And so could you. Give up the grip and the obsession and watch the money grow.

And the funny part about this is once you give up the grip—that tight hold of *I gotta have more* thinking, you open the valve to let money flow your way. Remember the old cliché, what you resist persists—by the focusing on what we don't want, we attract more of it. I saw this over and over in my quest to be skinny, where I focused on how fat I thought I was, which made me heavier and heavier, a vicious loop.

Another favorite book that helped me work through this negative thinking was *The Law of Attraction: The Basics of the Teachings of Abraham*, by Esther and Jerry Hicks. The message is you can deliberately create for yourself anything that you want to do, be, or have. The Law of Attraction states that 'like attracts like.' As in what you resist persists. That attempting to push certain experiences away only serves to draw more of the same to yourself. I read more and more books on how to move away from attracting what I didn't want—too many to name them.

In Frugality, Watch The Debt Fade

In time, I knew I could make my way out of debt. I could create for myself anything that I wanted to do, be, or have. To start the process, I lived poorly when I made money. I realized I knew how to live poorly well, so why not continue to behave as if I wasn't making money? Yes, I said I had been living above my means, but not in how I was buying fancy clothes and acting like I was rich.

No, I was living beyond my means through paying for education for myself, and my youngest son. I also had the horrible habit of buying a coffee and candies every time I went to the gas station and eating fast food and takeout—and I was knee deep in my eating disorders. Eating disorders when you binge-eat can be quite costly, dare I say.

And my husband, who also was carrying a debt, not because he lived lavishly but because he was starting off in a restaurant business and didn't have the start-up money to begin, so he bought everything on credit, and I mean everything. And of course the profits were slow to come, resulting in a steep debt.

The interesting thing about my situation was that I didn't come from poor as I've mentioned before, but I came from a father who was frugal and a mother who spent more than she had. I guess I took a bit from both of them, but in the end circled back to my dad's way of working with money, and that's living within or below my means. Please note living below your means does NOT mean you are suffering and living in rags, but it means you don't have to rush to the high-end store to purchase name-brand products to show you are living the rich life.

I remember a patient many years back who had inherited a great deal of money when her grandpa passed away. We'll name her Tanya. Raised by her grandparents as her mom died during childbirth, she lived a rich life—all her life. When she dropped a piece of clothing on the floor, a magical nanny swooped it back up and into a washed/pressed state once again. She lived her entire young and adult life without working or earning her own keep.

Tanya didn't know how to live frugally, nor did she know what saving money was like, let alone earning money. She was, however, kind and generous to a fault. She gave to every charity imaginable, and often assisted in philanthropic ventures. She always sought to promote the welfare of others, especially with generous donations of money to good causes. All good, until the money ran out; Tanya never thought the money could or would run out.

So Tanya, newly divorced, with no means to live up to the standards she had been, started dating—as if her life depended on it. She dated one wealthy man after another, admitting she needed to find that guy who'd provide for her.

One fellow comes to mind, Richard, aka Rich. He was rough around the edges, worked his entire life in construction to the point of becoming a very wealthy man. He still went out into the field to watch what his company was doing—though he didn't need to. He was very rich, the upper crust rich type—but quite down home and very real.

So Tanya took a real liking to Rich, who was intelligent and fun, and most important to her, wealthy, able to keep her above the level where she had been before. He was perfect. Perfect until they went shopping for a handbag that she had her eye on. When they arrived at the mall, she made a beeline to the posh handbag store and picked the one she wanted for several thousand dollars.

Rich noted the one she wanted, and they left. As the days wore on, Rich did his research and found the same bag discounted to five hundred dollars. Sharing the good fortune with Tanya thrilled him beyond words, but she hadn't prepared him for her response. She was furious, threw the bag on the floor, walked out of his home, slamming the door so hard pictures on the wall swayed, nearly falling off.

She surprised me when she shared the incident during one of our sessions. It was the same bag, same designer, brand new. Why in the world was she upset? She explained to me that if he loved her, he'd buy the one in the fancy store. Hmmm, I had to ponder that one.

We discussed how she came upon her money through inheritance, and how he'd worked from when he was a teenager, learning his craft and building it into a monumental company. His parents didn't hand the money to him, he didn't inherit it through some mysterious relative, nor did he live the high life. He had earned the money. He lived in a modest home, drove a modest car, and knew how to live thriftily. But he could spend—really spend when he wanted to, and surely he did.

And this is where differences of upbringing and how money is obtained can cause havoc in relationships. An interesting factor when letting go of an obsession with money and learning to be frugal is to agree with your significant other. If one is spending and the other is saving, this creates grounds for serious fighting, with one digging out of debt while the other is piling on the debt.

Tanya clearly was a wonderful person who gave to the less fortunate. Her grandparents hadn't groomed her the same way Rich's mom had brought him up. Tanya came from money, hung around people with money, and never worried about where it would come from. Rich grew up very poor. His single mom who raised him worked in a restaurant as a server to keep the lights on and a roof over their heads.

Rich helped early in life by delivering newspapers on his bike. He knew firsthand what having holes in his shoes and making do was like. He ate baloney sandwiches and a pickle daily for a cheap and filling lunch. Rich had loved his childhood. He had grand friends, a loving mom, and a huge extended family. He wanted for nothing.

As you can see, Tanya and Rich each came from unique backgrounds. A good relationship arises from working with the same core beliefs, which usually revolve around money, religion, and maybe today, politics.

In my situation, my husband and I are almost always on the same page with most of our decisions, and money doesn't stray far from the list of agreements. We both are prudent, but we also learned that if you are careful with spending, you can spend in other areas. One of Dave Ramsey's famous lines is "Live like no one else so you can live like no one else," which meant to me that if you don't spend foolishly and save, *then* you can indulge in some of the more decadent enjoyments in life.

My husband loves classic cars, so our driveway almost looks like a small car lot, and I like gold and diamonds, but this doesn't mean we spend beyond our means—but it means if we like something, and we've given it great thought, and it is within our means, and *if it's a superb deal*, we might just take the plunge. But not on credit, always paying with cash. Now that's the beauty of living like no one else, so you can live like no one else, I'd say.

Dave Ramsey sure knew what he was talking about when he spoke those very words, making it one of his themes in his money makeover strategies and radio show. I'm grateful beyond words for the advice and suggestions that I took and rode all the way to debt free. If you've never happened upon him, and you want to be one of those goofy debt-free kinda people, then Google his name. I promise what you find will not disappoint.

I see Mr. Ramsey as a simple guy with an amazing approach to digging your way out of debt. Dave has a story like I have a story, and so does Tanya. And so do you. Mr. Ramsey earned his money and learned from mistakes how to live debt free and to live like no one else because he lived like no one else. I have no affiliation with Dave, nor does he even know little ole me exists on planet earth, but he will forever be in my thoughts in living free from debt.

And Tanya, whatever happened to Tanya? Well, she continued her therapy, working on her own losses, grieving her way to a stable place. She loved and married Rich. She learned to respect and understand where he was coming from. She lives a very nice life but knows now that finding a bargain is okay, and that it's okay to look for the deals. She was equating bargains with being poor, but now she realizes how absurd that is, especially if the product is the same but at a better price.

Anxiety Be Gone

And then there was Carol, who began therapy because she had a general anxiety disorder. She was worried about everything, and I mean everything, from what to wear to go grocery shopping to what type of shampoo to use, to how heavy she *thought* she was. She feared being broke. She feared being fat. She feared living alone. Carol freaked over this spot on her face or this bump on her arm or this pain in her elbow.

Carol worried herself sick over the fears of things that were not happening and would never happen but worry she did. The one worry that was real was she was broke. She didn't have enough money to make it from one week to the next. Of course I didn't know this at first because Carol presented in high spike shoes, high-end workout clothes wearing some nice-looking diamonds.

When working with patients, the first step I take is to ferret out the issues, looking for what's real and what they imagine. Then we look at what is within the control of change and what needs to be accepted. That Carol had little money was quite real, but what shampoo to use was not as catastrophic as she made it out to be. What was real was if Carol kept living above her means and not earning more income, she'd be in serious trouble when she grew older and couldn't work.

So we moved out the little worries first, isolating the big one(s) to work on later. I tabled the big one of being broke for the moment. Often, little worries are knocking on our thoughts, so we don't have to look at the glaring big situations. We do this to minimize the fear or to distract our thoughts. It's sort of a bait-and-switch type of mentality. So, I saw that Carol had two big situations, followed by a swarm of petty annoyances.

Carol's actual problems were her health and her finances. She had retired early without a pension or savings, relying on her mere $700 a month from Social Security. She had spent on whatever she wanted in her younger days, not thinking about what it would mean in her older years. She brushed off the issue like swatting a fly, believing focusing on the moment was the way to live. And of course living in the present is a good thing, a splendid thing, as long as you don't negate the responsibilities from living frivolously as they will catch up with you.

And Carol was significantly obese on her short, five-foot, three-inch frame wearing most of her weight on her midriff where heart issues could become a concern.

Carol didn't own her home and leased her car. She didn't have an education beyond high school. She suffered from asthma and obesity and severe loneliness. We definitely had our work cut out for us. Though Carol had a mountain to climb, she did have one of the greatest gifts of all—faith. She believed in a higher source and that she would find a way.

Carol also had an amazing sense of humor. She always smiled and was quick to pass the heartiest of hearty laughs. She could put others at ease even when she herself was facing such challenges. She never complained, nor did she let anyone know the burdens she faced daily. She was kind and generous in responding to every situation that presented itself to her. She gave when she didn't have.

We looked at the endless possibilities to work through her challenges. Though money might have seemed like the glaring issue, it wasn't. Health was first on the major lists needing attention, and then the money fix later. So, the first on our agenda was to change her relationship with food. And funny, because once that area changed, it spilled down to the other areas, as you'll see.

Carol spent too much money on fast foods, take-outs, and home deliveries. She thought eating that was quick, cheaper, and less stressful than to shop for her foods and stand too long preparing in the kitchen. Her knees hurt and her back ached, so the last thing she wanted to do was cook, though everyone knew her to be a fabulous cook.

We slid through the easiest ways to build a grocery list with clean, healthy foods. We discussed working through the outer aisles in the grocery store to find real, wholesome foods and cook from home. Did you ever notice the junk foods are usually hanging in the center of the store? Of course lots of stores are growing wise to us savvy shoppers and putting the Ding Dong and Twinkies next to the succulent strawberries and apples.

Once Carol learned this simple little secret, she put the better foods in her cart and maneuvered through the store fast and efficiently. The savings were intense. The mistaken belief for most people is that eating healthy is expensive, but it doesn't have to be if you buy in bulk. To live conservatively, sometimes you have to purchase more in large quantities to obtain the good deals.

Next, we looked at the possibility of her finding a little part-time job to supplement her income.

Carol was more than open to living conservatively, as she always loved a challenge. We looked at the dreams and magic that could come her way if she lived below her means, way below. And she did. This was a fun game for her when she could file away twenty dollars here and twenty dollars there, to the point at which she had quite the nest egg in no time.

Carol gravitated to the frugal way of living, especially knowing that she could embrace a heartier way of living in no time at all. I assured her if she had the stash of cash, she most likely wouldn't even want to dip into it. Just knowing it was there and accumulating some interest would excite her.

Saving money became a game. The more she saved, the more she wanted to save. Carol didn't have any debt, which made the process of building her wealth much easier.

Carol gave up the obsession, and then the money flowed. Rather than wishing for money, she spent less, worked more, and saved more, and the results showed up just the way she thought they would after our discussions. As noted earlier, I'm not a finance person, I'm a therapist who understands how to move through the worries of another and finds suitable and practical solutions, which is what Carol learned to do.

Today, Carol sits in an enviable position. She still lives in her studio apartment and still works her little job four days out of the week. She now drives a car she owns and can go out and buy a nice outfit or something exciting *if* she wants to. And even when knowing she can, she doesn't. That's the magic.

Carol squirreled away nearly a thousand dollars a month, and with interest and time, she gathered over fifty-thousand dollars. Now to you this may seem like a lot or it may seem like a little. Given Carol was only making seven hundred dollars on Social Security and spending five hundred a month on her studio apartment, she was strapped for money and had no savings and no second job and was a worrywart.

Because she learned to make her own foods, she cut the expense drastically on her food bill, and the bonus was she lost weight, a lot of weight, to the tune of ninety pounds. Her worries vanished one by one, and now she's feeling mighty secure and hopeful about her life in the future. Her faith in herself and in the God of her understanding carried her to financial security. Living frugally became fun, not a drudgery because she saw the light at the end of the tunnel.

So living frugally can be a good thing—an excellent thing. It doesn't mean you are broke the way Tanya thought, and it doesn't mean that you are NOT the millionaire next door as the book *The Millionaire Next Door* touts. We can live debt free as Dave says and really be quite comfortable living in a simple way but big when we want to. And Carol, yes, Carol, learned she could dig her way out of her fears and live the rest of her life knowing she'll be okay. Look at Rich, a guy who grew up super poor and now is super rich.

If it can happen to Carol, it can happen to you. *Once you make a decision, the universe conspires to make it happen* (Ralph Waldo Emerson). Decide, and watch the changes take place—the universe is on your side. And the interesting thing is that money doesn't equal success, a concept hard for many of us to grasp, as you will see in Chapter 4.

Personal Inventory Questions

1. What is your decision? Do you want to obsess over money, or do you want to live in the land of plenty? Decide and let the universe plot to bring it to reality. As Ralph Waldo Emerson says, *Once you make a decision, the universe conspires to make it happen.* Do you think this is true, or a bunch of mumbo jumbo? What decision did you make that came into fruition? How did that happen?
2. I didn't have the funds to go to college, let alone graduate school, and certainly not the doctoral school I enrolled in. So what did I do? I borrowed student loan after student loan after student loan. Did you find yourself in the same position? And of so how did you climb out of it? What lessons did you learn?
3. As you've already read, I buried myself in one money book after another, looking for the answers. The first book I read way back in 1996 was *The Millionaire Next Door*, written by Thomas J. Stanley and William D. Danko. The authors started me thinking, planting the seed for the possibility of *me* being the millionaire next

door, and how I was going to move past this debt. What one book affected your way of thinking as it relates to money?

4. Though *The Millionaire Next Door* planted the seed as to the possibilities from now on, Dave Ramsey's *The Total Money Makeover* was what ignited the action for me. Everything we do starts with an idea, but to make the change we must put the idea into motion. What motion do you have in place? If none, what is keeping you from releasing your obsession with money?
5. Tanya's grandparents raised her since her mom died during childbirth. She lived a well-to-do lifestyle—all her life. Though she enjoyed a plush way of living, lack of funds caused a big scare later in life. What were your thoughts when you read her story? Did it make you mad? If so, why? Explore your feelings.
6. What did you think about Rich, the poor boy who became well-off? It's one of those stories you see in movies, but to know to go from rags to riches can be real makes an impression on most of us. How did his transformation affect your thoughts about money and riches? Do you share a similar story?
7. When you read about Tanya and the purse, how did it affect your thoughts? I know I was a bit surprised, myself, as I'm coming from the working-for-the-money perspective, and finding deals is almost a high for me. What's Tanya's sense of a bargain like for you?
8. That couples stay on the same page with their core beliefs is imperative for the relationship to grow in a healthy way. Do you and your significant other share the same important beliefs such as morals, money, religious faith, etc.? How is that working for you?
9. Carol was that patient who really moved me when I saw how she turned off her anxiety and became proactive in

moving her life from a place of fear to a confident journey. Do you have anxiety? How did her story impact you?

10. Do you see a connection between health, weight, and money? Carol did. She learned that her health had to come first in order for her to make her way through her other challenges. How is your health? What changes could you implement?

Chapter 4

Money Doesn't Equal Success

You can always be robbed of what you have,
But never of what you are.
~Persian Proverb

What is success? Is success making your way to millions and millions of dollars? Is it having the ability to purchase whatever you want whenever you want? Is it not having a care in the world because money will buy you out of your troubles? Or can you call what you have success because you went to the top in your company, or bought a company, or sold a million books or made it in the top ten of most-listened-to songs?

The Oxford Dictionaries define success as the accomplishment of an aim or purpose; or the good or bad outcome of an undertaking. So if you didn't achieve your goals and dreams, perhaps you didn't arrive at your success destination. But where does money fit into the equation? I read in Inc.com, a newsletter by Geoffrey James, his definition of success, "If you believe success is simply making (or having) a lot of money, you may be setting yourself up for failure."

Bingo. Money does not make you a success. Nor does reaching success status mean you have loads of money. This is a mistaken belief that most people hold near and dear to their hearts. I hear it all the time, "Oh, Johnny is a millionaire. He's so lucky." Or, "Betty has the mansion down the street. She has arrived." Or how about, "Did you see Lucy's Red Shoes?" Okay, if you don't know what Red Shoes are, you're not alone. They are a ridiculously expensive pair of shoes. Now I'm not talking Satanists who wear red shoes. I'm talking the high heel pumps with the red dot on the sole showing a brand. Lucy's pumps were $1,000!

Geoffrey James says how amazed he is at how many people define success as making (or having) a lot of money. I found this to be a jaw-dropper too when I spoke with students about identifying what success meant to them. They didn't mention the *meaning* part of success. You know, the touchy-feely part. They only looked at money as an indicator that you'd made it. When I'd question what about the love of what you do, they'd wave me off as if I was yesterday's news.

James notes, "It's very strange, because many of the people who think this way [having or making a lot of money is the meaning of success] are harried, stressed, and frankly, pretty miserable." Oh, is that the truth! If you obsess over money, or anything, you will stress, fret, and experience misery. I know I did when I chased skinny all those years. I was miserable, anxious, and downright depressed.

So back to the question at hand regarding success and money, or is it money and success? Enter Marla, a tall, lean girl of thirty-something who moved here from India to study law in New York, earned accolades such as landing on the

Moot Court and being named editor-in-chief of the law review at her university. Marla is not only attractive, kind, and super smart, she's quite likable. Yet, she circles around two issues, which brought her into therapy. The first, Marla binge eats and fears becoming heavy, though she's quite slim. Second, Marla feels like an utter failure because she's broke. She only started her private practice a few years back.

As I've mentioned earlier, seeing multiple obsessions within one person is not uncommon. In fact, it's more common than not. As Marla presented with binge eating and fear of growing heavy, she also twisted into a belief system that said she was no good because she didn't have money. So the two beliefs became intertwined. Marla studied for years and now works in a fabulous career, but she always feels she's not good enough.

Marla believes she's not a success story because she is in financial ruins. She has a massive student loan she put into deferment, and it's growing interest rate expense at lighting speed. Marla doesn't own her own home and rents her office space. She also spends money like there is no tomorrow. She wants the fancy name-brand clothes she buys with credit cards, the Porsche she leased, and the huge diamond rock around her neck to *show* she made it—she's rich. No, she's in debt up to her eyeballs.

James is spot-on the oddity among those who think having a lot of money means success. He's right: those on the money train are harried, stressed, and frankly pretty miserable. Why is that so? I ask myself. It's because people like Marla are not enjoying the journey, only want to arrive at the destination of piles of money, thinking that means success.

Marla is missing staying in the moment with this type of mindset. She's missing the moment. Marla intertwined her body image, though faulty, with her money image, swirling between the two belief systems implanted in her thought process. She was obsessed. Day in and day out, she lives and breathes the belief that she must get rich to be a success and she must be skinny to be a success, when neither will lead her to the road of success.

When I suggest to Marla money will not buy her success, she looks at me as though I'm sprouting two horns—that I just don't get it. But get it, I do. I know plenty of rich people who are miserable; I mean miserable and tightly holding on to every penny for fear of losing it, or spending like there's no tomorrow, for fear they may lose it. Neither situation is good. Earning money to become rich yet miserable makes no sense. If you're stuck in the loop of money will make your rich and happy yet you're miserable and broke because you're overspending or rushing the march toward success, you'll be a nervous Nelly, missing out on the joys of life.

Don't ignore the simple pleasures of life like witnessing the sun coming up, or hearing the birds singing morning melodies, or viewing the sky in its rich blue shades with white cloud markings throughout. Stop, and see what's around you. Really look. Perhaps gratitude for the wealth of having breath in and out and a heart beating *pump pump pump*, or eyes to see and arms to hug is the richness that leads to personal, soulful success.

Football, Anyone?

On Sunday, February 7th, 2021, Super Bowl 55 took place between the Kansas City Chiefs and Tampa Bay Buccaneers at Raymond James Stadium in Tampa, Florida. A game even those not into football could enjoy, moving away from the pressures of the coronavirus and politics in an uproar. And the commercials, yes the commercials, to pull you in and make you laugh and laugh. And as most know, Tampa won with Tom Brady and his team.

Now to be honest, I'm not much of a football person, but my husband and son Kris live and breathe the stuff, so it seeps into my world some. And of course writing about obsessions with money, I can't help but think about the millions of dollars these players are making to throw a football. And to be sure, I'm not the only one thinking about the gobs of money they are making throwing a football for sheer entertainment.

But what's amazing to me is how many people, hundreds and thousands of boys, young men, and mature men, too, are jaw droppingly amazed at the money these football players are making. And some feel envy. The belief they are successful because they make money is playing a key role. Now for sure many love to play football and would do it for free—I think. But the belief that one day they'd be rich as well if they could play football is a dream—though far-fetched.

Be the Gateway: A Practical Guide to Sharing Your Creative Work and Engaging an Audience by Dan Blank says, "We live our lives by a narrative. Everything is filtered through it. One person drives to Starbucks and sees it as their little escape, a sign that they have 'made it' because they can buy their personalized drink for $4.50 each day." I used to be that person spending on Starbucks until I became serious and went debt free and now brew my own coffee for just pennies.

Or that same narrative is becoming a famous football player, a status many would love to reach. But I ask, why such interest in becoming a famous something? Why wearing fancy shoes or carrying fancy handbags or a cup of coffee with Starbucks symbol to show you're a success because you can afford to buy this or that?

For sure the awe is clear regarding the sport of football with their exorbitantly paid players, perhaps because of the money. But do you think the players are in it only for the money? Maybe at first the money was the lure, but most are in it for the love of the game—which brings me back to my point that success is not about how much money you make, but the joy and pleasure you get from doing what you do. I'm guessing Tom Brady is quite wealthy, beyond most of our comprehensions, but do you think he's about the money? Was making money his way toward success? I'm thinking maybe not. He seems to be in it for the love of the game. He lives and breathes football.

Brady's success is living the life he wanted to live, doing what he wanted and loves. I would imagine going to the Super Bowl ten times and winning seven is quite a feat, but not what fills his success tank. His success is in doing what he loves and loving what he does.

So here we are circling back to money and happy, money which doesn't make you happy as noted in a previous chapter. It can provide security but not necessarily happy and for sure not success. Money is a necessity. We must have a roof over our head. And if money is a struggle for you, I'm not denying your need for financial security or for the basic requirements of food, shelter, and safety as important ingredients. Because surly they are.

But we are addressing the obsession with money. Marla obsessed over piling away money. She wants to be rich. She wants to live in a fancy house and drive a fancy car NOW. She didn't want to gather up money and pay off debt. She was rushing the process so that she could be rich, which leaves her poor.

When we discussed how she could live in a simple manner, below her means, she cried. She felt defeated. That she wasn't successful. That she *looked* poor. Marla bought thousand-dollar shoes and handbags that could pay most people's rent. She thought that made her a success—or at least let her look like a success. But having money is not being a success. Success is reaching your content phase. Not complacent, or giving up, but going for the ride in a present state.

Robbed

But if money is a success, and someone swindled you of all your money and belongings, then what? As a Persian proverb says, someone can always rob you of what you have, but never of what you are. It's not the money that makes you a success, but who you are. YOU are the success. But you might say, hold on, if I made the money and I'm a success, my success had to be the money as the prize for what I did, right?

No, the money isn't what makes you anything, it's you. You are the success. Your ideas, your courage to take steps in directions you never thought you could. You, who fell and stood back up, no matter what, no matter how hard, no matter how far you had to go. No, it's not the money that makes you a success, it's you.

I once heard a slaying, years ago, that if you can make a million dollars once and lost it, you can make it again. Why is that so, you might ponder? Well, because the money didn't make you, but you made the money. Drop the obsession for money and open your gates of creativity, and the money will come if that's what you so desire. But do it from the heart, from the soul, not for the almighty green stuff.

Mark Nepo, in *The Book of Awakening: Having the Life You Want by Being Present to the Life You Have,* writes: "Each person is born with an unencumbered spot—free of expectations and regrets, of ambition and embarrassment, free of fear and worry—an umbilical spot of grace where we were each first touched by God."

Whoa. This is heavy stuff. It reminds me of when I taught psychology we read a section on John Locke's blank slate theory, or tabula rasa as it's sometimes referred to. Locke's theory expands on an idea suggested by Aristotle in the fourth century B.C. Tabula rasa, or the blank slate suggests that beyond a very few basic instincts our experiences shape us entirely.

We are born with empty minds, this blank slate waiting to be filled with our experiences. What might these experiences be? They are the process or fact of observing, encountering, or undergoing something. You store in your mind every experience in your life—to pop up as needed.

Of course with any theory comes controversy. Do we really begin with a blank slate? Or do we have many lives like the Miami psychiatrist, Brian Weiss, writes about in *Many Lives, Many Masters: the True Story of a Prominent Psychiatrist, His Young Patient, and the Past-Life Therapy That Changed Both Their Lives.* Perhaps we've had many lives. Who knows for sure?

And if we had another life, or two, or maybe many, would that make a difference? Would you think of your life as a trial run this time around? Or is it an opportunity for a "do over," a chance to make the wrongs right? Who knows for sure? What we know is that we have instincts. And if you believe in something bigger and greater than you, perhaps we don't know much more that is here, around us.

So is it a blank slate or a spot? Nepo says, "It is this spot of grace that issues peace." And of course this spot has many names, as he points out. "Psychologists call this spot the Psyche, theologians call it the Soul, Jung calls it the Seat of the Unconscious, Hindu masters call it Atman, Buddhists call it Dharma, Rilke calls it Inwardness, Sufis call it Qalb, and Jesus calls it the Center of our Love." What do you call it?

I'd like to think the actuality is a compilation of all those beliefs; that we are each born with the opportunity to become our best self, even when we come from a low economic place. Many people go from rags to riches. Many have a story of how they went through tough times and made it big. Take Oprah Winfrey, a black woman who lived poor and now is one of the richest women in the world. I read she is the first African-American female billionaire.

But I still stand by the money doesn't make the person idea. Oprah was the one who made the money. I don't believe she was on the hunt to be one of the richest women in the world. I think she simply tapped into her successes. In the many Oprah Winfrey biographies, she is seen as the embodiment of American spirit and commercial success. Oprah is a noble example of a woman who moved from rags to riches. She rose from poverty to the top of the world—and she leaves behind a great legacy.

So if you want to release the obsession with money and live your best life, start with the core of you. Call it the spot, or the soul, the center of love, but know for certain that it is YOU not the money that makes you who you are. Yes, money is a pleasant thing to have, but it doesn't define you. It's all the fun things about you that define you. You have a magnificent gift tucked inside of you for the entire world to see and enjoy.

Do you have to ponder what people might think about you when you're long gone into the place beyond? Who will they know you as? I had the luxury of poring over old newspaper articles about my great-great-grandfather and grandmother on my mother's side to learn who these people really were as I prepared to write my first novel, loosely based on them.

I don't think of their successes as based in money, but about what they did. My great-great-grandfather, Charles Stark, was a newspaper guy who barely made it out of elementary school. He had a dream, and he chased it—to be a writer. And his lovely wife, Abbie, was known for her kindness to everyone she met, no matter their status, whether financial or social or racial or cultural. And this was way back in the 1800s.

And here I am this descendent, thinking about their lives so long ago. They paved a road that was their calling. They didn't start with loads of money or education. They started with a dream, a belief in something that lit the flame within.

Light your flame and become who you were meant to be. Do what you love and love what you do, and for sure the rest is easy. It's not about obsessing over becoming rich or having stuff. It's about being your authentic you in everything you do and everything you are.

Someone can always rob you of what you have, but never of who you are, as the great Persian proverb states. Stay true to yourself. You have no need to hide behind the pretense of success based on money earned but show yourself through what or who you are and what you stand for. Perhaps you're thinking it's too late for you, but I say it's never ever too late to carve out your authentic self. And it's never too late to build your finances by living within your means and putting some money aside for that rainy day. You'll see as you power through Chapter 5, It's Never Too Late.

Personal Inventory Questions

1. What is success? Is it making your way to millions and millions of dollars? Is it having the ability to purchase whatever you want, whenever you want? When you sit quietly with yourself and ponder the question, ask yourself, who am I? What great things have I done? What do I want people to remember about me when I'm long gone?
2. I read in Inc.com, a newsletter by Geoffrey James, as he puts forth his definition of success, "If you believe success is simply making (or having) a lot of money, you

may be setting yourself up for failure." Do you believe success is simply making or having a lot of money? If so, why would that set you up for failure?

3. I hear it all the time, "Oh Johnny is a millionaire. He's so lucky." Or, "Betty has the mansion down the street. She has arrived." Or how about, "Did you see Lucy's Red Shoes?" Does your belief system say that if you have stuff you've arrived? What stuff would make you feel successful? Does it really?
4. Marla, a tall, lean girl of thirty-something moved here from India to study law in New York where she earned accolades such as landing on the Moot Court and becoming editor-in-chief of the law review at her university. She has a fabulous career in front of her but feels like a failure. Can you relate to her fear? Is it realistic? What can she do—or you do—to turn that around?
5. Don't miss the simple things like the sun coming up, or the birds singing morning melodies, or the sky in its rich-blue shades with white cloud markings throughout. Stop, and see what's around you. Really look. When was the last time you connected to the natural gifts right out your window? What did you see? How did it make you feel? If it's been a while, stop reading, and look out the window. What do you see? Look beyond the usual things like your car, or messy yard or whatever else bothers out there and find a butterfly or hear the sounds of children laughing. This is real. Connect.
6. But what's amazing to me is how many people, hundreds and thousands of boys, young men, and mature men, too, are jaw-dropping amazed at the money the named football players are making. And some feel envy. Do you look with envious eyes at the famous football player? If so, why? If not, why not?

7. But if having money is a success, and someone swindled you of all your money and belongings, then what? As the Persian proverb says, someone can always rob you of what you have, but never of what you are. The money isn't what makes you a success, but who you are. Who are you? Money can disappear in a blink of an eye. But nobody can take you away from you. What do you think of that?
8. Mark Nepo in *The Book of Awakening: Having the Life You Want by Being Present to the Life You Have* writes: "Each person is born with an unencumbered spot—free of expectations and regrets, of ambition and embarrassment, free of fear and worry—an umbilical spot of grace where we were each first touched by God." What sprouted from your unencumbered spot?
9. Many have a story of how they went through tough times and made it big. Take Oprah Winfrey, a black woman who lived poor and now is one of the richest women in the world. I read she is the first African-American female billionaire. Of course Oprah's story is tremendous, and most will never reach her status, but is her money status what you think about when you think of Miss Winfrey?
10. I spoke briefly about the possibility we get "do overs" in this life. Do we have many lives as the Miami psychiatrist Brian Weiss suggests in *Many Lives, Many Masters: the True Story of a Prominent Psychiatrist, His Young Patient, and the Past-Life Therapy That Changed Both Their Lives.* And if we do have many lives, would that make a difference in how you live your life now? Explore the possibilities.

Chapter 5

It's Never Too Late

Daydreams are doable.
The turn-on is not in scale, spectacle, or cost.
It's in the doing.
Anything you haven't done is an adventure.
Wanting to is the principal requirement.
If you can do and want to, don't not.
In short, while alive, live.
~Malcolm Forbes

As long as you have breath in you, it's not too late to become your best self. It's not too late to live more penny-wise. And for sure it's not too late to save your money and live free. *The turn-on is not in scale, spectacle, or cost. It's in the doing.* Yes, it's in the doing. Remember the old cliché, if you always do what you always did, you always get what you always got. So take it a step further: *Anything you haven't done is an adventure.*

The adventure is in the doing. The adventure is in thinking with a different mindset. The adventure is in *believing* it's never too late. Maybe you're on a fixed income and you can't work and you're living above your means. This is real, and I'm not here to fluff it up and suggest you aren't trying because surely you might be. But, think outside of the box. Try to do something different. Rent out a room, offer to babysit or house sit or maybe you can work at home as few hours a week.

This book is about releasing the obsession with money. This book is about believing all things are possible with the right mindset. This book is about a spiritual awakening—to not lift money up as the most important thing in life. This book is also about letting go of the grip so that money can flow your way. This book is about living within your means, and if you need to save for that rainy day, then try to live below your means. But most of all, remember it's never too late to change your thought process.

Is My Thought Real?

When we change our thoughts, we can change our lives. How we think often becomes our reality, even if our thoughts constitute a false belief. Often, knowing what's real and what's not real is difficult—the rational versus the irrational. Thinking that is consistent with known facts is rational thinking. Irrational thinking is thinking that is inconsistent with (or unsupported by) known facts.

Irrational thinking is thinking in which the thinker completely disregards reason and logic in favor of emotion. The irrational thinker, overwhelmed by the emotional tension of the situation, decides without mental clarity or sound reasoning. An example of an irrational thinker is Lola, who once told me, "I'm always broke and I always will be," as tears flowed down her cheeks. No, this is not a fact; the thought is based on emotion. Lola is a respected, highly sought criminal attorney who actually makes a great deal of money.

So why does Lola feel she's too late to stop worrying about not having enough money? The answer is that she obsesses over the notion she's broke. She's not. Lola spends too much money and never saves, never. Once she changes her behavior with money, she will stop the inability to save. That's the fact. That she will always be poor is an irrational, unsupported belief —unless she continues to believe this thought.

Remember the old saying, change your thoughts, change your life.

Lola challenged her irrational thinking by changing the internal conversation to, *I earn plenty of money, and it flows right into my savings, only to grow.* Or she repeated in her mind, *I'm a saver, I have plenty.* And she had plenty when she saved and lived more simply. Lola thought because she was in her fifties, she was too late to achieve the life she wanted, but soon learned it was never too late to change her relationship with money by first changing her irrational thoughts to rational thoughts.

Self-inquiry

Byron Katie, an American speaker and author, teaches a method of self-inquiry known as "The Work of Byron Katie," a four-step method for questioning our thought. The practice is best described in Byron Katie's book, *Loving What Is: Four Questions That Can Change Your Life*, which was a godsend for me in my earlier years working through my own negative thinking. The suggestions she makes are not necessarily for turning negative thoughts into positive thoughts but rather for questioning how *accurate* these thoughts might be.

The four questions posed in Byron Katie's book are:

1. Is it true?
2. Can I absolutely know it's true?
3. How do I react when I believe that thought?
4. Who would I be without the thought? Or, how would I feel if I didn't have the thought?

These are simple yet powerful questions that ask whether a thought is an accurate assessment. Often after running through the questions, we will find the thought is not correct. It comes from our unconscious minds (drunken monkeys) whispering and at times screeching false information that we're accepting as real. We need mental "reset" buttons to turn around this negative chatter. The reboot questions the statement with another, more-probing investigation, free from faulty jargon.

How do you know if your thoughts are rational or irrational? Ask yourself. Is this thought based on facts? In Lola's case, she believed she would be broke for the rest of her life. I asked her if she could answer yes to this belief based on facts. If yes, it could be rational. She answered no.

My next question to Lola was, "Does this thought that you will be broke for the rest of your life achieve your goal?"

Lola paused for a moment then whispered, "No," realizing her goal was not to be broke. She understood if she continued to believe her irrational thought that she'd be broke all the remaining days of her life, she'd never achieve her dream of saving, buying a house, and living free of money worries.

I then asked Lola an ultimate question: "Does your thought of being broke the rest of your life help you feel the way you want to feel?" Another no. She wanted to feel good about her relationship with money and the life she'd be living in the future. She didn't want to feel defeated every waking moment as she had been feeling. She wanted to be free from this obsession.

Immediately, I saw the shift in Lola's eyes to a positive acceptance of this information. Lola realized her answers were repeatedly no, hence, irrational. Lola, for the first time, grasped the difference between irrational beliefs and rational beliefs. The concept suddenly made perfect sense to her. Lola couldn't answer as a positive fact that she'd be broke all the days of her life. She also couldn't bear the thought of being broke forever, as it wouldn't meet her goals. And this negative thought wasn't helping her feel the way she wanted to *feel*—relief from worrying about money.

So "I'm always going to be broke" needs to be transformed from a negative to a positive to turn it around, Lola learned. So, the "I am broke" belief made no rational sense because Lola was a top earner. She didn't know how to live within her means, however, or perhaps below her means to save and get out of debt. She made more money than she had bills. She learned this negative thought didn't make her feel the way she wanted to feel. Her thinking was negative and sprouted more negative thoughts.

Money Doesn't Make You Rich

I know plenty of people who, by most people's standards, live in poverty, and they are the richest people I know. They see and feel and embrace everything they face in their waking moments. They go to bed with a prayer on their lips and rise with gratitude and thanks, embracing what's in store for them each day. This is living rich. If you are in a depressed mental state, remember a positive thought can change that experience. *A thought can change your feelings.*

That a thought might change a mood seems so basic, but it can. If you polled the most-watched, lift-me-up videos on social media you'll find it's of kitties and puppies, cats and dogs, and little kids. Studies reveal watching children laughing and giggling makes a person shift from a down mood to a jovial mood. Watching cute cat and dog videos, or even looking at their pictures, shifts a mood in a nanosecond.

Now what does this have to do with it's never too late to alter your relationship with money? Well, our moods make a difference. If you're depressed and feeling bad, you're going to view life through the lens of doom and gloom. But if you turn to a video showing puppies, butterflies, and children laughing and giggling, your mood will improve, leaving you feeling upbeat—like everything is going to be okay. And it is.

What is amazing is the viewers' moods lift instantly. They don't go anywhere; they don't need money or to buy that fancy pair of shoes, but they immediately embrace the joy of what they're watching. They enter into the video and become a part of it. The rich experience of connecting with nature and the moment shifts their thoughts. They change their mood without realizing it has changed. It's never too late.

In addition, live animal camera feeds equally lift people's moods. From an eagle cam, to a shark cam, to a polar bear cam, we love watching live animal feeds. Millions upon millions of people tuned in to watch April the giraffe at the Animal Adventure Park in Harpursville, New York, during her pregnancy and when she gave birth (nearly 12 million). What drives the interest? Perhaps the escape for a moment from news, politics, and virus spread, and yes the worries about money. To take a pause and connect with nature is a stress reliever —an important theme you'll find throughout this book.

Go to your nearby park or beach or woods and watch what's there for you to embrace. Look at the life before you. It's not an expense; it's an experience. As Forbes says, *if you can do and want to, then don't not.* It's all in the action. It's all in the mindset. What is standing between you and your joy? If you can do and you want to, then do it. And if you don't want to, then don't, there's always tomorrow.

But remember the last stanza of the Forbes quote; *In short, while alive, live.*

When You're Dead, It's Done

When you pass on to the other side, you enter another place. Where? Who knows for certain? But what we know is that you are no longer here. And *the daydream is no longer doable.* Remember *the turn-on is not in scale, spectacle, or cost—it's in the doing,* says Forbes. Time is passing, so slow it down by staying in the moment, and stay present.

This past year many people I know, and loved, died. And I'm sure you, the reader, faced many losses as well. These individuals passed away, along with their dreams. But many I know lived—really lived, so they can pass on their dreams to others. They didn't waste time obsessing over money and having stuff. They lived—truly lived.

And because of these losses for many of us, we've had an awakening—a realization that life is short. That life is to be lived. Now. And it's never too late to dream and to dream big. To become what you always dreamt to be at whatever level right for you.

One of my longest and dearest patients unexpectedly died this year because of medical complications. I'm certain it was because she had medical needs and postponed seeing to them because she was afraid to go to the doctors for fear of contracting the virus. Instead, she neglected her heart condition, and without medical attention it got away from her. She was zany and full of spunk and spirit. I forever imprinted her laughter and Southern sayings in my mind. I can hear her voice and feel her love for life.

I know this patient had more life to live. She had stories to tell and experiences to experience. She always waited for a weight loss or for the timing to be just right to do things she wanted to do. She always wanted to visit France and test her ability to speak French. She dreamed of going but wanted to be thinner and stronger physically. Don't wait for money or to be skinny to be young again—do it now from exactly where you are. Tomorrow is promised to no one. What are you waiting for?

Live In The Dash

My sister shared this poem, which she heard at the funeral of a family member on her son-law's side. This was a painful loss for all. The poem, *The Dash*, is a reminder that we should make the moments between birth and death count.

The Dash
by Linda Ellis

I read of a man who stood to speak at the funeral of
a friend.
He referred to the dates on the tombstone from the
beginning…to the end.
He noted that first came the date of birth, and
spoke of the following date with tears, but he said
what mattered most of all was the dash between
those years.
For that dash represents all the time they spent alive
on earth and now only those who loved them know
what that little line is worth.
For it matters not how much we own, the cars…the
house…the cash.

What matters is how we live and love and how we spend our dash.
So think about this long and hard; are there things you'd like to change? For you never know how much time is left that still can be rearranged.
To be less quick to anger and show appreciation more and love the people in our lives like we've never loved before.
If we treat each other with respect and more often wear a smile…remembering that this special dash might only last a while.
So when your eulogy is being read, with your life's actions to rehash, would you be proud of the things they say about how you lived your dash?

Copyright © 2020 Inspire Kindness, thedashpoem.com

Cemeteries are a most interesting place. I find cemeteries to be a spiritual and powerful community with many stories buried in the soil. One cemetery in Berlin, Wisconsin, always speaks to my pondering and wandering mind when I look at all the dates of my family members on my mom's side, dating all the way back to the early 1800s.

This little poem eloquently hits on living in the moment between your birth and your death. It's that time we spend alive between are birth and our death that counts.

The *Dash* was given freely, for all those who hear/read it to share—so I share with you. And if you share, please use the credit lines to give credit where credit is due.

I hope this little poem with a big punch gives you spiritual food for thought. Often we waste our days, our precious moments, being angry, irritated, and irritable. Sometimes a little poem with a punch is required to shake us out of our "I-isms" and embrace all that is around us. It's never too late.

Live In The Now

We only have this moment now to live to our fullest and love with all we got. Life really isn't about the big fancy car, or how much money we have, it's about how we live our lives. What do you want to be remembered for? It's never, ever too late to kick up your heals and really live. What you'll find is if you dig into the story of someone's success "back in the day" … or in the cemetery filled with stories, you'll find interconnected relationships filled with persistence, perseverance—and yes, even failures.

But through the tough stuff, they got back up and fought for all they were worth to travel where they arrived—the ones who dared to daydream and put their wishes into action. Their lives were not about obsessing over money, but in the doing, and becoming, and knowing it was never too late.

At the end of our journey, when we are deep in the soil, or turned to dust lies a budding of a fresh experience. As Mark Nepo writes in *The Book of Awakening: Having the Life You Want by Being Present to the Life You Have*, "There is very little difference between burying and planting. For often, we need to put dead things to rest, so that new life can grow. And further, the thing put to rest—whether it be a loved one, a dream, or a false way of seeing—becomes the fertilizer for the life about to form."

These are powerful words. I remember a lovely British man I saw years back who made a profound statement regarding endings. I had said something about a situation that was ending and how sad it was, and he burst into a million-dollar smile and said, "That was a season—everything has a season. It served its purpose." I never really had thought about that. Endings had always been tough for me, but this new insight makes a lot of sense. Everything has its season.

I never was good at goodbyes. Even when I close one house of mine to go to the other, I feel a sadness—a yearning at the end of a weekend. And here was this mega statement that it's a season. A season changes four times a year—at least for many states. In the winter, everything is ice and cold and the green leaves are gone, but soon the birds will begin chirping in spring as the babies are born, and the blossoms will bloom and the summer warmth returns—for a season. But when that summer ends, the new season of fall blossoms with the orange hues from trees of all sorts. And the blanket of leaves saturates the ground, making the scene breathtaking for all to embrace. And then there we are, cycling back to winter once again to prepare for holidays and festivities. So one ending blooms into another opening.

Nepo says, "As the well-used thing joins with the earth, the old love fertilizes the new; the broken dream fertilizes the dream yet conceived; the painful way of being that strapped us to the world fertilizes the freer inner stance about to unfold." Life itself is waiting for a birth of another opportunity. We have to clear out the old in order to bring in the new. This is sage advice for all of us to hook into.

We need to move into that phase of doing, stir up the daydreams that are doable, as it's not in the scale, spectacle, or cost. Remember, it's in the doing. Let's pave the way for something spectacular—it's never, ever too late. Think about your dash in life—what you want it to look like for you. One way to get to that place of doing and becoming is to think of measurable intentions, as revealed in Chapter 6.

Personal Inventory Questions

1. Daydreams are doable. It's not in the scale, spectacle, or cost. It's in the doing. This powerful stanza strikes a great point I'm trying to hit home in this book, and Forbes delivers it spot on. Are you waiting to make your dreams come true? What's standing in your way? Is it in the scale, spectacle, or cost? NO, often if not always, it's in the doing. What's holding you back?
2. As long as you have breath in you, you're not too late to become your best self. You're not too late to live more prudently. And for sure you're not too late to save your money and live a freer life. Are you a saver or a spender? A dreamer or a planner?
3. When we change our thoughts, we can change our lives. How we think often becomes our reality, even if the belief is false. Often, the important thing is knowing what's real and what isn't real—figuring out the rational versus the irrational. Are you able to sort through what's real and what is not? How do you know? What mind knots do you have stirring in your thoughts?
4. Irrational thinking is thinking in which the thinker completely disregards reason and logic in favor of emotion. The emotional tension of the situation overwhelms the irrational thinker so that they decide based on this. Lola's emotional tension revolved around believing she'd always be broke. What emotional tension drives your thinking?
5. I know plenty of people who live in what is poverty by most people's standards, and they're the richest people I know. Do you know people who are rich in ways besides money? What is it about being rich in life rather than money that's appealing? What doesn't appeal to you regarding rich in money?

6. That a thought can change a mood seems so basic, and it can. If you polled people on social media to find the most watched lift-me-up videos, you'll discover they are of kitties and puppies, cats and dogs, and little kids. What was the last cute video that stirred your heart? Was it an animal or kids?
7. When you pass to the other side, you enter another place. Where? Who knows for certain? But what we know is that you are no longer here. And *the daydream is no longer doable.* When you just read this, what was your first thought? Did the idea make you nervous? If so, why? What is it you aren't doing that you wish you were?
8. Cemeteries are most interesting places. I find cemeteries to be spiritual and powerful sites with many stories buried in the soil. What runs through your mind when you're at a cemetery, besides the grief you may have felt for someone you just lost? Do you look about at the other stones and markers? Stories, many stories, lie beneath the soil. What story do you want to leave for others to tell about you? Is it about money, fancy cars, or things you gained?
9. As Mark Nepo writes in *The Book of Awakening: Having the Life You Want by Being Present to the Life You Have*, "There is very little difference between burying and planting. For often, we need to put dead things to rest, so that new life can grow. And further, the thing put to rest—whether it be a loved one, a dream, or a false way of seeing—becomes the fertilizer for the life about to form." What did Mark's words mean to you?
10. The poem, *The Dash*, is a reminder that we should make the moments between birth and death count. What line in the poem hit home most for you? Why? What did it make you feel?

Chapter 6

Think Measurable Intentions

No one has ever become poor by giving.
~Anne Frank

Releasing your obsession with money doesn't mean living in poverty or that having money is a bad thing. What it means is you will no longer let money control you. And one way to accomplish this feat is to think about measurable intentions. Rather than thinking about goals to motivate you, put your attention on measurable goals with clear intentions to accomplish releasing your obsession with money.

With a specific goal in mind, you can decide what you need to do to achieve your measurable intention—and you'll know for certain if you've accomplished it or not because it's precise. And within your intentions, think about giving some of your money away. As Anne Frank says, "No one has ever become poor by giving."

When we hold on to every penny, we block the flow to return to you, a theme you'll hear throughout this book. So as you are working through your measurable intentions, plug in a plan of giving to open the valve to receiving. To start your intentions think SMART.

The acronym SMART, which stands for Specific, Measurable, Achievable, Relevant, and Time-Bound are the ingredients needed to help set intentions so you can continue staying on course with long-term goals. Within your SMART intentions, plug in a place to give, and you will receive twice-fold. Think of it like tithing.

This type of planning is NOT with grit teeth, filled with worry, but that flows along neatly and gently, guided by you. You are in control. When you're writing measurable goals, you want to work through each of the SMART terms to ensure your plan is realistic and achievable. This differs from having a doable dream. A doable dream is an idea of what you'd like, but intentional measures are putting into action the doable dream.

And you already know from the previous chapter the difference between rational and irrational beliefs. So I say dream big but dream real—and watch the formula manifest into something intentional and measurable. So your goal is an intended outcome you want to achieve, and your objectives will help you understand what needs to be done in order to achieve the intention. Then from there, you leap to the measurable aim, which is tracked with numbers and figures.

So let's work SMART, which as noted stands for Specific, Measurable, Achievable, Relevant, and Time-Bound intentions. Now reiterating: you're building specific and narrow goals for more effective planning. These goals become measurable when you define a plan that is plain and clear—that will prove to you you're making progress.

The best part is that it's YOUR plan, which means you can go back to the drawing board and reevaluate when necessary. Ask yourself, is my goal attainable?—can I reasonably accomplish my goal within a certain time frame?

And the most important question to ask is whether your goals align with your values and long-term objectives. And are your goals realistic, designed with an eagerly desired intention of achieving the success of your goal with an end-date in mind.

You can devise a solid plan with concrete and measurable goals that leave little to chance. Remember to write your goals in the most simplistic language possible while you home in on one specific outcome.

When I was in debt up to my eyeballs, I took small bites toward becoming debt free, which was my specific goal. I wasn't seeking to buy a house or car or anything of that sort. I specifically wanted to eliminate all of my debt except as required for the necessities, such as food, electric, and the basic needs to stay alive, secure, and safe.

So, how was I to put this goal of becoming debt free into action? Well, I needed a plan. And as you know I was a disciple of Dave Ramsey, so I started with the small debt first, which once paid snowballed into the next debt, which also was measurable and achievable. I intended to be out of debt in three years from start to finish, including home, cars, credit cards, and student debt. My plan worked with my values and I knew the plan was a rational one that I could master with slow and steady steps.

I knocked out the credit cards first, then the cars, and then the student loan, respectively. But at that point I needed a pause from the effort, so I granted myself a one-year break from the push and then hit it hard from the ground again, running like a banshee, and slid into debt free. My SMART worked because I worked with intention but not panic. I adopted the "slow and steady wins the race" attitude with the goal to become debt free. I was debt free in four years.

When you work with measurable intentions, you can see the light at the end of the tunnel. You're inching your way to the finish line. As long as you're moving toward your goal, you psychologically release the mental anguish of feeling as though you have a mountain to climb.

Within the process, I wore my badge of faith, believing I had that higher energy moving me along. Napoleon Hill in *Think & Grow Rich* nailed it when he penned, "FAITH is the head chemist of the mind. When faith is blended with thought, the subconscious mind instantly picks up the vibration, translates it into its spiritual equivalent, and transmits it to Infinite Intelligence, as in the case of prayer."

Every accomplishment I've ever made in this life has been with measurable intention and a *belief* it was going to happen. It's true that the subconscious mind instantly picks up the vibration, translates it into its spiritual equivalent, and transmits it to infinite intelligence—like a prayer.

The only time I had a snag was during the decades-long battle I had with binge eating disorder brought on by a food addiction. In that case, I had a mental, physical, and spiritual war going on in my head, which blocked me from any spiritual vibration. I blocked my subconscious mind from believing I could beat this addiction and live a complete life of prayer.

And if you read my first book, *Release Your Obsession with Food, Heal from the Inside Out*, you learned I had to first remove the toxic foods in order to produce the healing from the inside out. I couldn't put my mind right if my disease was roaring.

Here, we are talking about the toxic thoughts in the head rather than ingesting toxins with the foods. With the food addiction, I had a trilogy of issues to clear out of the way. But with releasing your obsession with money, you clear out the negative thoughts and tap into your faith base, and presto, the magic pops. And the magic kicks into top gear when you have the faith and the belief, combined with the measurable intention in place.

A Little Autosuggestion Please

In order to ignite a measurable intention, you need to have a belief in place that you can realize your goal. Autosuggestion is one way to change thoughts and behavior to ignite a belief in a measurable intention. Alex didn't believe in anything but gambling his way to wealth—and you know how that story ends. Well, maybe you don't.

In Alex's situation, he got in over his head trying to earn winnings to live the rich life, which soon turned into a full-blown addiction. He was riding high—so to speak. He won sizeable amounts of money—and in his search for love, he met one girl after another looking for deep pockets.

His desperation became so intense that he shifted money from his employer's accounts to toss the dice and pull the levers, and when he hit it big, he returned the money. This went okay at first. He thought of this as borrowing, not embezzling money.

The girls were swirling around, and he felt rich and important. He felt like the spotlight was on him. The casinos comped hotel rooms brought him drinks and free foods. Everyone, especially the hot chicks, wanted to be near him. He was dashing in looks, and he threw money around as if it were confetti.

Napoleon Hill says the emotions of faith, love, and sex are the most powerful of all the major positive emotions. Alex was missing faith and love. He was high on money, sex, and the hope for love. Alex needed to have faith in himself without the bells and whistles. He didn't believe he could earn enough money on his own, that he had to win it. And he didn't believe he could find love or sex without the money. This set up a vicious cycle of activity for him.

And with the casinos praising him every time he entered an establishment, being somebody fed his ego. This went on for quite some time until Alex hit a losing streak and couldn't return the money fast enough and was caught. This was when I met Alex.

Alex was a good fifty pounds over his desired weight. He ate whatever he wanted, whenever he wanted, to fill emotional deficits. And emotions feed behavior as we learned earlier when we examined rational versus irrational. Feelings propel irrational thoughts.

So, Alex had some work to do to remove his emotional attachment to money and all that he thought came with it, and replace it with something solid, manageable, and of course, measurable with intentions. He needed to implement a plan that wasn't backed by magical thinking, which is what the gambling became. His feeling was that he was being given presents, as though this were Christmas with gifts falling from the slot machine and from the quick roll of the dice. Winning the money felt real. It felt good until it didn't.

So, where does the autosuggestion fit in? First, what is this autosuggestion, and how do we plug it in? And isn't this possibly magical thinking? No, autosuggestion is a psychological technique related to the placebo effect, developed by Emile Coue in the early 20th century. It is self-induced suggestion in which individuals guide their own thoughts, feelings, or behavior.

When an improvement of symptoms is experienced, the placebo effect kicks in, despite the fact that one is using a non-active remedy. For instance, suppose one group took sugar tablets for a headache while the other group took aspirin, but neither group knew which pill was real and which was sugar. Often both the sugar (placebo) pill and the aspirin work to relieve a headache because all those treated feel faith in the treatment.

Researchers believe the placebo effect works because of an expectation the remedy will work. They observe an improvement of symptoms despite using a non-active, "look-alike" treatment. The fake treatment often can produce a very real response due to the expectations of the patient. If you expect it to work, it will.

I use this same technique with self-hypnosis, which I've been conducting with patients for nearly thirty years. I help the patient work through a list of changes they want to implement through their subconscious mind, expecting it will work to change the behavior or the thoughts. A person can do self-hypnosis on their own without a hypnotist, but I find my patients prefer the guidance of another, especially one with experience.

I've also found when working with patients that combining psychotherapy with hypnosis delivers a powerful punch toward realizing the desired outcome. Again, manifesting through thought and belief, from my view, is not magical thinking of any sort. Rather it's a way to put into motion that which one wants to create from now on.

We are creating reality-based manifestation. For example, if your dream is to be a writer, you can't simply compile a list of ideas, such as "I want to be a writer; I can see myself with a bestseller lining the shelves at Barnes & Noble; Money is flooding into my bank account." This is a good start, but the person also must have understood how to construct a sentence and how to put together information that is cohesive and entertaining and leaves the reader wanting more. Understand money doesn't just find its way into your bank account without you making this happen.

Or say your dream is to be a brain surgeon and you wish to have a load of patients and become famous for a technique you created to save lives. Outstanding! But, you can't just grab the scalpel and start digging into someone's brain. NO, complete high school, go to college and then medical school. And prior to medical school take courses that will push you forward in your dream to become a surgeon. This is a long but doable process, but not without work to prepare you to live your goal.

Now with that said, this very person can begin the autosuggestion process in high school or college to plant the seed of want and momentum. The autosuggestion can instill the confidence and drive that is needed to power through to the dream. The preparation in the mind prior to beginning the process can be nothing short of propelling the dream into reality.

So when Alex and I compiled autosuggestions revolving around the things he wanted to change, we built a list of wants. He wanted to earn money, save money, and live within his means. This was huge compared to the way he had been living. The list of changes he wanted needed positive words and sentences used repeatedly in order to change his perception. We explored in psychotherapy what he would feel like if he was debt free with no money worries and a newfound respect for money.

We know this as a self-development method used to create new, positive beliefs about one's self along with ending bad habits. In Alex's case, he believed he was nothing without the money. We needed to clear out this belief first, and Alex came to understand that money does not define him. It simply provides security.

During Alex's gambling days, he developed the dangerous habit of eating and drinking whatever he wanted, wherever he wanted. This behavior made him feel as though he'd arrived! But had he? Alex's understanding of success, stemming back to his childhood, was that if you could buy whatever you wanted, you were somebody. He had grown up in a rented apartment as an only child. His father was a waiter, and his mother cleaned houses. They didn't speak English. They had come here from Bolivia looking for the American dream.

To Alex, the American dream was to buy things his parents couldn't because of their fixed income. All too often, he had heard, "NO, Alejandro, we don't have the money." He hated hearing no, so in his mind buying whatever he wanted whenever he wanted, without hesitation, meant he'd arrived.

After we looked at the reality, he embraced the understanding that he hadn't arrived. What he thought living big meant was an illusion. He wanted to erase his Latin heritage and be American to the point he dropped the last part of his name and called himself Alex. Alex seemed right, like an important name that didn't sound as though he came from another country. That his parents spoke broken English and what they did for a living embarrassed him. He wanted something different.

Moreover, in Alex's case, we were dealing not only with this false belief system about what arriving meant in America, but also with his idea of how he was going to obtain this money to live big. Alex earned his first money by selling World's Finest Chocolate bars at school, and he had a knack for persuading kids to buy his candies. After he realized he was good at selling candy for the company and school, he decided he could do this on his own.

Alex started selling candies he bought from the store, but raised the price to make a profit. This sustained him at first, but then he found playing cards was a faster way to make money. And from cards, he went to betting on high school football games.

Soon, Alex found his way to the casino and fell for the slot machines at first, then graduated to poker. He became a full-blown gambler and was food addicted as well. As time wore on, he became more and more hooked. He began scrounging around for money to play more. Winning exhilarated him. And with each win, he became more and more excited. And with each win, others noted what he was doing. He was on fire for casinos.

Again, he thought he'd arrived! This was being rich enough to buy what he wanted and eat what he wanted and to have girls of all sorts crooning for his attention. Life was superb. He drove a fancy gold Cadillac, had expensive black suede shoes on his feet, and wore a Rolex. He bought a house resembling a governor's mansion on the corner overlooking the bay, and to go with this look, a standard-sized poodle. He was living high on life. But with the winning streak, he experienced a losing streak as well.

He was in deep trouble with the law on both a civil and criminal level. They were coming after him in a big way.

So why use autosuggestion? Well, it's one of the quickest ways to redirect the thinking from the subconscious base. We wanted to turn around Alex's faulty thinking so he might develop his measurable intentions toward the dreams he was striving for—but with a reality twist.

Now autosuggestion only works if the subject believes the ideas placed in his subconscious mind are true. Alex had to believe he could change his situation. He knew he had to regroup and admit he was at fault and own his errors. This was a tough one as he justified his behavior as being okay because he was paying back the debt. In his mind what was the harm if he borrowed and returned the money. He didn't believe he was wrong.

Now you, the reader, might scratch your head, thinking how in the world could Alex think taking colossal sums of money from his employer to the tune of $100,000 might not be a problem. He never asked permission. Nobody knew he was borrowing money over a period of years and returning it. But people have a way of convincing themselves and justifying behaviors that are inappropriate and immoral, which is what Alex did.

Let The Healing Begin

The process we underwent before we could make headway and look at the issue straight on was a long one. I asked Alex if it would be okay if his daughter Alicia siphoned money out of his wallet from time to time but always put it back until what she had taken surpassed what she could return. Would that be okay? When using an emotional question regarding his child, the truth of the matter really hit home.

Alex squirmed in his chair. Sweat sprouted on his forehead, dripping down his face to his chin, while his face turned tomato red. How this would feel if the money were his, taken by his daughter, was registering within. The twist of events made him squirm because such a situation didn't feel right. This was exactly where Alex needed to be in order to apologize and make amends for what he did with the owners of his company, regardless of whether they still would prosecute.

Once Alex could put himself out there and own his behavior, the healing began. He realized for the first time he wasn't borrowing money, but stealing it. He had no right to that money. It wasn't his, and he didn't have permission to take it, which was exactly how he responded when Alicia entered the scenario.

The thought of his daughter taking his hard-earned money made the entire situation change. He looked up at me and said, "That wouldn't be right if she went into my wallet.

Why that's stealing." And then the understanding clicked. He was stealing. And stealing is wrong.

Through autosuggestions or self-hypnosis we carved out a plan for change implementing SMART. We plugged in Specific, Measurable, Achievable, Relevant, and Time-Bound intentions. Alex sold his home and paid off his debt. He worked on abstinence from gambling of any sort and let go of foods that ignited his toxic eating. He needed years of therapy, hypnosis, and time to pay off his debt and clear his name. And then the healing came in droves.

Alex no longer has to look like the big shot with money. He realized he wasn't happy in that imaginary role. Now he lives in an authentic way. He saves money and gives money to help causes that mean something to him, like giving money toward scholarships for education for those less fortunate, particularly those coming from another country and adjusting to the American language and ways. He learned firsthand *no one has ever become poor giving* (Anne Frank). Rather the opposite happened as the more he gave, the better he felt, and the freer from debt he became.

Money has a way of coloring the reality of life sometimes, as you will see in Chapter 7, You Are Not Your Money. Money may be something we need to survive, but it is not who we are. We are so much more.

Personal Inventory Questions

1. *No one has ever become poor giving,* as Anne Frank said. Giving has a way of opening up the flow to receiving. Do you find this to be true in your life? Giving can be time, clothes, love, service, and of course money. What did you give and how did it make you feel?
2. With a specific goal in mind, you can decide what you need to do to achieve your measurable intention—and

you'll know for certain if you've accomplished it or not because it's precise. What is your measurable intention?

3. The acronym SMART, which stands for Specific, Measurable, Achievable, Relevant, and Time-Bound are the ingredients needed to help organize intentions so you can continue staying on course with long-term goals.
4. The best part of drawing up an intention is that it's YOUR plan, which means you can go back to the drawing board and reevaluate when necessary. Ask yourself, is my goal attainable—can I reasonably accomplish my goal within a certain time frame?
5. And the most important question to ask is whether your goals align with your values and long-term objectives. And are your goals realistic, designed with an eagerly desired point of achieving the success of your goal with an end-date in mind?
6. Napoleon Hill, *Think & Grow Rich*, nailed it when he penned, "FAITH is the head chemist of the mind. When faith blends with thought, the subconscious mind instantly picks up the vibration, translates it into its spiritual equivalent, and transmits it to Infinite Intelligence, as with prayer." What is your vibration? And how did it translate into its spiritual equivalent for you?
7. In Alex's situation, he got over his head trying to accumulate winnings to live the rich life, which soon turned into a full-blown addiction. He was riding high—so to speak. Do you know of anyone riding high? How did that story end? Gambling addictions are growing leaps and bounds as are the casinos offering opportunity in almost all cities.
8. Autosuggestion is a psychological technique related to the placebo effect, developed by Emile Coue in the early 20th century. It is the practice of self-induced suggestion

in which individuals guide their own thoughts, feelings, or behavior. Do you believe you could autosuggest a change of thought, belief, or even action in your own life? What would you change?

9. During Alex's gambling days, he developed a dangerous habit of eating and drinking whatever he wanted, whenever he wanted. It made him feel as though he'd arrived! But had he? Alex's understanding of success, stemming back to his childhood, was that if you could buy whatever you wanted, you were somebody. What is your belief stemming from your childhood? Has this belief been a positive or negative in your life?
10. I asked Alex if it would be okay if his daughter Alicia siphoned money out of his wallet from time to time but always put it back until it surpassed what she could return. Would that be okay? When using an emotional question regarding his child, the reality of his behavior really hit home. What emotional question would you use for a situation you might be in?

Chapter 7

You Are Not Your Money

Giving is better than receiving because giving starts the receiving process.
~Jim Rohn

Money, money, money—it seems to take on a power greater than its reality. A funny thing about money is that the more you give away, the more that flows back to you. As the great motivator Jim Rohn wrote, *Giving is better than receiving because giving starts the receiving process.* No doubt giving blocks the resistance when you turn it loose and lighten the grip. This doesn't mean spend crazily, this means be charitable.

And regarding charity, money can be a touchy subject, especially for those with a strong faith. A funny thing happens when you talk about money—people become uncomfortable, especially when money and Christianity are spoken in the same breath.

Charity is one of those things people don't want to talk about, especially if the topic points directly to the person.

This seems to be so especially when the individual is trying to be a good person and do good works, as talking about money seems to be unspiritual or maybe even unclean.

So how do we talk about giving money away when talking about money is uncomfortable? I think the answer starts with the reality that you are not your money. You and your money are not the same. You are you and what you gained is what you gained. If you dress you up hiding behind money to prove something or to be showy, you are losing sight of you. And then you become tied with the money.

The money talk is not so uncomfortable when it's not about keeping but about giving, which removes the greed attached to money. The type of giving can be uncomfortable, however. If you feel you must give out of guilt, that's not giving freely. Or, if you give to earn brownie points with God, that too is not giving freely. To give from the heart without applause or recognition is to give humbly to receive the gift of giving, no more or no less.

I've sat in many pews in church and felt bad when the preacher talked about giving money away, especially when I was broke and deep in debt. I had a friend once tell me she quit going to church because every time she went she felt the priest was manipulating her to give more—that if she didn't she was bad. To give or not to give is a choice. But when *Giving is better than receiving because giving starts the receiving process,* you open the flow.

Giving money is about you, not about guilt or what others do or what others tell you to do. When you read about in his earthly ministry and money, he had much to say throughout. One thing that comes to mind is "He who is faithful in what is least is faithful also in much; and he who is unjust in what is least is unjust also in much. Therefore, if you have not been faithful in the unrighteous mammon, who will commit to your trust the true riches?" ~Luke 16:10-11.

We often know this as the principle of little and much. In simpler terms, whoever I can trust with little, I can also trust with much, and whoever is dishonest with very little will also be dishonest with much. Julie is a perfect example that comes to mind. She's a young girl living simply with little extra money by cleaning houses, caring for children, and dog walking and dog sitting. She works in fancy homes with diamonds and piles of money lying about, and she watches children for free with people who have no money to pay her. Julie is trustworthy in the smallest of situations to the grandest—for those from the poorest to the wealthiest.

In the parable of the unjust steward, Jesus calls managing money the "least" of our responsibilities. Some believe Jesus was saying money is the first thing we need to sort out. That if we can't handle our money properly in godly ways, then we're going to have problems in all other areas of our lives. Having the money isn't the issue; the question is how you accumulate it and what you do with it—and how it plays into your overall life.

Alex, who I discussed in the previous chapter, defined his worth by his money. He wasn't trustworthy with other people's money, as he took it without permission. Nor did he handle his money winnings properly, either. He spent frivolously, without concern, perhaps because the money wasn't his to begin with. He thought of it as "borrowing" rather than stealing. He wasn't trustworthy and needed to sort out his money beliefs before he could live an authentic life.

If Not My Money, Who Am I?

So many ask this question, "If not my money, who am I?" They're placing money as their worth, which isn't really who you are. You are first your self-worth over and above your net-worth. Money is a number; it doesn't have a heartbeat.

It's a thing. You are much more than your money. You are a thinking, feeling, caring human being.

Some would argue this point. But let's go back in time. A decisive moment in U.S. financial history took place on Black Thursday, October 24th, 1929, when the United States stock market crashed. People, especially investors, soon began panicking over their financial future. One of the biggest impacts reported during this Black Thursday was that investors jumped out of the windows of their high-rise office buildings. Now this was thought later to have been a mere rumor, that in fact, scores of people were *not* leaping to their death because of the crash, but the financial devastation left many weary in its path.

What happened, however, behind 1929's building-jumping myth was that the onset of the Great Depression correlated to an increase in suicides. Based on statistics reported by John Kenneth Galbraith in *The Great Crash 1929*, the suicide rate in the United States increased from 17.0 per 100,000 people in 1929 to 21.2 in 1932 during the worst of the financial calamity.

Now of course these times must have been quite frightening for all, but to take your life or to consider taking your life because of money is even more frightening. We are not taking the money with us when we go to the land of beyond. It stays here. We are not permanently of this earth—at some point we leave behind the house, diamonds, and goods we've accumulated. The goal of this book is to find your inner worth, not your net worth.

The definition of net-worth is our total assets minus our debts. Our net worth is the value of all our non-financial and financial assets that we own as an individual or institution, minus the value of all our outstanding liabilities. That sounds cold, doesn't it?

The financial world describes your net worth as *the most important num*ber in your personal finance life. It's not about your heart or your soul or the meaning of your life. It's a number in our personal finances that we often confuse with our self-worth. Self-worth is deep with meaning. Your self-worth is the quality of being worthy of esteem or respect. To be regarded highly or favorably not by what you own or acquired but by who you are as a person.

Sadly, people compare themselves to others. And often this comparison is about who has what. And to think someone is worthy based on their clothes, cars, homes, and paychecks is absurd when we consider it. Our worthiness is not about our possessions. I think of Laura, who felt unworthy and unsuccessful because she didn't have the possessions her friends had.

Laura interacted with people well beyond her financial means. Her friends were wealthy—really wealthy. Most friends lived close to the ocean in sprawling houses with high-end cars glittering in their driveways. At the drop of a hat, they could go out to the fancy restaurants and drop five-hundred dollars for a meal without hesitation. Laura couldn't do that. Laura watched her money carefully in order to pay her bills.

But Laura wanted to be friends with them. She dreamed of being rich like they were. She believed that with money she could be worthy, too. She was insistent that this was the remedy that would bring her happiness. I reminded her often that the wages that we earn provide for our lives, but they don't define our lives. When I made these comments, she looked at me as though she wanted to hit me with a wet noodle.

Back then, Laura rolled her eyes, wrinkling her nose, waving me off to say I wasn't "with it," that I just didn't get it. She turned blood red with anger when we had these conversations, refusing to own what I suggested as truth. What was really interesting about Laura as well was that she never—and I mean never—paid her bills on time. She often needed reminding several times before she made a payment. Yet she was irate when her clientele didn't pay her. A synergy existed in this situation. If someone isn't paying their debt they send the same vibe out in terms of receiving payments.

So I brought this observation forward to discuss the possibility that maybe if she paid her debts promptly, others would pay her promptly in turn. That maybe she could open a flow of helping each other reach that place where both were getting what they wanted. During a long, quiet pause of silence, Laura thought about what I was saying. She really thought about it.

Over the next several months we talked about honoring others and honoring self. That what we put out is what we receive. And that self-love puts out opportunity to love others. That self-respect puts forth respect of others. After a while, Laura grasped the reality under what was being said and the great meaning behind this idea. She, in time, paid her bills promptly, sending lovely notes or a quick text to follow.

This was a huge turnaround for Laura. She had always neglected her bills until the person owed was deeply irate. And she was irate because nobody, it seemed, paid her on time. She was in a spin going nowhere—just dreaming to be like her rich friends. We then looked more closely at her friends and their money habits. Yes, at times they went out and spent big money, but such was actually not a daily occurrence.

Most of her friends respected their hard-earned money, spending it wisely. They held the belief system that if they saved, lived debt free, then they could enjoy a splurge from time to time. Laura wasn't doing that. She was spending long before earning and saving. Laura was only thinking about the glitz and glitter defining who her friends were. She wasn't looking at them closely.

In fact, Laura's good friend Paula was someone Laura described as a very considerate friend with self-awareness. One day when they were lunching, Paula expressed to Laura that she felt most people were on the wrong side of the track in today's world. Laura, with raised eyebrows, didn't follow what Paula was saying. Paula proceeded with the idea that people weren't living, really.

Now you can only imagine what Laura was thinking, given Paula was totally rich beyond imagination. What did she mean people weren't living, really! Living really was having money and living the life, thought Laura. Paula expressed the importance of being authentic with oneself. That money and things were not all that they're cracked up to be. Paula embraced the idea that life and purpose have so much more to them than things.

Paula, in fact, is spiritual and whole, looking for the realness in people. She is proud of the work she does helping drug addicts get clean. She charges a mere pittance and delivers tons more. "We are missing community, spirituality—that higher source," she told Laura. Laura later turned to me as she was relating the story negatively, swaying her head back and forth, clucking her tongue, saying, "What is she talking about? Paula is rich."

We looked closer at the person Paula really was. Laura had to move past the glitz and glitter to see her friend. Upon a closer look, wide eyed, she nodded, recognizing all the work Paula does in her community to help soften the drug crisis. She works tirelessly to assist the unfortunate, asking for nothing in return. Somehow Laura missed this.

She missed the fact that Paula is soulful, believing the universal self wants to be happy—that a path to bliss exists, but money is not the path. Laura missed the kindness and generosity that flowed out of Paula freely. She only saw the diamonds and fancy car but realized little of Paula's authentic self.

Paula feels the new earth is being born, that we ought let things flow and stop holding onto the belief that money is the path—that we need to have this or that. She feels the much bigger picture is about prayer, connecting to nature and community.

Laura isn't particularly a religious person, so she wasn't sure what all of this meant. Paula, too, is not religious, but she has a strong faith in a higher source. She believes in prayer, that prayer groups can change the world's intentions, as can meditation groups, especially through the authentic self. Laura and I explored ten steps towards the authentic self.

Ten Steps Toward Your Authentic Self

1. **Self-Awareness.** Self-awareness, awareness of the self, coupled with the self-being, is what makes you unique. This self-comprises thoughts, experiences, and abilities. You are only one you. Who are you? Who are you really? Know who you are. As you tap your conscious knowledge of your own character and feelings, you connect to self. Most of us walk through our days in a daze, not connected to the now—to the self. Begin this step by increasing your self-understanding of how you think within your inner world. Once you tap into your self–awareness, you are open to look at your self-worth.
2. **Self-Worth.** What is your worth? And of course your first thought might be monetary—but we are not our money, as you've learned. The self is grander than that. Self-worth defines the level of importance you place on yourself. The knee-jerk reaction to self-worth taps into the emotional outlook that determines how and what you feel about yourself, compared to how and what you

feel about other people. We derive our worth by believing we are a good person who deserves to be loved—that we make the world a better place being in it. And worth is you beginning this process by starting with you respecting you. How do you do that? Well, it's through self-acceptance…

3. **Self-Acceptance.** Self-acceptance is one of the most challenging of all because it's exactly what its label suggests: The state of complete acceptance of oneself. Whoa. This means true self-acceptance—embracing who you are right now as you are. This is a critical step because you are taking a direct look at your awareness of your strengths and weaknesses. Merriam-Webster defines self-acceptance as: The act or state of understanding and recognizing one's own abilities and limitations in each moment you're practicing self-acceptance—or you're judging yourself. When you enter the stage of harsh judgment of self often, it blocks the ability to self-love.
4. **Self-Love.** This step is to have "love of self." This is a tough step for most because to love thyself is to have regard for one's own happiness or advantage, which might look like an ego trip to vanity and selfishness. This is not the goal here of self-love. This is about having a high regard for your own well-being and happiness by taking care of your own needs and not sacrificing your well-being to please others. It's about not settling for less than you deserve.
5. **Self-Value.** Self-value regards believing in your worth, but not by comparing yourself to others. This step is more about how you act toward what you value. This value includes you, yourself, and of course others. How do you feel about yourself? How do you value others? In this step the upshot is about self-care. In self-care the implication is of intrinsic excellence or desirability. It's

not only about the grooming side, which of course is important too, but also about taking care of your psychological health along with spiritual qualities of mind and character—your moral excellence in growth and development. What are your inner thoughts, your inner dialogue? Are you kind when you are in your quiet space in your mind?

6. **Self-Esteem.** Self-esteem is a function of how we feel about ourselves—based mostly on comparison to others. We are better than some, but not as good as others. Self-esteem is what we think and feel and believe about ourselves. An artificially high self-esteem can create a sense of entitlement. The dark side of a high self-esteem is when the world does not meet an individual's entitlement needs, leaving the person feeling wronged, which can lead to retaliatory manipulation, abuse and even violence. Of course a low self-esteem has the opposite effect in that the person holds back from succeeding at school or work because they don't believe they're capable of success. The goal here is to find a healthy self-esteem in order to navigate through life with a positive, assertive attitude with a belief in the ability to accomplish goals, which is where self-confidence takes center stage.
7. **Self-Confidence**: Though we can't be good at everything, we want to be good at the things that are important to us, that add to our personal sense of self-worth overall. A lack of confidence characterizes a low self-esteem. People with low self-esteem often feel unlovable, awkward, or incompetent. Some signs of a low self-confidence are when the person is hesitant or unable to accept compliments. They worry about what others think about them. They can't decide even about the simplest of arrangements. They do not trust themselves or their

judgment. They may even blame others or make excuses for why they can't do something instead of owning their mistakes. The way to turn this around is for them first to be nice to themselves and recognize nobody is perfect. We all err and we all need some fine-tuning from time to time. Let's always focus on what we can change and get moving in a positive direction to lift ourselves up and out of the darkness.

8. **Self-Reliance.** Self-reliance is relying on one's own powers and resources rather than those of others. Not that we need to live in an island mindset, but we want to plug into the ability to sustain ourselves, not banking on what others will give us—or what we might inherit. Yes, working with community in mind in order to work together is optimal but with that said, nothing's wrong with being self-reliant. In this context, self-reliance is about being a warrior for self so that no matter what's happening, we're still standing. Self-reliance doesn't mean not helping or supporting others, because the reality is actually the opposite. Self-reliance means positioning ourselves to be a giver, because we can. When we're self-reliant, we open the door for self-appreciation, encompassing all that we are and all that we do.
9. **Self-Appreciation.** This type of appreciation is to recognize and see ourselves exactly the way we are. It's a compilation of all the previous steps, allowing for valuing ourselves for the person we've become. To walk tall and feel good about how not only we see ourselves but for how others see us. This step moves our negative understanding of self to positive, nurturing self-beliefs. Self-appreciation opens the floodgates of love to self and freely to others. If we feel good about self, we can invite good from others into our realm. This mindful

awareness of who we are allows us to remain conscious of good works for self and others. By embracing this appreciation for self, we are showing ourselves compassion and gratitude, which leads to the ultimate step ten.

10. **Self-Compassion.** This last step toward the authentic self is the kindness directed to self when we decide we are worthy. Compassion is the ability to show empathy, love, and concern to people who are in difficulty—which begins with us, ourselves. That this life we live is precious and we are deserving of all the good it offers. Self-compassion means releasing all self-criticism and the self-defeating mindset to become the best we can. We often are cruelest to ourselves, which splatters and taints the surrounding goodness. This overall self-compassion allows us to change our thoughts and create positive emotions and let the healing begin from the inside out—which is the message in all my writing. Self-compassion signifies the inner relationship with ourselves, and the desire to ease our own pain and suffering, instead of putting our own needs last. Above all else, we must guard our hearts, for everything we do flows from it. Self-compassion is the self- love and self-recognition for all that we are and all that we do. As Oprah Winfrey says, "When you undervalue what you do, the world will undervalue who you are."

Laura now values her worth. That said, we are now ready to move into Part II, the realignment phase beginning with the psychology behind money.

Personal Inventory Questions

1. As the great motivator Jim Rohn wrote, *Giving is better than receiving because giving starts the receiving process.* No doubt

it unlocks the resistance when we turn it loose and lighten the grip. Do you find giving is better than receiving? What does giving starts the receiving process for you?

2. A funny thing happens when we talk about money—people become uncomfortable, especially when speaking of money and Christianity in the same breath. What happens to you when you mix money and your faith? Does it make you uncomfortable? If so, why? If not, why not?
3. When you think in the terms of the principle of little and much, what reminders pop into view for you? In simple terms, whoever we can trust with very little we can also trust with much, and whoever is dishonest with very little will also be dishonest with much. Does this concept resonate as a positive or negative emotion with you?
4. In the parable of the unjust steward, Jesus calls managing money the "least" of our responsibilities. Some believe Jesus was saying money is the first thing we need to get sorted. Is your money sorted? Where do you place money in the line of importance?
5. So many ask this question, "If not my money, who am I?" They consider money as their worth, which is not really who we are. You are first your self-worth over and above your net-worth. So who are you without your money identity? What is your self-worth?
6. In order to dig deep into your self-worth, you need to plug into your self-awareness. Self-awareness is awareness of the self, which coupled with the self-being, is what makes you unique. This self-comprises thoughts, experiences, and abilities. There is only one you. What awareness about yourself are you most connected to? Do you find discomfort looking closer into your self—your being side of you?

7. Take Laura, who felt unworthy and unsuccessful because she didn't have the possessions her friends had. Laura interacted with people who enjoyed life well beyond her financial means. Her friends were wealthy—really wealthy. Most lived close to the ocean in sprawling houses with high-end cars glittering in their driveways. Do your wealthier friends make you feel less-than? What about those who are less privileged than you? How do you work between the two spectrums?
8. Paula and Laura engaged in a discussion on the realness of people over lunch one day. Paula expressed the importance of being authentic in expressing the self. That money and things were not all that they're cracked up to be. Laura wondered, *What does Paula mean people aren't living in a real way! Real is having money and living the life.* Paula was spiritually embracing that life and our purpose is so much more than things. How would it strike you if your wealthiest friend made such comments, while you were striving to keep up with those who have more?
9. The ten steps toward your authentic self-explores the idea of self-reliance, a touchy topic to consider when also embracing your spiritual self. Self-reliance signifies relying on one's own powers and resources rather than those of others. Not that we need to live in an island mindset, but self-reliance means plugging into the ability to sustain ourselves, not banking on what others will give us—or what we might inherit. What makes you self-reliant?
10. This ultimate step ten, self-compassion, moves toward the authentic self and consists of the kindness directed to self when we decide we are worthy. Are you worthy? Do you embrace self-compassion?

Part II

Realignment

Chapter 8

The Psychology Behind Money

Poverty just like happiness
is primarily a state of mind.
Giving someone money
will not make him or her rich,
though it will make YOU feel rich.
To help someone get rich,
simply help them become more conscious.
~Soren Lauritzen, the Personal Development Guy

To help someone get rich, simply help them become more conscious. Being conscious is the key to staying present—to staying aware in the moment. Often, as noted throughout these pages, becoming numb walking through life, missing opportunities, is easy. And as an addiction psychologist and a professor teaching psychology for many years, I find our personal psychology is the root of all our thoughts and behaviors. And within our psychology, often the nemesis behind *our stuck* is fear.

What is psychology? And how does it fit into money and releasing our obsessions? Psychology is the science of mind and behavior. According to Merriam-Webster, psychology is the mental or behavioral characteristics typical of an individual or group, or as a particular form of behavior, may be characteristics typical of a mob. So, how we think and how we behave is critical to releasing the obsession with money. Often, individuals follow a group-think or their family's behavior as it relates to money.

The major reason I wrote this book about how to release the obsession with money is that millions of men and women are paralyzed with the fear of poverty. And, of course, when that fear is looming overhead, it can crush the spirit and cripple our ability to move forward. The fear induces desperation rooted in fear of criticism and inferiority, among other types of suffering, which can lead to the obsession.

As I researched the psychology behind money, I was astounded to learn Morgan Housel, author of *The Psychology of Money: Timeless Lessons on Wealth, Greed, and Happiness,* shared many of my thoughts. He points out, "People from different generations, raised by different parents who earned different incomes and held different values, in different parts of the world, born into different economies, experiencing different job markets with different incentives and different degrees of luck, learn very different lessons." This hits the mark for sure—but to release the obsession with money requires a new relationship with money to see the powerful change, regardless of differences, though they truly exist.

My father was on the path to building his wealth at a very young age. He came from a family that emigrated from Italy to America with very little money. My Grandfather Nonno wasn't wealthy by any means, nor was he educated, and he could barely speak English. He took whatever jobs came his way, some not always in tune with the law—like making alcohol.

Yes, Grandpa was a bootlegger—he illegally worked his own "liquor stills" in his basement, supplying anyone who had money to pay for the moonshine during his early years in America in the 1920s. My grandfather, consequently, spent time in jail. Bootlegging surged in popularity once Prohibition spread nationwide in the United States, with the 18th Amendment taking effect in early 1920.

Though my grandfather dipped into some sketchy areas to make money, he simultaneously was a devout Catholic living life in prayer. This division in his lifestyle seems a surprising dichotomy when you ponder it at face value, but if I step back and consider, here was a man who didn't speak English well and wanted to provide for his family. Yet, he had a faith in God to guide his steps.

And my grandfather passed this strong faith down to his three children. He also passed down the importance of education and a strong work ethic. Nonno wasn't afraid to work with his hands doing physical labor, but he didn't want that for his children. He wanted a better way of life for them. He pushed music, and my father became an accomplished accordion player, then pianist, eventually opening a chain of music stores.

So, yes, we all do come from different walks of life with our own stories of trials and tribulations as to how we've developed our belief systems around money. Though I don't have the financial expertise of Mr. Housel, I do share many of the same basic understandings of acquiring wealth as I teach how to release the obsession. As an addiction psychologist, I look not only at obsessions, but try to understand where addiction and compulsion fit into the mix.

What Are Obsessions?

Many of us who are filled with obsessions of some sort become lost in the twists and turns between obsessions, compulsions, and addictions. These illnesses are so twisted that they connect. And what are these pesky obsessions? Obsessions are thoughts, images, or ideas that won't go away. They are unwanted and may well cause extreme distress.

For sure, everyone has unusual or even disturbing thoughts that pop up from time to time, but this is about a mesmerizing obsession that won't let up—and it takes over and interferes with your daily life.

Our obsessions, most often not desired or needed, seem to pop up, regardless. They consist of intrusive thoughts, images, or urges that can trigger intensely upsetting feelings. Often the obsessions connected to compulsions result in repetitive behaviors or thoughts that a person engages in to neutralize, counteract, or make their obsessions go away.

What Is Your Obsession?

So many of us are saddled with an obsession over something, or perhaps someone. When I first began my recovery from my obsession with food, I realized I had a food addiction, which led me to binge eat, which constituted a long haul of hard days.

That crazy obsession ride I engaged in brought me to earn my master's degree in mental health and open a practice intending to help others suffering as I did. But that was not enough for me, so I earned a doctorate (PhD) in addictions, with the focus on food at first. But this area of concentration morphed into my studying a range of obsessions. I saw with patients that so many struggled over different compulsions.

I found, first with myself and then with others, the more we try to ignore or stop our obsessions, that effort only increases our distress and anxiety. What happens then is that the discomfort drives the person to perform compulsive acts to ease their stress. Despite efforts to ignore or disperse bothersome thoughts or urges, they keep coming back. They are pesky grips that won't release—at least not until we learn how to let them go. Until a resolution is affected, the obsessions often turn into ritualistic behavior—hence, the vicious cycle of obsessive-compulsive disorder (OCD).

Obsessive-compulsive disorders center on certain themes, for example, an excessive fear of gaining weight, a fear of being contaminated by germs, or a focus on the phone (my next book to launch in the fall). And to ease the person's fear, they diet or wash their hands. Let the obsessions begin…

Addiction or Obsession or a Blend?

Addictions are another form of an obsession. Or are they the same form? The major difference between an obsession and an addiction is the question of pleasure. I believe that an obsession usually refers to compulsive behaviors or streams of thoughts that the individual feels driven to perform or to follow mentally. Even though we might know engaging in this behavior or thought pattern won't benefit us, or may even cause suffering, we're compelled along that track, anyway. But with an addiction, the addict is seeking pleasure—a relief from pain of some sort.

Deciphering the difference is a slippery slope. Often a person thinks they are suffering from an obsession when they have an addiction, and vice versa. The lines between the two blur. When obsessing, the individual finds that the ritualistic routine becomes part of everyday life, while when one is addicted, that person never feels satisfied unless using the substance or engaging in the behavior (such as some sexual act).

Sorting through the two is tough as they often coexist together—kind of like the chicken or the egg argument. Rather than focus on the ritual, as the obsessive will, the substance abuser (addict) is seeking a mental escape from reality. In my practice, however, I find obsessive and addictive behaviors co-mingle regularly.

I've written about these experiences. In fact, I opened a website, Weightcontroltherapy.com, to help people remove their obsession with dieting and their weight, along with visitors who may be addicted to food. To see the issue as weight control, whether it's weight up or weight down or a compulsion or addiction, was and is my quest. The goal I have in mind with these sufferers is for them to stabilize and move away from the obsession—or addiction—or both.

But of course the obsessions don't stop with relief from food addiction, dieting, or mind chatter. No, they continue to morph into other areas. At first on my website, I carved out different recipes and content on food addiction and binge eating disorder. But again, I realized those who experience some kind of food addiction or eating disorder also are caught by other obsessions.

At this point I wrote books to address obsessions and addictions from different angles. Obsessions come in multiple packaging. Some obsessives suffer from OCD (obsessive-compulsive disorder) while others engage in full-blown drug addictions. Fear drives obsessions, but I found they all could cross into each other.

I saw patients obsessing over their body parts (dysmorphia) or aging or fear of becoming an adult. At this point I birthed my series on obsessions. All my books revolve around obsessions, and all circle back to body image or weight issues of some sort—coming from that sense of not being good enough. And this book is no different. So many obsess over money, which stems most likely from other obsessions.

One obsession often transforms into another. Patients may come to me for gambling addictions, but then as we look more closely, we find weight obsessions and money obsessions, along with aging obsessions, and other compulsions or rituals taking up residence in their heads and behaviors.

I have found that one obsession is just an opening to another obsession, which is why we need to release our obsessions, which is the major theme of every single book I write and every single blog I post. Clinging to an obsession blocks you from your authentic you. It keeps you in the grip of grasping for something that is not real—not real in the sense of who you are and what's important.

We all obsess over something. **What is your obsession?** Maybe you're a germaphobe, and squeamish about catching something. Of course, with the coronavirus, fears of becoming sick popped up for many. Please explore your obsession—you're in good company. What are your recycling thoughts taking up residence in your head? Tap into them and you'll find your obsession.

What Is Your Mindset?

If you're seeking riches and you live in America, the land of opportunity, you are well on your way. "America provides all the freedom and all the opportunity to accumulate riches that any honest person may require," says Napoleon Hill in *Think & Grow Rich.* If you're reading this book, and you live in America, you can create riches within your means.

Mr. Hill remarks that "America is a country whose citizens are so rich that women, alone, spend more than half-a-million dollars annually for lipstick, rouge, and other cosmetics." Author Hill pointed this out in the 1960s—so what is the amount spent nowadays? Today, we live in a country where little kids, and I mean *little kids,* are walking around with smartphones, iPads and other high-tech items to play very expensive games.

And women (men too) are spending loads of money on cosmetic surgeries and products to look young, fresh, and appealing to the onlookers. Hey, we have to, with social media competitions baked into every post. Yes, we have far surpassed money spent in the 1960s on lipstick, rouge, and other cosmetics by the millions, and more probably billions.

So in this land of abundance, we can change our thoughts to change our lives, allowing the floodgates of money to flow. How? Well, fine-tune your mindset. Mindset, from the context of this book—and as it relates to psychology—refers to your belief system, regarding whether you understand your intelligence and natural abilities to be fixed or changeable traits. If you believe your capacity for learning, reasoning, comprehending, and similar forms of mental activity are set in stone, then that mindset will prevent you from moving into the realm of change.

As the skilled master in motivational speaking, Soren Lauritzen, the Personal Development Guy, cleverly states, *Poverty, just like happiness, is primarily a state of mind. Giving someone money will not make him or her rich, though it will make YOU feel rich. To help someone get rich, simply help them become more conscious.* Again, if YOU believe your capacity for learning, reasoning, comprehending, and similar forms of mental activity are set in stone, that mindset will block you from change.

But if, instead, you're open to learning alternative ways of seeing the world through a different mindset, you will stir up and manifest an understanding that all things are possible. This is a shift in thinking—and the concept is not new by any means; the idea has been around for eons, only growing in popularity. Do a Google search on "the power of the mind," "mindset," and "manifesting," and you'll find book after book, blog after blog, along with programs and videos teaching you how to transform your thoughts.

The message is we ALL can change the way we think—wanting to change your belief system from a negative "I can't have" to a positive "all things are possible" mindset, you are well on your way.

In order to plug into this positive mindset then, you want to set a plan of action to go with your intended mindset. You have nothing to stop you, or anyone else, from engaging in any portion of the effort necessary to move into the land of opportunity. The only one stopping you is you.

Yes, perhaps you are in a pickle at the moment, with debt piled high. Or maybe you don't have a job or you're scared. I could write an entire book on how fears block successes, but I'll save that for a later date.

No matter where you are financially, you can dig your way out. I was talking to Earnest, whom I'm working with about this very topic. One day, he surprised me when he shared a personal story about his father. Earnest is very closed off concerning his personal life, but on this day he let spill the lessons he'd learned from his father, Jeddah.

Earnest didn't have a close relationship with his father. Jeddah left all eight of his children when they were under seven—one set of twin boys, followed by three girls, two more boys, and Mom with baby Earnest in her belly. These were trying times. Earnest was the unborn baby, so he had no recollection of a father figure in the household and was subject to hand-me-downs all of his childhood.

But though his dad never gave a monthly contribution of money to the family, Jeddah did show up when a serious problem arose and paid whatever the cost.

When Earnest's dad was elderly and frail, he spent more time with his grown kids, particularly Earnest. The neighbors knew Jeddah as the garbage man. He wore worn baggy pants, sneakers with holes in them, and a crumpled black t-shirt. This was his uniform. People felt sorry for Jeddah as he collected their junk with his old pickup truck that burped and gasped as it chugged along, leaving a trail of smoke.

Earnest always thought of his dad as this poor guy gathering garbage, but in his later years, he discovered a shocking surprise. His father was far from broke. When he went home—away from his pickup route—he changed into an expensive pair of slacks, crisp shirt tucked in and held in place by an alligator-leather belt and snake-leather shoes. He wore a large gold nugget ring, a thick gold chain, and an expensive classic gold watch.

Earnest hadn't known Dad lived a double life. Now, where does mindset fit into all of this? Well, Jeddah always told his kids if they saved, they could have whatever they wanted in life. They didn't understand because they saw Dad as this smelly, unshaven guy driving a dilapidated old truck.

The secret sauce was that Jeddah picked up junk—dryers, refrigerators, old cars—you name it. He then took his stash home and repaired the pieces. He painted, restored, and otherwise fixed everything he picked up. And then he sold his "junk" for top dollar. Every penny he made, he saved except for basic living expenses and when he bailed his kids out from this problem or that. Earnest recalled Dad calling him, "a no-good bum." Jeddah thought Earnest was lazy and told him so.

But in those later years as they bonded, Earnest saw his dad through fresh eyes. He realized this was the land of opportunity, as his dad had always told him. Jeddah explained to Earnest that you have to get creative in your way of earning, and then save. He made it all sound so simple, but

Earnest didn't want to be his dad driving in an old truck wearing smelly clothes. He wanted the best and spent everything he made, only to wind up broke. He hungered for new things because he always had the hand-me-downs and felt poor.

Yet once Earnest realized his dad wasn't poor but in fact quite wealthy, his eyes opened to life's possibilities. He wanted what his dad had—the mindset to save money so you have security for those times when you really need it. This was how the father could help the family during seriously dire times.

Earnest often found himself in horrible scrapes with the law and was in and out of jail for crimes he swears he didn't commit. Jeddah always bailed him out. Now, Earnest lives his father's mindset to save money to have security for those times when he, or his kids, really need it. He lives simple to live rich.

Crippled Independence

I recall many years ago when my son Benjamin was a few years old. I was broke. I was single. And I had debt piled up to the ceiling along with a mortgage that was four months behind. My good friend Helene and I were sitting on the front porch, trying to figure out how we could make some money. For a nanosecond we thought we could be bug exterminators. We lived in South Florida, and bugs were plentiful. We could have started a business, two young women killing bugs, and it would have been a hit. Of course, when we gave the idea a deeper thought, it was a no go. We both hated bugs and chemicals and dirty hands. So, on we went to sell real estate for a few years.

Poverty, just like happiness, is primarily a state of mind. Helene and I felt poor—and perhaps part of this was true, as we both were seeking independence. We both wanted to know we could make ends meet, whether married or single. We both had little children and no career to support our expenses on our own, independently. I learned in life, watching my mom and her good friend Miah (not her real name) leaning on their husbands to survive financially, that it crippled their independence.

One beautiful breezy Wisconsin summer, a group of us piled in my sister's boat taking a slow cruise around Silver Lake, visiting and looking at the landscape. It was a warm summer evening; the stars were twinkling with meteorites shooting through the sky. My toddler son was sitting on my lap wearing a bright-orange life jacket, swinging his legs, pointing up to the sky as each meteorite swept across the sky, and then disappearing.

My mom was along for the ride and talked about "poor Miah," and how she was struggling financially since she had left her husband. Miah was a best friend who spent much of her time with my mom, as she was adjusting to her single life.

I leaned forward with an incredulous shock that she was concerned about "poor" Miah, who was not taking in enough alimony since she'd left her husband. I was broke, no alimony, no child support, a mortgage four months behind, and Mom worried about poor Miah who had no children, a teaching degree, and a home that wasn't in arrears. Oye! At that very second, I realized the state of mind was the key to change. If I believed I was "poor" Lisa, destitute Lisa, I would never climb out from under my rock. I didn't have degrees, and selling real estate wasn't really my cup of tea, so I had a long haul ahead of me but *poverty just like happiness is primarily a state of mind.* I chose happy and erased poverty from my thought process—and change took hold.

The lesson I learned is that I am responsible for myself. I learned not to depend on another, that I could make it psychologically, financially, spiritually, and in how I needed to be on the right path. Back in that summer of 1991 in the boat I had my "ah ha" moment, and I became my cheerleader. As you move on to Chapter 9, you will become your own cheerleader too.

Personal Inventory Questions

1. Consciousness is the key to staying present—to stay aware in the moment. Often as noted throughout these pages becoming numb walking through life, missing opportunities, is easy. What opportunities are you missing?
2. As I researched the psychology behind money, I was astounded to learn that Morgan Housel, author of *The Psychology of Money: Timeless Lessons on Wealth, Greed, and Happiness,* shared many of my thoughts on money. He points out, "People from different generations, raised by different parents who earned different incomes and held different values, in different parts of the world, born into different economies, experiencing different job markets with different incentives and different degrees of luck, learn very different lessons." What is your "different" and how has it affected your psyche as it relates to money?
3. The major reason I wrote this book about how to release the obsession with money is the fact that millions of men and women are paralyzed with the fear of poverty. And of course, when that fear is looming overhead, it can crush the spirit and cripple our ability to move forward. Are you paralyzed with the fear of poverty? If so, when did this start?
4. My Grandfather Nonno wasn't wealthy by any means, nor was he educated, and he could barely speak English. He took whatever jobs came his way, some not always inside the law—like making alcohol. What lessons did

you learn from your grandparents about money? Were they moral lessons or on the edge of illegal?

5. Many of us are filled with obsessions of some sort, so that often the meaning of an obsession gets lost in the twists and turns between obsessions, compulsions, and addictions. The differences are so convoluted, in fact, that they connect. What are these pesky obsessions? Obsessions are thoughts, images, or ideas that won't go away. They are unwanted and cause extreme distress. What are your obsessions? Do you have constant thoughts that won't go away? How are these thoughts standing in your way?
6. I found one obsession is just an opening to another obsession, which is why we need to release our obsessions. That's the major theme of every single book I write and every single blog I post. If you obsess over something now, I'm certain you obsessed over other things before this newest obsession. Do you have a long string of obsessions? List them and look closely at how one connects with another, and how they began and how they faded, you'll learn much about yourself.
7. As Napoleon Hill points out, "America is a country whose citizens are so rich that women, alone, spend more than half-a-million dollars annually for lipstick, rouge, and cosmetics." Imagine, author Hill noted this in the 1960s, so what is the amount spent to beautify the fairer gender now? How much money do you spend primping and for non-necessities? Do you find you overindulge, or do you find you go the opposite way and spend very little on yourself?
8. The story about Earnest and his father, Jeddah, is quite interesting. Earnest always thought of his dad as this poor guy gathering garbage, but in later years, he discovered a shocking surprise. His father was far from

broke. When he went home—a distance from his pickup route—he changed into an expensive pair of slacks, crisp shirt tucked in, and held in place by an alligator-leather belt, and snake-leather shoes. What were your thoughts when you read about this father/son duo? Did it make you angry?

9. In those later years, as the two bonded, Earnest saw his dad through fresh eyes. He realized this was the land of opportunity, as his dad always told him. He told Earnest, you have to get creative in your ways of earning and then save. He made it all sound so simple, but Earnest didn't want to be his dad driving in an old truck wearing smelly clothes. Do we have to live poorly to become rich? Do you live poor, rich, or somewhere in between?
10. My good friend Helene and I felt poor—and perhaps part of this was true, as we both were seeking independence in those early years of being thirty-something. We both wanted to know we could meet our expenses, whether married or single. We both had little children and no career to support us on our own, independently. Are you independent? Is that important to you? What does independence mean to you?

Chapter 9

Are You Your Own Cheerleader?

One person with a belief
is equal to a force of ninety-nine with only interests.
~John Stuart Mill

What do you believe? Do you believe you will always obsess over money without making headway in a positive direction? Do you only have a passing interest in building your financial wealth? How you answer these questions are the building blocks toward your financial freedom. Financial freedom is your release from the obsession. It offers a lessening of the grip, opening up the flow toward riches within your reach.

Riches Are Within Your Reach

Sometimes, when life is hard, and it knocks you down, and you struggle to meet your needs with the basics, believing riches are within your reach seems impossible. But they are.

Plenty of people will tell you their rags-to-riches stories—and possibly you are (or will be) one of them.

Some rags-to-riches individuals lose the riches only to gain them back again. A wise person once told me that if you earn your money once, and lose it, you can earn it again, and again, and again. And I've heard many stories about this too. So where do you fit in the rags-to-riches saga? Are you in the rags, or are you in the riches? I've traveled between both spheres a few times myself and know firsthand you can climb out of the rough patch, if you *believe* you can.

Robert Collier, in his *Riches Within Your Reach*, suggests, "Visualize this thing that you want. See it, feel it, believe in it. Make your mental blueprint and build."

If you believe all things are possible, then fulfilling this want is possible too. Often our negative naysayer mind-chatter enters in doubts. Doubts get in the way and cancel out your belief. I say, add to the seeing, feeling, and believing with the senses of taste, touch, and hearing. Tap into all of your five senses, then with the *believing,* hint on the sixth sense, which connects to our conscious mind first, followed by the subconscious mind. Your extra sense, the sixth, is there for a reason.

The sixth sense is the sense that is always ready to be activated—we perceive via this sense that something is about to happen, call it a hunch, an instinct, or maybe an intuition. But is this sixth sense one of those woo-woo (supernatural) ideas? NO. Lets unpack it and understand it. First, let's look at how the conscious information travels to the unconscious—and then we'll add in the aspect of belief so you can ignite the cheerleader in you.

We all have stored facts and impressions in the deep wells of our subconscious mind. This information comes from our conscious minds. Perhaps you saw something as a small child and filed the incident in the subconscious. I remember when I was a small child my sister Mickey let me tag along with her when she went to the drugstore to pick up a prescription for our mother. Funny, but you couldn't have little kids pick up prescriptions today, let alone walk a long distance that has them crossing a major highway. We crossed a very busy street from the sidewalk in the center of the road—today known as jay-walking. I only looked to my right, not my left. Cars were whizzing by as they moved with the traffic.

A harsh, shrill sound was followed by blood-curdling screams (mine and Mickey's) as an olive-green car came to a screeching stop inches from running over my toes, my face plastered on his passenger door. Had my sister not pulled me back at the same time as the car stopped, I'd not be writing this. I'd be somewhere in the beyond, or worse, in a wheelchair for life.

I smelled the rubber hitting the road. I heard the screech of the tires. I felt the cold metal of the green car. It tapped me into the four senses of smell, sight, hearing, and touch, skipping taste. *And I never ever forgot about it.* To date, I always, with some angst, look both ways when I cross a busy street. I have a slight panic within me that I won't make it to the other side before the light changes.

Just thinking about it now raises my heartbeat, increases my breathing, and leaves me feeling uncomfortable. Why? Because I stored these sensations into my subconscious mind from my conscious mind on that chilly spring morning as we made our way to the drugstore.

As we move through the present, our senses remind us of situations of the past. Maybe you tasted your grandmother's homemade blueberry pie that was baking for an hour, emitting the fresh aroma of blueberries and buttery crust. Perhaps that was a very safe time in your life, and every time you taste, see, or smell a similar pie, you're taken back in time to a fond memory, leaving you giddy with joy.

These very sense impressions we've stored are what bubble up when we need them—and sometimes when we don't. We use these senses to understand the inner and outer world we live in. Using these past impressions, we make sense out of the senseless. Add to that thought that in order to see it, feel it, along with taste it, touch it, and hear it, to believe it, you must become your personal advocate, *the cheerleader*.

Once you mix your *belief* with your cheering, you can believe all things are possible. But *you* do it; nobody else is going to do it for you. Nobody. You are the believer in self, and you are the earner and saver to build your wealth. The process isn't about obsessing over it, but about releasing the obsession and letting the money pour in.

Perhaps you're bubbling over with anger as you're reading this because your mortgage is behind, the gas tank in your automobile is empty, and you have only two dollars and some change in your wallet.

And perhaps you have no clue what you'll do to make your way to an interview, because you don't have a job, or the right clothes, and your two-year-old is looking up at you with wondering eyes, trying to read your face of fear. I get it. I was that person, really.

Okay, maybe you're thinking about the money Sally inherited, and how she's enjoying the riches within her reach. Yes, lucky Sally was handed a break. But what Sally does with this lucky financial break is more telling. She could blow her good fortune in a nanosecond, thinking further riches will fall from the tree of inheritance. (But then will they?)

You may inherit some money, and that's well and good, but that's not the same thing as earning it yourself. And often it slips through your hands like sand between the fingers when you don't make your personal mental blueprint, and build. Think about making this your mission, not relying on someone else. If someone else leaves you money, outstanding. But don't sit around expecting it because then you miss living in the moment.

Invest In YOU

When you invest in *you,* the change happens. In Chapter 6, through autosuggestion, and in Chapter 8, mindset, we see that both key ingredients work through the changes using the subconscious mind. What are you suggesting to yourself? Recently, I got off a tele-health session with a patient who said she was sick, and that she was *always* going to be sick. Now that is autosuggestion you don't want. Why? Because you *can* make yourself sick if you *believe* you will be sick.

And as I'm writing this, we are barely coming out of the coronavirus pandemic, during which time all of us have been a bit on edge, wondering if we're going to get this thing. Inevitably, this patient I'm telling you about became sick—and ended up in the hospital for months. And her illness wasn't Covid.

Napoleon Hill defines autosuggestion as a term that applies to all suggestions and all self-administered stimuli that reach one's mind through the five senses. Autosuggestion is self-suggestion. And to set self-suggestion, you change your mindset into the belief that you can achieve the thing that you want (hopefully not the thing that you don't want). That's why I say be your own cheerleader to attain your dream. *One person with a belief is equal to ninety-nine with only interest.*

And where does this belief come from? Is it part of the sixth sense? What do I mean by belief, or a hint of the sixth sense? The sixth sense I'm referring to is about trusting your feelings, perceptions, and intuitions, even when you can't figure out with scientific certainty how you sense them. The sixth sense is a knowing. It's more than a hunch; it's an internal knowing.

A knowing, in this case, that when you do your part, earning, spending carefully, and saving, the rest will work itself out. Knowing this comes from your belief within, a faith within you. I'm not referring to extrasensory perception, or the "third eye" as the sixth sense, which is a topic for another time. This is a sense that you will build your wealth without the obsession, fear, or internal doubt.

Your belief in your ability to change your life is the key to achieving your goal. Collier speaks to this inner ability for change. Gems fill line after line, page after page, in *Riches Within Your Reach: The Law of the Higher Potential*, but the one that opened my eyes and toned down my inner negative rant was: "In every man there is a Seed of Life, with infinite power to draw to itself whatever it conceives to be necessary to its expression. It doesn't matter who you are, what your environment or education or advantages; the Seed of Life in you has the same power for good."

You have the Seed just as I have the Seed as the guy down the block has the Seed. What is this Seed? Some see the Seed as God, while others see it as the Universe, and maybe you see it as your Higher Source within you. Whatever or however you see it, it's for you to see, feel, hear, smell, taste—and believe. You and you alone make this happen. What you do with the seed is the ingredient behind the power of change.

Collier's book came to me when I was only a kid and didn't understand what it meant. I speak to this at great length in my book, *Release Your Obsession with Diet Chatter: Heal from the Inside Out* so I won't repeat the story here. What I can tell you is that through no accident at all, this book ended up in my collection as one of the most important books I own—

it has guided me across much of my journey through life to date.

But what I will repeat is I had that book from my early teens to this very day and didn't grasp the meaning until I was well into my forties. The old truism that when the student is ready, the teacher will appear was my actual experience. The book was my teacher, even if for many years I wasn't ready, though I tried and tried and tried again to understand one of the most powerful books I've ever read in my life.

In time, I realized that the only one who would make my life into a life with purpose was me, that I had the seed of opportunity within—just as you do. I had to kick-start my seed by becoming my own cheering squad. Attaining my dream wouldn't have happened just by wishing upon a star. I had to let the seed fester in my conscious mind first, then send the message to my subconscious mind.

Just Click Your Heels

Simply click your heels three times and repeat, "I can make my wishes come true," just like Dorothy in *The Wizard of Oz*. Well, maybe you can, but clicking her heels wasn't really what made Dorothy's objective come to life.

The Wizard of Oz is a 1939 American musical fantasy film produced by Metro-Goldwyn-Mayer. I view it as one of the greatest films of all time—a commercially successful adaptation of L. Frank Baum's 1900 children's fantasy novel.

As you no doubt recall, the story chronicles the adventures of a teenage farm girl named Dorothy in the magical, vibrant Land of Oz after a cyclone swept her and her pet dog, Toto, from their Kansas home.

On her journey to find her way back home, Dorothy meets up with a couple of characters as they follow the Yellow Brick Road toward the Emerald City to meet the Wizard. In route, Dorothy and Toto meet a Scarecrow who needs a brain, a Tin Man missing a heart, and a Cowardly Lion who wants courage.

All four are hopeful each need will be filled once they arrive in Emerald City and meet the Great Oz, but of course, as in life, they must first contend with the Wicked Witch of the West who is out to revenge herself on Dorothy after the girl accidentally killed the witch's sister, the Wicked Witch of the East.

Isn't life just like that, presenting us with one obstacle after another? And maybe for you it's "if only I had money," rather than if I only had a heart, brain, or courage, or in Dorothy's case, wanting to find her way home. All four really didn't need the Wizard to grant their wishes, but they *believed* they did. They depended on another rather than their own God-given gifts within to obtain what they needed. They missed cheering for their personal wants.

This is the reason your mindset is so crucial to the outcome of your opportunities. Think of it as planting the seed in your conscious mind and then it sprouts in your subconscious mind, working behind the scenes. Think of it as the Wizard standing behind a curtain orchestrating the delivering of what his visitors wanted.

Toward the end of this tale, the foursome make their way to the Wizard, who they believe will make their wishes come true. At the end, Dorothy clicks her heels and repeats, "There's no place like home," three times and voila, soon enough she's back home in Kansas.

What Dorothy learns at the end of the story is that she had it all along within, that she didn't need the Wizard to make her wish come true. You don't need the character Oz behind the curtain either; you just need to adjust your mindset and cheer for yourself. All you need are the five senses to activate your autosuggestion and restructure your mindset. Tap into your sight, smell, touch, hearing, and taste, and of course that sixth sense and believe, which is what you're working on right now with your subconscious mind awakening the seed you planted in the conscious mind.

Each of the five senses teaches us something about an item, person, place, or whatever that is near us. We tap into these senses to understand our world. We have a memory bank where all our experiences are filed for later use when we need them.

You may remember Aunt Nancy by the scent of her perfume you just smelled while strolling through the mall. Or when I look up in the night sky and see a sequence of meteors shooting across the path, I recall a moment with my mom in the boat all those years back. Let the Wizard *in you* show you the way.

Back to the Wizard. In *The Wizard of Oz*, the Wizard turns out to be an old man who resembles a professor pulling levers and speaking into a microphone pretending to be the Wizard of Oz, who can grant you your wishes. Turns out, he was no wizard after all. At the end, Dorothy clicks her heels together three times, repeats "There's no place like home," and the ruby slippers take her and Toto back to Kansas where she wakes up in her own bed with Auntie Em and Uncle Henry fussing over her.

And of course, the other cast of characters in her dream stop by to see her, to see how she's doing. Every person, every dream, every experience connects us to our conscious and unconscious self. And just like Dorothy, we always had the power all along. Our self-doubt, our inability to cheer ourselves forward is what results in our being stuck in the many challenges of life—and in terms of this book, obsessing over money, when we can have an ample amount. Just click your heels, and you'll see.

The Imposter Syndrome

How can we be our own cheerleaders when we don't believe in ourselves? Many feel they aren't who they say they are or didn't accomplish what they say they accomplished. When you doubt your abilities or feel like a fraud, the condition is now known as the imposter syndrome. Originally called the Capgras syndrome, sufferers believed that someone they knew had been replaced by an imposter. This imposter syndrome as it's seen today, however, is a psychological condition in which self-doubting disproportionately affects high-achieving people who find accepting their accomplishments difficult.

Many years ago I was lecturing for Weight Watchers of Greater Miami when my sister Debbie was in town visiting. She tagged along for the lecture. I asked her to be silent because I needed to pretend she wasn't there. The idea of my sister listening made me very uncomfortable. She was my sister—who thinks of me as her baby sister, not someone giving lectures on how to eat healthy and release weight.

Something about giving a talk when a family member was sitting right there made me half-expect her to stand up and scream, "Hey, that's not true—you're an imposter!" when I talked about weight loss and how I achieved mine. But of course, she didn't. In fact, she was so excited about my talk that to this day over three decades later, she still speaks of that lecture and how impressed she was. The imposter syndrome is a made-up syndrome you impose upon yourself.

Sometimes when I look at all the books I wrote, I have this fear that I wasn't really the one who wrote them. My internal chatter says, *Who do you think you are? You can't write.* I really didn't have the talent to write these books and somehow faked my way through it.

So many of my writer friends suffer from the same syndrome—this fear of being found out as a fraud. In fact, this fear is one of the primary reason people stand in their own way. How can you cheer for yourself if you internally question your own validity?

If you don't get a handle on this fear of being discovered as a fraud, it can have devastating effects on your ambitions and your ability to tap into your Seed within. The syndrome can lead you to agonize over your mistakes and blunders in life. This fear of not being good enough will squash all your ambitions.

Much of my work as a clinician is helping patients to find their inner strength, so they can bolster their outer dreams. If you don't remove this block, you have no chance to be your personal cheerleader. Instead, you'll develop a pattern of doubt concerning your skills, talents, accomplishments, relationships, and so much more.

If I could count how many times I've heard someone say they'd like to write a book, but they're afraid, the number would be endless. I was afraid too. In fact, my first book was in the works right out of my doctoral program but never came to fruition until nearly twelve years later. I was paralyzed with fear. I questioned, who am I to write these books? Who would want to read them? And what if they flopped?

But then, many profoundly wise persons reminded me that all writers have these fears. Many of the greats questioned their works even after they soared high. In fact, I was recently listening to Joanna Penn's podcast, *The Creative Penn*, featuring Steven Pressfield, the author of *The War of Art: Break Though the Blocks and Win Your Inner Creative Battles* (and many other books), which I've read and reread more times than I care to admit—and here he was saying he doubted himself.

Steven Pressfield with imposter syndrome! Just this book, *The War of Art*, alone to date has over nine thousand

and thirteen almost five-star reviews. The entire book is about breaking through your blocks with your inner battles, *and he has doubts.* This was eye opening and actually a relief to learn I'm not alone—and nor are you. And Joanna too has spoken of this as well, and she's big—huge in the writing world.

So how do you become your own cheerleader in your quest to release your obsession with money so that you can heal from the inside out? Well, to start, you feel the fear and do what you're called to do, anyway. Pressfield says in *The War of Art*: "Most of us have two lives. The life we live, and the unlived life within us. Between the two stands resistance." Stop resisting and move forward.

Trust that you have to start somewhere, anywhere—just start. If you stay stuck in the life you live, but wish to connect with the unlived life, you must push past your resistance. If money is what's keeping you up at night, then trust your start button. Believe you can be your own best cheerleader. To start the money flow, plug in earning followed by saving. Believe in the Seed within you, that it will prosper and grow. See this Seed as you need to.

My Seed is God within me, above me, around me, beside me at all times. I turn over my doubts and trust my desired outcome will occur.

I started with my autosuggestions that propelled my mindset. It worked. I believed and turned over the result, and life took on purpose that was on point with my belief system. Like Dorothy, I had it all along—and so do you.

Click your red slippers in your mind, repeat three times your planted want and let the universe, God, or whatever your belief system is, to take it to that next level. But keep in mind your want is NOT magical thinking. Do the work as you manifest these wants. You do have to believe it will happen, but not in a magical capacity, as you will note in Chapter 10.

Personal Inventory Questions

1. What do you believe? Do you believe you will always obsess over money without making headway in a positive direction?-Do you only have a passing interest in building your financial wealth? How you answer these questions are the building blocks toward your financial freedom. Take a moment and ponder the questions, writing out your thoughts. Tap into how you feel about your perspective as you answer. Check in with your five senses.
2. Our five senses lead us to understanding so much more about ourselves. The senses are an internal tracking of every experience with our taste, touch, smell, hearing, and seeing. And of course we want to look at the idea of a sixth sense. Do you believe in a sixth sense?
3. Robert Collier in his *Riches Within Your Reach* wrote, "Visualize this thing that you want. See it, feel it, believe in it. Make your mental blueprint, and begin to build." If you believe all things are possible, and you're willing to see it, feel it, and believe it, perhaps this want can become yours. Do you visualize this thing that you want? Can you feel it? Do you believe it will happen? What is your negative mind chatter telling you?
4. We all have stored information in the deep wells of our subconscious mind. Based on impressions, this information comes from our conscious minds. Perhaps you saw something as a small child and filed the perceptions in the subconscious. I remember when I was a small child my sister Mickey let me tag along with her when she went to the drugstore to pick up a prescription for our mother. As you read, that experience stayed with

me. What do you remember from your five senses that stays with you? Is the memory a wonderful one or one that cripples you with fear?

5. Maybe you're thinking about the money Sally inherited and how she's living the riches within reach. Yes, lucky Sally, she inherited a break. But what Sally does with this windfall is more telling. Do you wish for an inheritance or would you like to take a stab at earning your wealth yourself, whatever that means to you? Does earning, spending less, and saving sound daunting?
6. When you invest in *you,* the change happens. In Chapter 6, through autosuggestion and Chapter 8 mindset, we see that both are key ingredients to work through changes using the subconscious mind. What are you suggesting to yourself? And how does your mindset fit in?
7. Gems fill line after line, page after page in *Riches Within Your Reach: The Law of the Higher Potential*, but the idea that opened my eyes and toned down my inner negative rant was: "In every man there is a Seed of Life, with infinite power to draw to itself whatever it conceives to be necessary to its expression. It doesn't matter who you are, what your environment or education or advantages; the Seed of Life in you has the same power for good." How do you define your Seed of Life? Do you believe you have such a Seed?
8. Just click your heels three times and repeat, "I can make my wishes come true," just like Dorothy in *The Wizard of Oz*. Well, maybe you can, but clicking her heels wasn't really what made her wish work for Dorothy. What would your wish be if you clicked your red slippers? What was your understanding of the message for Dorothy and her friends?
9. How can we be our own cheerleaders when we don't believe in ourselves? Many feel they aren't who they say

they are or didn't accomplish what they actually did accomplish. This is known as the imposter syndrome. Do you have imposter syndrome? What is your question about yourself regarding being an imposter?

10. Thinking back regarding *The Wizard of Oz*, the Wizard turns out to be an old man who resembles a professor pulling levers and speaking into a microphone pretending to be the Wizard of Oz who can grant you your wishes. Turns out, he was no wizard, after all. Often we put our faith in something that doesn't exist. We rely on someone other than ourselves to grant our wishes. Do you have a fake wizard to grant you your wishes? If so, what does your wizard look like—and how's it working for you?

Chapter 10

Money And Magical Thinking

Success is neither magical nor mysterious.
Success is the natural consequence
of consistently applying the basic fundamentals.
~Jim Rohn

Often when conversations revolve around manifesting, autosuggestion, and mindset, the naysayers think it's all magical thinking. It's not. Britannica.com states that magical thinking is the belief that one's ideas, thoughts, actions, words, or use of symbols can influence the course of events in the material world. Magical thinking presumes a causal link between one's inner, personal experience and the external physical world. That if someone wishes for it, something magical will happen.

The idea seems to be a bit of a conundrum, given you just read a complete chapter above about believing something first to spark that Seed within, and now I'm saying it's not magical thinking, and yet Britannica is saying this type of thinking is a belief in an idea that can influence the course of events. Okay, hold your horses, what is this magical thinking, anyway?

Well, yes, for sure if you want to release your obsession with money and you want to be free of a financial concern at the same time, you need to tap into another part of yourself, which is your belief system. You do have to believe your ideas, thoughts, actions, words, or use of symbols in order to influence the course of events, but I say not in the material world—in your internal world. That belief is a faith that if you do x, y, and z, you'll attain the outcome you're seeking.

Thoughts Plus Actions Equal Consequences

As Jim Rohn says, success is neither magical, nor mysterious, but rather, success is the natural consequence of consistently applying the fundamentals. What does that mean? It means you have to consistently apply the fundamentals to wind up with the natural consequence. For example, if you want to release weight, you need to believe that you can. Then you need to eat whole, natural foods in the amount your body requires. Add to the mix is exercise. What's the consequence? You will release weight naturally.

Now let's do the opposite. You want to release weight, but you're eating cakes, donuts, and cookies for breakfast and fast-food tacos with French fries and a malted milkshake for an afternoon snack. While relaxing on the couch, you down a bag of potato chips. Oh, and for dinner you eat half a Domino's pizza, washing it down with a couple of beers. And oh yes, exercise is just not your thing. Yep, the consequence is for sure weight gain and overall awful health even if you believe in and visualize a thin body.

What are the basic fundamentals you might wonder? And you may also wonder how magical thinking branches from manifesting, mindset, and believing something will happen. Yes, there's that *belief* thing.

Fundamentals include the basic qualitative and quantitative information that contributes to the financial or economic wellbeing and the subsequent financial valuation of a company, security, or currency. (investopedia.com/terms/f/fundamentals.asp).

For the purposes of this book, the company is **you**. I'm not a financial advisor, nor do I have experience or degrees in this field. But, what I do have is common sense. And so do you. Fundamental, from the perspective of this book, is forming a necessary base or core, of central importance. A fundamental is a central or primary rule or principle on which something is based. That's not magic. You are the foundation of your want, building structure for what it is you want to achieve, which at this point is to be free of your money worries from an obsessive perspective.

You are the generator of making this happen, not some magic force. When I think of magic, I think of a trickster producing illusions for entertainment—you know, pulling the gold coin out from behind his ear sort of trick. Such magic is deceptive, causing you to believe something is really happening when it isn't. This implementation of a fundamental isn't based on using deception but rather on using your thoughts and actions backed by the belief that you can release your money worries and live happily without fear of poverty.

In implementing this process, you aren't creating and transforming your relationship to money as if by magic—no sir/ma'am, you are creating and transforming the relationship because you believe and put forth action to make the result happen. You are rolling up your sleeves and taking a good, long, hard look at your thoughts and behaviors as they relate to money and security.

This type of process reminds me of a young student I knew many years ago who was going to build his empire on an island. Well, good, but how are you going to pay for this island? I asked the young man. And what will you do on this island? He shrugged his shoulders and said, "I don't know, but I'm going to live on an island that I own, while running an amazing company." Oh, how lovely. I feel the ocean breeze, and watch seagulls flying about to dive for their lot of little fish, and hear waves crashing on the shoreline. I can hear the island music and taste the pina coladas. Oh yes, I'm there.

I wonder what happened to that young man. The last I knew he quit school because he decided working for a business degree was a waste of time, that he was going to make his success happen fast and on his own, and with no rules. Now that's not incorporating fundamentals unless you want the consequences to be unemployment or a job that's less than what you dreamed—or perhaps the young man chose an occupation as a bellhop on a wonderful island. At least that's getting closer to the dream without magical thinking.

Okay, all kidding aside, I hope this young man realized his dreams. But I'd be willing to venture his dreams didn't come to fruition because he was relying on a magical whim. This student presumed a causal link between his inner, personal experience and the external physical world that would magically make it happen. This isn't how we manifest something. This isn't setting a realistic mindset, nor is it kicking on a reality-based autosuggestion.

Can We Manifest?

Now the waters become murkier when the idea is that personal thoughts can influence the external world without acting on them, or that objects causally connect if they resemble each other or came in contact with each other in the past. The problem with this type of mysterious inner chanting is that you're expecting the happenings without acting on them, or that they somehow link together.

What is confusing is when the idea of manifesting often can vary depending on who's using the term, and in what context. From the viewpoint of psychology, the belief in manifesting is a belief that one's thoughts *by themselves* can bring about effects in the world, or that thinking something corresponds with doing it. In the contexts of this book, I'm not referring to that. Manifesting cannot happen by itself; you must be *doing* something to prompt it to happen. Remember the acronym SMART we talked about in the previous chapters?

SMART is going to prompt you as we power through the remaining chapters, along with your mindset and manifesting. SMART is Specific, Measurable, Attainable, Relevant Time-based goals. These elements all go hand in hand to bring you to your goals. You can manifest, but you want to be specific and clear about what you're manifesting. And what is this manifesting to you?

Now I have this eerie ability to think about someone, and voila, soonish they call. Or I can scroll through my files in the file cabinet and happen upon a patient I hadn't seen in a very long while, and that person calls me. I'm always amazed. It really does happen—and often. Or when I first graduated from my master's program, I visualized lots of checks coming—and they did. What is this?

With a little Googling, I found an abundance of information on manifesting. The common definition is: To manifest something is to make it appear. Seemingly out of thin air. Did those people call or contact me because I manifested their actions? Did I push those checks my way?

Did I manifest these things out of my thoughts, making them happen in actual time? It seems so.

But how could I do this? Honestly, I have no clue. I knew the checks would come because I planned to work vigilantly and diligently. I planned to work on skills to add to my degrees. And this I did. I studied everything I could about eating disorders, low self-esteem, depression, anxiety, addictions, and hypnosis. And within all of those areas I found glued to the disorder an obsession—every time.

It is possible that the universe works with our thoughts, though we can't sit idly by and just wish upon the star and poof it happens. That is for sure what I'm not referring to. But to manifest something means to first see it in your mind. Plant the seed. Visualize what you would like to manifest, but you must first harness and use your imagination. And of course plug in SMART.

Is it possible we can *connect* with some other side, and things will come to us? Yes, maybe, but I'm not certain. This manifestation is from a spiritual dimension, not just magically thinking Uncle Bart is going to bring it to you from the beyond, and you don't have to lift a finger. My understanding is that we manifest or connect through energy, which is a physical reality—but not through magic, which is an illusion.

I was reading a book a friend of mine wrote about her ancestors who were prominent in Jamaica. At the start, the book consisted of loosely connecting stories the author had heard while growing up, which made for an excellent read. But as the narrative went on it, the account became more and more magical in regard to events that had occurred to her forebears.

At this point, when the tale became more improbable, the book took a turn from reality to wishful fantasy. Though the anecdotes were super fun to read, the reader clearly is to understand this is a magic carpet ride—which was the logo my friend had on the book. Was this a coincidence? Maybe, but highly unlikely.

Coincidence Or Miracle

As a "cradle Catholic," I was taught about the various saints and angels that will guide us through our lives. I attended St. Anthony Elementary School, and remember a nun directing us to sit to the left of our seat to leave room for the angel on our right. This could explain my poor posture or continuous sore back and also my sense of never being alone, always having that *knowing* I was okay as the angels and saints, not to forget God and Jesus along with the Holy Spirit, were there for me.

Whether you believe in angels, saints, and the Higher Source is up to you, but to consider magical thinking without exploring coincidences and miracles seems to be ignoring a common type of experience. Did you ever drive around looking for a parking spot and pray to God He'd lead you to one? I have. And I've had a parking spot waiting every time. Did God open the spot or perhaps I manifested it, or maybe it's a coincidence? In any event, I always find a spot and I always know I'll find a spot.

So is my finding a spot a miracle, or a coincidence, or heck, just good ole luck? I guess how you see this matter is up to you. For sure this is tough to answer. It's certainly possible that what's termed miracles could be coincidences—or maybe even a hallucination or even a delusion.

I recall when I worked on the psychiatric ward my second year of interning, this fellow who was up for discharge wasn't released because they considered him delusional. He talked about these happenings that sounded so real to him—and to be honest they sounded real to me too, based on the way he presented them. At that moment I wondered about the differences between such thinking and what occurs to some of us.

I remember sitting there, thinking possibly that with some patients the psychiatrists and other practitioners could be wrong. I realized, of course, that we have to know the difference between real and not real. I had a patient who saw Bobby, her late husband, behind my chair during our sessions. She'd be talking to me and then suddenly she'd look past me wide-eyed, stunned because Bobby was there. She'd point and begin shaking from tremendous fear.

I don't think Bobby was there, but rather she imagined he was there. She had undergone years and years of trauma imposed on her by Bobby, so that she still feared he was coming to get her though he had passed on years before made some sense. But the guy in the psychiatric ward was different. He was clear, concise, and consistent when he spoke. I found him intriguing.

He told me he "was on fire" with his feelings and how things were unfolding. That he could see what was happening with the government and that we were in for a big change. He said one day we would have money aside from the national currencies, that perhaps money as we knew it wouldn't exist. He seemed to know something.

This patient spoke about crypto-currency long before such an idea was part of our world. He spoke of this back in the early 1990s, a few years before computers landed in everyone's homes. He said that banks wouldn't create this new currency. He said it was a type of encrypted electronic money, but I had no idea what that meant. E-cash wasn't something people talked about at the time.

I didn't think his was magical thinking, but that he was a guy who had insight and studied things that *could* become a reality. He wasn't delusional; instead, he was at the genius level, well beyond our small minds to comprehend what he was saying.

And what about miracles? Are they real or delusional? I believe in miracles. I believe in prayer. Pray for what you want, believe you'll receive it, and most of the time your request comes to fruition. Prayer and miracles go hand in hand. Pray for what you need and believe our God of understanding hears our prayers while we wait with faith.

Matthew 19:26: "But Jesus looked at them and said, 'With man this is impossible, but with God all things are possible.'" So, the manifestation of what is prayed for isn't magic, it's a result of turning the want over to our higher understanding of God, or whatever your belief is. If you believe that with God, all things are possible, then all things are available to you.

I find miracles to be a personal, subjective experience, and many are affirmed by physical, objective truth. When I was pregnant with Benjamin, I meditated about how the birth would be. I practiced breathing exercises and relaxation techniques the whole pregnancy. I listened to classical music and imagined how I wanted my birth experience.

On that morning of December 14th, I popped out of bed, waddling my way to the stove to make a hot tea. I felt something trickle down my leg, not sure if I'd had an accident—but then quickly I realized that my water broke. I called the doctor's office. He instructed me to go to the hospital immediately. I primped with makeup and donned a nice outfit. The phone soon rang with Dr. Danoff yelling on the other end. "Where are you?" He scolded me, reminding me I didn't need makeup or to look cute to have a baby, that I'd be the worse for wear.

I believed I would have this baby without a hitch and with no medication. I'm not afraid of much, but I am afraid of needles. The not-so-nice nurse said, "Honey, you're having a baby, far worse than this little needle." I disagreed. While I was giving birth, I 'please' and 'thank you'd the entire way. I never screamed, except once when I was catching my breath—not from pain.

I prayed the Hail Mary, a Roman Catholic prayer, in my mind and rode one contraction after another like a wave in the ocean. I rose above and saw myself having my baby. The doctor and all the staff were there. I wasn't dreaming, nor was I delusional. I wasn't making magic, and that I had this miraculous experience wasn't by luck or a coincidence. I *believed…*

Another time, I was driving to Miami to take the Law School Admittance Test (LSAT). I'm not only afraid of needles, but I'm not comfortable with timed tests either, so I was a total nervous wreck. On the highway, unbeknownst to me, a car was coming up the ramp into my lane while the lane to my left was merging into my lane. I closed my eyes to brace myself for the crash, only to rise above and not be hit. I have no clue how this happened. I was a goner, and yet nothing touched me. I call this a miracle not coincidence or luck.

One of my favorite quotes is from Albert Einstein, who wrote, "There are only two ways to live your life. One is as though nothing is a miracle. The other is as though everything is a miracle." Every breath we take, every morning we wake, and every step we make is a miracle. We ignite the miracle when we believe.

According to *Dangerous Prayers: 50 Powerful Prayers That Changed the World*, Harriet Tubman is said to have recited, "I'm going to hold steady on YOU. You've got to see me through." She recited this prayer when she led runaway slaves to freedom in the North. Tubman was born into slavery, escaped, and subsequently made thirteen missions to rescue seventy enslaved people, including family, networking with antislavery activists and safe houses known as the Underground Railroad. She believed in the power of prayer.

Riches Begin With Thought

Thought is an idea or opinion produced by thinking or occurring suddenly in the mind (Oxford Dictionary). Taking it a step further, in *Psychology Today*, Ezequiel Morsella, PhD states, "Thoughts can be idea-like, memory-like, picture-like, or song-like." (Psychologytoday.com, "What Is a Thought?"). For sure these thoughts are spurred on through our brain function, which gives rise to them, but that's about all we really know. How thoughts and the brain truly function is controversial at best, and a complete mystery at worst.

But what we know is that we all have thoughts. We think about *stuff* all day long, and in our dream-state too. Some of these thoughts are random, while we center others on situations we're in. Regardless of how these thoughts come, they're important to our functioning.

Thoughts can be positive, negative, motivating, or even crippling. We can use these thoughts constructively when we set our belief, desire, imagination, and persistence to what we are out to accomplish. Or we can be the Debbie Downer and set destructive thoughts that send us spiraling down in doubt and fears. Which do you prefer?

Set your definite goal. Make the goal realistic and attainable, not magical and full of illusions, and it will sprout your set intentions. Though all things are possible through God, that doesn't mean all things are right for you. And it certainly doesn't mean money completes you, as you will see in Chapter 11.

Personal Inventory Questions

1. Often, when conversations revolve around manifesting, autosuggestion, and mindset, the naysayers think we're

talking about magical thinking. Do you believe this idea of manifesting autosuggestions as you reset the mindset is magical, wishful thinking?

2. You do have to believe your ideas, thoughts, actions, words, or use of symbols will influence the course of events, though I say not in the material world, but in your internal world. Do you believe your ideas, thoughts, actions, words, or use of symbols to influence the course of your events are regulating your material world or your internal world? What's the difference to you?
3. As Jim Rohn says, "Success is neither magical, or mysterious but rather, success is the natural consequence of consistently applying the basic fundamentals." What are your fundamentals? And do you consistently apply them in your daily life? Is success the natural consequence for you if you apply your fundamentals?
4. You are the generator of making this desired end to manifest, not some magical force. When I think of magic, I think of a trickster producing illusions or entertainment— you know, pulling the gold coin out from behind his ear kind of trick. Such magic is deceptive, causing you to believe it's really happening. Do you believe in using such magic in making your wants come to fruition? What about luck?
5. I spoke of the young student who dreamed he would own an island. He didn't have a plan in place, but this was what he wanted. Is this kind of "want" realistic? Was he magically wishing upon a star? Maybe you saw his situation differently than I did. How do you plug into that type of thinking?
6. SMART is going to prompt you as we power through the remaining chapters, along with changing your mindset and manifesting. SMART is: Specific, Measurable, Attainable, Relevant Time-based goals.

What is your SMART? Spell out your goals using this acronym to deliver your money wants without obsessing over them.

7. To manifest something is to make it appear—seemingly out of thin air. Did I manifest people to call or contact me? Did I push those checks my way? Did I manifest these things out of my thoughts, making events happen in actual time? What is your understanding of manifesting? Do you manifest things? Do you think about someone and voila, they call you? What is actually happening?
8. As a "cradle Catholic," I learned about the various saints and angels that guide us through our lives. I attended St. Anthony Elementary School, where we were taught to sit to the left of our seat to leave room for the angel on our right. So for me, miracles are not so farfetched. What about for you? How do miracles fit into your life and your financial wellbeing?
9. One of my favorite quotes is from Albert Einstein who wrote, "There are only two ways to live your life. One is as though nothing is a miracle. The other is as though everything is a miracle." How does that quote factor into your way of thinking? Do you live your life as though everything is a miracle?
10. Set your definite goal. Make the goal realistic and attainable, not magical and full of illusions, and it will sprout by way of your intentions. What are your intentions? Are they realistic? How attainable are they?

Chapter 11

Money Does Not Complete YOU

The essence of all art
is to have pleasure in giving pleasure.
~Dale Carnegie

So we covered you are not your money, but what about money completing you? Yes, money can motivate you to obtain more of it, but it can't complete you—because if it did, that would mean with the green stuff you're lacking nothing. Having money would mean you are whole, and all parts to your life are unbroken, lock, stock, and barrel. I'm guessing that's not your story—nor is it mine.

Money does not complete you, but it does give you an opportunity to do things you might not do without it. For instance, you can be charitable, giving to those who have less. "The essence of all art is to have pleasure in giving pleasure," Dale Carnegie wrote, which could *complete* you. Let me repeat, giving pleasure breeds more pleasure, which can lead to an organic wholeness.

Think about the last time you freely gave something to someone. Did it give you pleasure? Now, of course, if you're giving out of guilt or "musts," then it won't hit your pleasure button, but might leave you feeling frustrated. Anything we do out of guilt alone isn't feeding your soul or your wellbeing.

But by giving freely, scientists believe, this altruistic behavior releases endorphins in the brain, producing the positive feeling known as the "helper's high." By giving, we spread goodness, cultivating gratitude on the part of both the giver and the recipient.

The givers are grateful that they can give, making life a little better for someone else. And receiving also feels good.

I can think of many ways to give. We can give time, food, money, clothes, attention, and a host of other gifts. Whatever you give increases personal happiness resulting from the opportunity to lend a helping hand.

The Takers And The Givers

Now you may be reading this and thinking, *Wait one minute. My kids are always asking for money, and they're ungrateful brats.* Of course, this wouldn't feel too good.

Ted called me years back beside himself about his eighteen-year-old daughter Belinda, who not only was skipping school, she was flunking out and two years behind her graduating class. She smoked weed, brought friends who had sticky fingers into the home, and was promiscuous.

Ted's daughter had an entitlement issue that was making him pull his hair out. She wouldn't find a job to pay for her lovely well-manicured nails, hair, and feet or gas for her Range Rover Jeep that *he bought her* when she turned sixteen. This kind of giving does not beget pleasure but rather rage. Ted didn't instill in his precious daughter a work ethic, let alone gratitude. In fact, she was furious that he wasn't doing more for her.

I believe part of the problem was Ted's daughter didn't feel good about herself. She thought money and stuff would complete her, but it didn't; it made her feel awful about the person she'd become. She even said so. She was trying to buy friends, but people aren't for sale. They used her and stole from her and her family when left to roam in the house.

Ted's situation was the opposite of feel-good giving; his giving was creating a toxic household with unhappy inhabitants. They had a six-bedroom home equipped with a full-sized pool, and with two Mercedes-Benz cars in the driveway, along with the Range Rover that was dented because of one too many accidents from drinking and driving. At her father's insistence, Belinda joined therapy sessions.

She expressed there that her parents always doted on her because of a heart condition she was born with and which required many doctor's visits. She was told she couldn't overly exert herself; hence she didn't run and play like the other children. She was always kept away from anything that seemed fun, according to her. They forbid her to do even the household chores, as her parents didn't want her to overexert herself. So she let them wait on her hand and foot.

As she grew older, she felt different from the other children. She fed her sadness with all the luxuries her parents gifted her, along with eating whatever she could sneak when they weren't watching her. Belinda was on a special healthy diet and kept from the sweets and treats she yearned for, so she snuck downstairs like a thief in the night to find sugary treats to port back to her room where she ate and read stories well into the night.

Belinda developed into a young adult, and with that passage grew to be overweight, which triggered her eating disorder of dieting and bingeing to the point of gaining fifty pounds on her five-foot, three-inch frame. She felt not only ostracized by her heart condition, but now she was encased in a body that made her feel ugly and fat. Her only solace was to beg and scream for money to buy the things she wanted, hoping her purchases would make her happy. And they did—at least initially.

But as Belinda learned, money and stuff did not complete her. She felt broken, like a misfit in society, which attracted her to the less fortunate kids who liked to come to her home filled with luxuries. This was where the rubber met the road, and her dad's worries began. Belinda was out of control with food, drugs, boys, and her impulsive wants.

I suggested Belinda get a job and earn her luxuries—no more handouts. I also suggested she volunteer one day a week in a community of choice. She picked the nursing home where she could read her beloved books to the lonely elderly. Giving begets pleasure, and Belinda blossomed as proof of that. She didn't have grandparents, and the residents adored her doting love and gratitude instead of money.

Belinda no longer had time for her unruly friends between work and her community service hours. She also changed schools, finding one designed for special needs as she had missed so much school during her sick times she couldn't catch up to the other students. Instead, she attended a school that met her learning needs exactly where she was in her education experience. As her grades improved, her social life changed, and her weight corrected because she was more mobile and more confident and felt better about herself.

Ted no longer feels frightened about Belinda's future because she's thriving as she heads in a positive direction. Giving makes a difference because it feels good. Not only giving money, but also giving time can have an impact on other people's lives while the benefit boomerangs back to the giver. Belinda is feeling the joy of being needed by others.

Pay It Forward

I recall many years back, 1990, to be exact, I was on my way to the west coast of Florida with a toddler in tow to visit my mom for the long Thanksgiving weekend. I ransacked my can of loose change to pay for gas to drive from one coast to the other, not even thinking how I'd have enough money to return. I was driving a dilapidated 1985 gold Mercury Topaz—a compact car produced by the Ford Motor Company.

Back then, Alligator Alley was a one-lane road, meaning one lane went west while the other lane when east. There were no stops along the way for a good 80 miles on I-75, stretching between Fort Lauderdale and Naples. The road had opened in 1968 after many years of construction and felt antiquated twenty-two years later.

Alligator Alley gets its name from the nearby swamps that alligators call home. In those days they didn't fence the roadside to protect the driver, nor the wildlife that freely roamed. Warning signs were up everywhere that should you need to stop, to pop open your hood and turn on your lights and remain in the car for roadside help because of the panthers, alligators, and other wildlife out on the road.

I'd heard stories as far back as I could remember of dead bodies disposed of in the swamp. This was no place to be stuck and no place to pass a slow driver ahead of you for fear the oncoming lane would cause a head-on collision, which was another known risk. To be sure, Alligator Alley was one scary road to be on when alone, and for sure scary when your car breaks down, having a toddler and Oscar the Pug in tow.

This day, as we nibbled on our travel goodies, bobbing and laughing, listening to music, we made our way across the alley. When we happened upon the tollbooth, the woman waved me through without taking my money. She explained when I gave her a perplexed look that the car in front of me had paid my toll.

I couldn't believe my luck. Nobody had ever paid my toll before. I couldn't get out of my head the question of why someone would pay for me to travel this road. At first, my mind wandered, as it might, and I thought the other driver was a mass murderer who was going to run me off the road and kill me. And then after a pause, the idea occurred to me that she was a kind person passing on a good deed. I could do the same with the money saved due to her generosity. And I did.

Giving is good for you—good for your health. Giving has far-reaching arms. Thus, maybe I could learn from the person who'd paid for my toll, so with the saved money, later on during the drive, I paid for the person behind me. I saw that "paying it forward" could be a good thing in many situations, and I did this more regularly.

For years, I didn't have extra money, but I found when I gave, being generous seemed to open up more opportunity in a variety of ways. The very day I paid for someone else's toll, I had a flat tire only moments after giving and an hour from receiving from the woman ahead of me. I pulled over and followed the protocol by popping open my hood, turning on the fog lights and waiting. I was frightened because my little one had to go to the bathroom and no way were we leaving the car where wild animals roamed, waiting to eat us.

Not long after, a driver pulled over to help us. At first, I thought he could be a murderer who would stuff our bodies in suitcases only to throw them to the alligators, as rumor suggested. But he wasn't dangerous at all—instead was kind and helpful as he changed my tire, risking his own safety between the danger of wild animals and the cars whizzing by, known to swerve and hit those out of their car on this one-lane road. Further, this is an incredibly remote part of Florida where at the time they had no hospitals, and ambulance service was sparse. In short, this was no road on which to drive a dilapidated car in an area where help was scarce.

When the gentleman finished fixing the tire, he waved me off when I tried to give him the few crumpled dollars I had. He was glad to help and wanted nothing. I had been the object of two generous acts in one compact frame of time and had myself paid forward for one. The lesson I found was in the gratitude of kindness, not in a pocket full of money.

Money is a touchy subject. On the one hand, it can bring us security, but on the other, some can mistakenly believe it will exhaust all worries. It won't.

Winning BIG

The idea of money completing me, or you, reminds me of George who lives in an economically depressed area. He received the stimulus checks of the past and more recently as part of the Covid relief packet. He, of course, was grateful to receive his check(s) and really needed the help. But he snickered, thinking about a few people in his neighborhood sporting new hairdos with matching pedicures and manicures and expensive perfume as if they had hit the jackpot.

The fact people were blowing their checks as though it was their new identity astounded George. They were acting in anticipation of more that would flow their way. I found this interesting, as I knew of some who, cashing their checks, went out for expensive dinners with a bottle on the table. Bottle service happens at tables in well-defined, elite, super VIP areas of nightclubs or lounges. They usually separate these areas from the general public. In South Florida ordering a bottle is a BIG deal.

When as a patron, you order a bottle, usually of some sort of high-priced liquor, you've *arrived.* You are somebody. You are rich. You made it. Money now completes you. When you order a bottle you're treated special; you don't wait for your table like everybody else. Oh no, they usher you to a designated area. You are big.

A sweet friend of mine, Michael, won a lawsuit and came into a small pile of money. We were in our early twenties, both working in a restaurant/bar, paying our way through school. Michael even drove horse-drawn carriages through the city of Chicago to make ends meet.

Ah, such fun days. But when he received that check, he went wild. He ordered a limousine, and out we went to a fancy dinner at a French restaurant, spending an insane amount of money. I wore a faux black leather dress and high heels, feeling pretty spiffy for sure.

I remember on our way to the restaurant; Michael had the limousine driver pull into the 7-Eleven so he could buy a pack of gum. Mind you, the time was ticking with the expense adding up for every minute that the driver waited while we dilly-dallied in the store. Michael was on a high. As a tagalong, I too was on a high, imagining what being uber rich would be like, even if it was only for one night. Kids were peering in, trying to get a sneak peek at the *celebrities* in this limo. I had never been in a limo before, so I felt pretty cool, as though I were somebody—at least for a moment.

Our evening was short-lived, and back to reality we went. At lease, I went back to reality. Michael loved the rush of feeling rich. He believed this was what rich people did, spend money on whatever whim they had. He felt complete. For sure, the very rich might do this, but most of us don't spend like no tomorrow, unless we want to live broke and in debt, which is exactly what Michael did.

And then I think of the guy who won the lottery. His name escapes me, but not his face. He was dishwater blond with a strong accent, Romanian I believe. He was a regular at the bar I tended. Anyway, he won a boatload of money on one lucky ticket. He made the news big, as our area never saw such winnings. My lovely customer swapped out of his jeans and t-shirt for a pair of leather slacks, silk shirt, and a snazzy cap to go with the outfit.

Almost every girl gave him attention whereas before they didn't give him the time of day. He was spending money on drinks for everyone, smiling and nodding like a movie star or a big tycoon of some sort. Watching this was fun, as I knew him when he had nothing, and I mean nothing. And then one day I noticed I hadn't seen him in a long while. I found out he'd died—that he hung himself.

I was sad, because he believed that money completed him, made him more than some guy living from paycheck to paycheck from his parking cars job prior to his big winnings. In time, though, he learned people only wanted to be around him for his money. This is familiar story to me, and to you by now as you power through these pages. Money is for survival and security, but it doesn't complete you as a person. You complete you, by what you do, the thoughts you harbor, and the belief within your core.

But the best part of the lottery win story was something I learned many, many years later: My Romanian friend didn't die after all. He had an awakening. He had an insight, realizing he could find better ways to feel the fullness of life than walking around like a hotshot with deep pockets spending and splurging at every turn.

He learned that embracing his fullness of life would arise out of authenticity and genuine relationships. He loved life and lost sight of that with all the attention he was receiving. For the first time in his life, he felt big, important, puffed out with this notion he now was *somebody*. But was he? He now realized his love of life and others had nothing to do with money. It had to do with kindness and generosity.

He didn't like the feel of being rich when it wasn't fulfilling the core of his being. So he faked his own death, changed his name, and took on a simpler life. He learned money didn't complete him.

A salutary lesson for all is that money and winnings don't complete the person; in fact, they can do quite the opposite. This lottery winner wanted to taste life in a relaxed manner, with authenticity. He eschewed his fancy clothes, donning a nice casual look of blue jeans and polo shirts, swapping out his leather shoes for a nice pair of sneakers.

He stopped flashing his money and lived a simpler life. Not as simple as pre-winnings, but simpler than the rich guy he had become known as. He moved to a small town, bought a farmhouse equipped with a barn and one hundred acres. He filled his little sanctuary with horses, goats, and his beloved hound dogs. He found genuine love and had many children to satisfy his yearning heart. He was happy.

So, money doesn't complete you but rather buys security. The focus needs to be placed on more important things such as relationships, values, and meaning. But with that said, a stash of money for security can bring relief. This is not a book on let's be poverty stricken and sing cumbayá. NO, this is about releasing your obsession with money and living SMART, as you will see in the remaining chapters.

Humble Down

Of course, though money is unlikely to buy happiness, it may help you feel confident in sustaining what you do have and value. And maybe the things you would like to have. Dave Ramsey's quote is my motto. "Live like nobody else so you can live like nobody else." I live simply, but when I want that big splurge, I can have it. I don't obsess over the money; instead, I follow my simple rule—very similar to our granddaddy's rules. I work, save, and spend cautiously, and avoid debt at all costs, which equaled for me financial freedom.

When the coronavirus hit, and my husband had to close the restaurant for six months, leaving me as the sole earner, I cut back. I had lost my housekeeper in December 2019 and cleaned myself, saving a good pile of money each month—and getting quite the workout on my cleaning day. I even created my outfit of black capris and a sleeveless red top to wear, designating "the housekeeper has arrived" to set my mind and tone.

Because of the pandemic, I let go of the hair salon, pedicures, and manicures. I'm sure you made such changes too. I stopped the once-a-month facial and the massages. Yes, these were luxuries afforded to me because I lived like no one else, so I could live like no one else. All stopped. And to this day, as they now have opened things in Florida, I haven't resumed my old ways.

We could power through the six months without fearing we'd lose our home, cars, or other essentials like *food.* For those of you who read my other books, you know I love food…to the point I binge ate as a true food addict and suffered from bulimia through exercise because I obsessed over staying thin. Spending money on food is expensive, which leads me to my next chapter, Eating Disorders and Money, as you move toward releasing your obsession with money—so that you can heal from the inside out.

Personal Inventory Questions

1. So we covered you are not your money, but what about money completing you? Yes, money can motivate you to go after more of it, but it can't complete you because if it did it would mean that with the green stuff you are lacking nothing. Are you lacking nothing? Do you believe money would complete you? If you do, how so?
2. "The essence of all art is to have pleasure in giving pleasure" (Dale Carnegie), which could *complete* you. What do you give that delivers pleasures to others and to you? Are you an artist, or perhaps a writer with fun stories, leaving others feeling good? An artist who gives merely to make money might miss the essence of all art, which is to have pleasure giving pleasure. Think about what that means to you.
3. Now if you're reading this and thinking, *Wait one minute—my kids are always asking for money, and they're ungrateful brats,* this is not the giving I'm referring to. Of course, this type of giving wouldn't feel too good. Remember Ted, who called me beside himself about his eighteen-year-old daughter, Belinda, who not only skipped school, she was flunking and two years behind her graduating class. Do you have a Belinda of some sort squeezing you dry for something? How does the situation serve you? How does it serve him/her?
4. Giving is good for you—good for your health. Giving has far-reaching arms. And I found a lesson in the person who paid for my toll, the lesson being to pay it forward. So with the money saved, I later paid for a person behind me. Paying it forward could be a good thing in other situations, too, so I did this more regularly. What about you? When was the last time you paid it forward? How did it make you feel?

5. George, who lives in an economically depressed area, was grateful for the stimulus checks received as part of the Covid relief packet, as he really needed the help. But he snickered, thinking about a few people in his neighborhood sporting new hairdos with matching pedicures and manicures and expensive perfume as if they'd hit the jackpot. What are your thoughts about how individuals spent their relief checks? Did you judge? How did you spend yours?
6. A sweet friend of mine, Michael, won a lawsuit and came into a small pile of money. We were in our early twenties, both working in a restaurant tending bar to pay our ways through school. Did you ever receive a large amount of money? If so, what did you do with it? If you didn't, but you know someone who did, how did they spend their windfall? What did you learn through your (or their) experience?
7. And then what about the Romanian guy who won the lottery? He struck it big, winning a boatload of money on one small ticket. He swapped out of his jeans and t-shirt for a pair of leather slacks, a silk shirt, and a snazzy cap to go with these. How did his story impact you? Sometimes we have to die to live…
8. Of course, though money is unlikely to buy happiness, it may help you feel confident in sustaining the things you have. And maybe the things you would like to have. My motto is Dave Ramsey's quote, "Live like nobody else so you can live like nobody else." What are your thoughts about living like nobody else so you can live like nobody else? What does it mean to you?
9. I don't obsess over money, but I follow a simple rule—very similar to our granddaddy's rules—that idea Dave Ramsey suggests. I work, save, and spend cautiously, and avoid debt at all costs, which equaled for me financial

freedom. What rules did you learn from your grandmother or grandfather? How is it working for you?

10. When the coronavirus hit and my husband had to close the restaurant for six months leaving me as the sole earner, I cut back on spending. How did the shutdown impact you and your spending? What did you learn about yourself?

Chapter 12

Eating Disorders and Money

Our main business is not to see
what lies dimly at a distance,
but do what lies clearly at hand.
~Thomas Carlyle

One way to make a change is to pay attention to what *lies clearly at hand, not to see what lies dimly at a distance.* We want to stay in the now—to live in the present. And while in the present and on the discussion of releasing your obsession with money, I would be remiss if I didn't touch on eating disorders and money. Why, you might ask? Well, as an eating-disordered person in recovery—who was in tremendous debt because of spending money on food, along with other spending(s) to strive to be skinny—I'd like to discuss a topic many can relate to.

I work in eating disorders, which always touches on depression, anxiety, and other obsessions—and many times money. So here we are at this juncture of my writing where the time has arrived to look at how much money we spend on food, restaurants, and the fast food drive-thru. Remember SMART, where you align your goals to be Specific, Measurable, Attainable, Relevant, and Time-based. This area is not only for the binge eating-disordered person but for anyone who spends money on low-quality foods that take a tremendous hit on the wallet not to mention your health.

Parts of this chapter are excerpts from *Release Your Obsession with Cheat DAZE: Heal from the Inside Out* (Chapter 15) and *Release Your Obsession with Diet Chatter: Heal from the Inside Out* (Chapter 5), briefly addressing eating disorders, but also weaving in a discussion of the expense that comes with spending without a SMART plan lined up. But before we go there, let's take a quick peek at the different eating disorders.

Eating Disorders

As we navigate through this chapter on eating disorders and money, we'll start by discussing the different eating disorders before integrating the goal of releasing the obsession with money, as an explanation of both is necessary and appropriate. Though many types of eating disorders exist, and often one blends with another—or one ends while another appears—I'm going to look at the four most common types of eating disorders defined in the *DSM-5*, the guide to diagnoses.

These four most common eating disorders are: anorexia, bulimia, binge eating, and lastly, other eating disorders characterized by some variants of the first three.

Briefly, anorexia, or Anorexia Nervosa, can often exist in a person of a low body weight that is unhealthy for their body type, height, or activity level. The anorexic restricts food, with achieving thinness as the primary goal. This person harbors an intense fear of becoming fat. The inner chatter concerns the fear of "getting fat," and such persons believe they are viewed as being fat. This population is hyper-focused on calorie intake, body shape, and weight.

Bulimia Nervosa, a second eating disorder, can be diagnosed in an individual eating large amounts of food, often in hiding/secret, and then purging through vomiting, laxatives, or extreme exercise. This type of eating-disordered person more often than not will binge and purge cyclically. They eat compulsively, binge eating well past the point of comfort. This group typically practices a cycle of bingeing followed by fasting. They diet constantly while obsessing over their body weight and how they look. Those with this disorder can be of normal weight or overweight. They are not underweight, which is one difference between anorexia and bulimia.

The third eating disorder is Binge Eating Disorder, often referred to as compulsive overeating—eating well beyond the point of fullness. This group of people may be overweight or obese and definitely feel out of control during a binge. Not uncommonly the binge eater will experience depression, anxiety, and feelings of isolation.

The fourth classification of eating disorders is a "catch all" category for all other eating disorders (and is called Other Eating Disorders). The practices of those in this group are excessive practices, including extreme exercise and restrictive diets used solely to lose weight, such as veganism, raw food diets, and/or liquid only diets. Other Eating Disorders also includes late night binge eating, the use of diet pills, or any stimulant addiction with the purpose of speeding up metabolism in order to lose weight.

I, myself, jumped between Bulimia Nervosa, Binge Eating Disorder, and Other Eating Disorders—with food addiction as my primary affliction. Yes, you read that right. I'm a food addict, that is, a food addict in recovery. And yes, I had bulimia and used exercise to rid myself of the consequences of excess eating, and on rare occasions, I restricted and over-exercised. Admitting I had such disorders was hard—*very hard*. But I did!

Not uncommon for me was my going on a huge bender with food, eating enough for ten in a scant hour session, and waiting a bit to start the process all over again. Can you imagine the expense! On a bender, I could easily spend $75 in one outing for one person. I would bounce around in weight, weighing as much as 234 pounds at the top end, while other times as little as 115.

Today I'm a comfortable weight and my inner negative chatter has decreased at least 85 percent. When the drunken monkeys (negative mind chatter) do rear their ugly heads, I knock them down with an arsenal of weapons such as meditation, prayer, reading positive words, and so forth—and they retreat.

So whether you suffer from anorexia or bulimia or binge eating, or perhaps dance between these, and/or other types of extreme food behaviors, you may legitimately have hope and you can find help. And simultaneously, you most likely are spending a great deal of money to feed your habit, which is the focal point of this chapter, as you are releasing your obsession with money so you can build your wealth.

I began my healing process using a combination of Cognitive-Behavioral Therapy while changing my thoughts and behaviors; accepting I was a food addict and using a Twelve-Step program designed for food addicts; and of course, worked my recovery through a spiritual connection. I don't believe I'd be where I am today without a mixture of all three. But as President Lincoln so eloquently stated, "Most folks are as happy as they make up their minds to be." I've attached to happy.

Food is the key to wellbeing in every respect. So true that "One cannot love well, think well, or sleep well, if one has not dined well," as writes Virginia Woolf, who was spot on. And one way to insure you dine well is to have the right foods with you whether you are home, on vacation, or even in another country. And it's a way to keep the cost down too.

How can you do this, you might ask? The answer is, through preparation. If you prepare to fail, you will fail, but if you prepare to win, you will win at managing your food and your money, regardless of where you are.

On this note I've heard, "But I don't have the money to eat well, or to travel, for that matter. So I turn to fast food for the bit of enjoyment I can find in life." Sounds dismal, yet this is something often said by patients working through their body, weight, and food challenges. But the situation doesn't have to be that way. Let's look at food and then money to see why I believe so.

First, we'll explore packaging and portions, and then move into money. Who doesn't like to talk about money?

Small Packages Are The 'In' Thing

The other night during dinner, my husband, older son, and I discussed foods, packaging, and cost-effective shopping. I went into my rant regarding how food is a necessity for sustaining life, and how, for the food-challenged person, food is ominous and frightening, as they have to face dining four times a day, including a half-meal—or snack as some call it.

My son said something like, "The millennials don't like to buy enormous packages of foods, but rather go for the smaller package." His understanding, from a news report he'd heard earlier that day, was that the younger population isn't prone to stock up on foods. The story said that they prefer teeny packages rather than to buy in bulk. For them, spending money on smaller was okay. I couldn't wrap my brain around this concept. Buying smaller packages isn't cost effective, for sure.

I found this most interesting since I need to have a full fridge, freezer, and pantry to feel safe—as without these I fret I might go hungry. This stems from my early twenties, when I was quite broke and knee deep in my food addiction, and feared to stock an abundance of food, worrying that I'd then binge eat. My best friend, Yvonne, marveled at the fact I only had a jar of peanut butter, a head of lettuce, and skim milk in the fridge. I thought the less food you had in the home, the less risk of overeating.

Wrong.

A filled pantry, fridge, freezer, and now a deep freeze I've added to the mix, bring great peace and calm to me because I know I have food to eat at all times. A plentiful supply of edibles lessens my fear of not having enough to eat. So I've swung from the fear of having any food at all in the house to oversupplying. Perhaps this need for abundance stems from being the youngest of six children, and Mom tending to others first, maybe. And the skimpy selection I maintained for many years definitely arose from the fear of getting fat.

But for sure the necessity of having more food stems from years of chronic dieting. At times I was so hungry I could have chomped on tree bark to fill my stomach. I hopped from one diet to the next, a definite ingredient in binge eating and the dread of not having enough to eat.

So, not only are we working on changing our relationship to money, but we're also looking at our spending on food, which is a necessary staple in everyday life. Looking at shopping together now, we want to make certain you buy enough quality food to eat at a price that makes good sense.

Yes, that money part again. But hang on, more to say before we look at money abundance, and its connection to food.

So here we were at the dinner table, and I pondered, *why is it* the younger generation doesn't stock up on food? Is the reason that they're transient—or are they perpetually broke? Or perhaps they eat out at restaurants more often than at home?

I was watching television the other day, a rare treat, and what did I see but a commercial showing peanut butter cups, pointing to how thin they now are—and promoting that this was a desired, outstanding feature for the consumer. As an advocate for saving money and time, I'm thinking, *But then they receive less of it for the same price, so how can that be good?*

This made me think about Kris at the dinner table, saying smaller portions are the "in" thing these days. My mind wandered to the small popcorn and chip bags, and the tiny peanut butter containers promoted at all the supermarkets and the club stores such as Sam's Club, BJ's, and Costco, and I thought perhaps this was a ploy to manipulate us consumers into believing less is more.

Or perhaps the strategy is to appeal to us to save calories. You know, the 100-calorie bag of chips, cookies, popcorn, etc. The approach seems to be the advertisers saying we can't be trusted to portion out the exact amount we need from a larger—more cost-effective—package.

But being the money-conscious person I am (*The Millionaire Next Door*!), I think buying in bulk is much more efficient. Why not buy the ginormous bag of Skinny Popcorn and divide it into smaller zip-locked portions yourself? Or what about popping it from its raw version yourself at home and then divide that into portions?

I've given many talks and presentations that revolve around the cost of eating clean and healthy. I often hear from patients and attendees at these talks that only the rich can eat clean and healthy—but I beg to differ. Or I hear eating clean is time consuming or they don't cook. Or how about "After I worked so hard all week, now you want me to cook on the weekends too?" The best excuse I hear is "Why would I go on a vacation and look for a grocery store? *I'm on vacation!!*"

I get it, really I do. But if your goal is to live like no one else so you can live like no one else (words of Dave Ramsey, the Christian finance guru), then shopping for your foods and preparing your foods is one of the first steps. I find those struggling with money are often struggling with their food issues too. Somehow, dollars and calories go hand in hand. In 2007, I noted my food intake relationship changed when I began the debt-free quest. I ate less and spent less. I became debt-free on 11-11-11 (yes, I'm a numbers girl).

What's Money (Calories Too) Got To Do With It?

A few book launches back, I was sitting pondering a chapter for my book on releasing the obsession with cheat days and food fest(s)—fests meaning festivities such as birthdays, weekends, long weekends, holidays, and traveling—events filled with food—and my mind drifted to thoughts of how much my life changed when I became debt free.

Okay, you say, what the heck do celebrations and festivities have to do with breaking free from money worries? Well, once upon a time I was broke. Yes, I mean so broke and so in debt I should have been shaking in my boots. I wasn't. My inner self told me I'd find my way out.

And I did.

In 1998 I began reading books like *Don't Worry, Make Money: Spiritual and Practical Ways to Create Abundance and More Fun in Life* (Richard Carlson), and I became a disciple of Dave Ramsey, reading his *Total Money Makeover: A Proven Plan for Financial Fitness*, and Thomas J. Stanley's *The Millionaire Next Door*, along with Napoleon Hill's *Think and Grow Rich*, and many more that would take pages to enumerate. At the same time, I was working my way out of my food addiction—and somehow I noticed similarities.

In what way? you might ask.

Well, I saw I was spending money on total junk food, and that was costing me a fortune. I was eating at every donut shop, stopping at the store to buy poor quality food, and grabbing a coffee laced with cream and sweetener, along with candy bars, at every gas stop—and of course, all went on the credit card, with interest charges in the background eating away at my money every second.

After reading money books, I understood I wasn't respecting my money. I had student debt of at least $300,000, plus a mortgage, car payment, and credit card debt. I was up to my eyeballs in total debt—and because of out-of-control binge eating, I was gaining back the hundred pounds I'd lost.

When I took a step away, and looked at my spending and my eating, I had a revelation… an aha moment. I realized the two went hand in hand, and if I worked on the money, I'd probably get a grip on the food.

I did!

I wrote down every morsel of food I was eating, and every dollar I was spending—at the same time working on Dave Ramsey's snowball idea… paying down my smallest credit card and working my way up. Eventually, I saw a light at the end of the tunnel. Every time I paid off a credit card, I had that much more money to throw at the next card… on and on… until I paid off all my cards, and then moved on to the car… then the STUDENT LOAN, which was enough to choke a horse.

After nibbling away at the other debts, the money I then had to throw at this debt became enormous. *I lived poor so that I could live rich.*

When I freed myself from the student loan, I went all out and paid off the house mortgage, and to date I live debt free. **Debt Free!!** And my food bill is not massive because I learned to buy actual, real foods in bulk, and store them in the freezer, and pantry, and divvy them out in pre-made packages.

You can do this too.

If you're drowning in debt, and your weight is climbing, you, too, can take a step back, work toward eating clean and healthy and letting go of your debts—and watch the magic happen. Buy books on managing money or check them out of the library, and learn to eat actual (natural) foods, and life will become a whole lot better.

And the funny thing is that when you practice working toward becoming debt free, and then living debt free, you thereafter stay in a frugal way of living, which we delved into in Chapter 3, Living The Frugal Life. At the same time, when you want to go on that vacation, or you want to buy that piece of jewelry, or you're ready for a new car, you buy it in cash, and don't feel the financial strain.

A favorite quote of mine from Richard Carlson's *Don't Worry, Make Money: Spiritual and Practical Ways to Create Abundance and More Fun in Your Life* is "One of the most severely limiting beliefs that many of us have is that the person we were yesterday is the person we have to be today." Not so. If you hang onto this type of belief system, you will remain heavy, addicted to foods—and perhaps broke. That you can't be a different person is a self-defeating belief, which goes against the self-love and self-care I speak of in this very book you're reading.

What do you think? Do you see a correlation between your consumed calories and your financial status? Examine this interrelationship closely and see if you can change your belief system. Having more money isn't about how much money you make, but about how much you save. And losing weight isn't about how many calories you eat, but how much *quality* food you consume.

Perhaps you started this book diet driven, financially shaky, overweight, and in desperate need of a makeover. Perhaps you want to travel, but you fear clothes won't fit, money is lacking, and you need to start your diet first. Stop that thinking now. You're beautiful as you are.

Save Big—Shop In Bulk

Shop in bulk at a "club" type store to save a good thirty percent, roaming the aisles for only *real* food, steering away from processed and packaged foods. Think natural; think free of sugar, flour, and wheat; think quality fats, protein, veggies, fruit, and dairy, and starchy carbs—and you are more than on your way.

Shopping at a Sam's Club or Costco in bulk—whole foods, of course—is much more efficient than going out to a fast-food restaurant. I recall in my binge-eating days, before I read *The Millionaire Next Door,* stopping at Miami Subs and buying a giant tuna sub, a bag of baked chips, and a Diet Coke. At the time, I thought that was healthy eating. The cost was over ten dollars, and this was years, and years, and years ago.

Had I gone to the store and purchased the tuna and fixings, and a large bag of baked chips, portioned out, along with a tumbler of crushed-ice water with a wedge of lemon, the cost would have been less than a few bucks. We don't have to spend tons of money to eat clean.

I have a generic list of "must haves" that I purchase and stock at all times. First, I always have eggs on hand. Eggs are a versatile protein eaten in a wide variety of ways, such as boiled, poached, and scrambled, which are the basics—but expand your mind.

You can make vegetable omelets, muffins, pancakes, etc. with eggs. So yes, eggs are a staple, as are: almond milk, spinach, spring salad mix, bananas, strawberries, apples, oat bran, old-fashioned oatmeal, chicken, salmon, cod, lean hamburger, olive oil, avocado oil, and coconut oil, to name a few must-have items.

But what about organic foods you might ask? Well, yes, that's another thing, and I agree organic can be quite costly. I admire those who can afford to purchase from an organic venue, but I choose not to. Yes, if I can buy at a farm market, I'm in, but if I'm going to pay triple the amount for the food, I'm not.

I'll buy fresh, and real, but maybe not organic every time. A part of me always questions how organic the organic is. Isn't the field still receiving rainwater from the pesticide-laced soil next door? And isn't pollution in the air moving from one field to the next? Again, if I can buy organic at a trendy farmers market at reasonable cost, I'm all in.

You can release your obsession with money too, whittling down your debt and Working SMART (Specific, Measurable, Attainable, Relevant, and Time-based). Goals are part of every aspect of winning in whatever you set your mind to accomplish. Our goal is to release the obsession with money and to heal from the inside out. The healing part is inescapable when you work smart. The SMART questions you want to ask yourself are:

1. **Specific:** Are your goals clearly defined and specific?
2. **Measurable:** How easily can you identify your accomplished goals?
3. **Attainable:** Make sure your goal is achievable, not impossible to achieve. For example is your money goal something you can accomplish, such as getting out of

debt and living free versus purchasing an island when you don't have a job or money in the bank.

4. **Relevant:** Are your goals within reach, realistic, and aligned with your other goals?
5. **Time-based:** Do your goals have a clearly defined timeline, including a starting date and a target date. Remember, the purpose is to create some sort of urgency linked to a timeframe.

In Chapter 13 we'll look at food, mood, and how money fits into the equation. You'll meet Melanie and see firsthand how specific foods impact mood and how eating out drains the wallet.

Personal Inventory Questions

1. What are your thoughts regarding Thomas Carlyle's quote, "Our main business is not to see what lies dimly at a distance, but do what lies clearly at hand." What lies clearly at hand for you?
2. I work with people who have eating disorders, which always touches on depression, anxiety, and other obsessions—many times money. Which of these conditions resonates with you? Do you find you're experiencing a combination of a few, or all, or none?
3. Whether you suffer from anorexia or bulimia or binge eating, or perhaps dance between these and/or other types of extreme behaviors, you most likely are spending a great deal of money to feed your habit. How much money do you spend on food? How is that spending affecting your savings? Your debt?
4. I began my healing process using a combination of Cognitive-Behavioral Therapy while changing my thoughts and behaviors; accepting I was a food addict and using a Twelve-Step program designed for food

addicts; and of course, working my recovery through a spiritual connection. I then took many of these techniques and supports into releasing my obsession with money so I could heal from the inside out. Which of the combination might you employ to conquer your needs?

5. My son said something like, "The millennials don't like to buy enormous packages of foods but go for the smaller package." His understanding, from a news report he'd heard earlier that day, was that the younger population isn't prone to stock up on foods. Is this true of you? Are you a small package person? Is it an illusion to keep you from eating more, yet spending more?
6. Okay, you say, what the heck do celebrations and festivities have to do with breaking free from money worries? Well, once upon a time I was broke. Yes, I mean so broke and so in debt I should have been shaking in my boots. I wasn't. My inner self told me I'd find my way out. What's your inner self telling you? Do you *believe* you can find a way out of debt?
7. After reading money books, I understood I wasn't respecting my money. I had student debt of at least $300,000, plus a mortgage, car payment, and credit card debt. I was up to my eyeballs in total debt—and because of out-of-control binge eating I was gaining back the hundred pounds I'd lost. Are you eating your money?
8. And the funny thing is that when you practice working toward becoming debt free, and then living debt free, you actually thereafter continue in a frugal way of living. How could that be? Are you thinking that if you only were debt free then you could buy this or that? How are you processing the concept of living debt free and being frugal?

9. A favorite quote of mine from Richard Carlson's *Don't Worry, Make Money: Spiritual and Practical Ways to Create Abundance and More Fun in Your Life* is "One of the most severely limiting beliefs that many of us have is that the person we were yesterday is the person we have to be today." Are you the person you were yesterday?
10. You can release your obsession with money too, whittling down your debt and Working SMART (Specific, Measurable, Attainable, Relevant, and Time-based). Goals are part of every aspect of winning in whatever you set your mind to accomplish. What is your SMART? Examine your goals and see if they measure up to Melanie's in chapter 13.

Chapter 13

Food, Mood, And Money

It is never too late to be who you might have been.
~George Eliot

It's true: It's never ever too late to be who you might have been, as George Eliot states. So, who you might have been is still right there within you, ready to show him/herself. Ask yourself, who was I supposed to be? Perhaps you are right now doing exactly what you were meant to do. Great! Are you your authentic self? Often people look back with regret for not living their life as they thought they would.

Well-intending parents ushering us to become more, often to fulfill their dream of who *they* might have been, may put a stop to our personal wishes. This is fine if their dream is our dream, but often it's not. Take young Melanie, who dreamt of being a psychologist. Sadly, her mom thought she'd be better off as a web designer because she could learn in a program developed by her high school to give graduates solid tools to keep up with the needs and expectations of employers.

Melanie grew up quickly with a single mom and with siblings out of the home before she turned six years old. Not uncommonly, she would be alone hours on end while her mom worked two, sometimes three jobs to keep a roof over their heads, food in the fridge, and gas in the car. She wanted better for Melanie. She wanted Melanie to go to a trade school instead of high school to lock in her career by the time she turned eighteen. Melanie was whisked away from her childhood friends and a school she loved to attend a tech school that focused on skills to build a career right out of high school.

Working To The Bone

The tech school she attended was not quite what Melanie had in mind to shape her future. She didn't want to be an information technology (IT) specialist working with computers, telephones, and fax machines. The work felt cold and distant, more of what she had grown up with. She wanted a career helping people.

Fast forward, Melanie is now in college, working two jobs to make ends meet. She's been working since she was of age. Melanie never took a break. Now in college, she finds her grades plummeting, her weight inching up, and she's irritable beyond recognition. And of course with work and no play comes burnout. Burnout is one of those words thrown about like it's a quick passing fancy, but sometimes it's not.

Burnout means physical and mental exhaustion—and with it comes a sense of dread about work, and frequent feelings of cynicism, anger, and often irritability. Burnout comes from an extended period of stress that feels as though it cannot be mitigated. Melanie is in a state of emotional, physical, and mental exhaustion caused by excessive and prolonged stress.

She's juggling school and two jobs and has been operating as an adult with little to no supervision since she was a young child. She's tired. And she's moody. Nothing eases her discomfort. She's mad at the world. She's mad at herself. She can't sleep and eats out of control for some relief—though the relief is only temporary.

Working to make money is great, but when we work to the sacrifice of our health, it's no longer a good thing. Too often work becomes a be-all and end-all, and balance is gone with the wind. When this happens, everything sours, as it did for Melanie. She no longer wants to attend her classes or do her homework. "Why go to school? It's a waste of time when I can work more and make money!" she exclaims.

Melanie doesn't want to quit her two jobs. The money motivates her, for she has a car payment, car insurance, and food expense, gas expense, and basic grooming expense. So as a result, she's stress-eating and spending money on take-out, leaving her with $20 in her bank account. Melanie is swirling in a vicious cycle, seeing no way out but to quit school.

Melanie can't see into the future; she only sees this moment. She's not plugging in SMART. She can't tend to her **S**pecific goals because she hasn't clearly defined and detailed what she wants in the future. She's looking for immediate relief, which in her mind is to quit school rather than the two jobs. She has earmarked bringing in the money, now. In her mind, money will solve *all* of her problems. She won't have to go to school. Mom will be proud of her. And she'll be able to pay her bills and buy things.

Melanie joins a host of other people with the same idea. But, her goal is not **M**easurable because she didn't identify what she wants. Yes, of course she said she wants money, but how is she going to get it? Her jobs combined bring in approximately $150 a week. With taxes, she's lucky to clear $500 a month. What is she going to do?

Melanie needs a plan. Once she has a plan in place, she'll be able to make her goal **A**ttainable, and watch the magic happen. What's missing is her goals are not **R**elevant because they don't align with her other goals, and of course she's not time-based because she didn't find a plan to link to a timeframe.

Melanie can only see this moment. And at this moment, she's dead tired. She's not having downtime. She's upset she can't go to her yoga classes because she's too tired, and she turns over when the alarm blares, only to go back to sleep. Clearly, Melanie suffers from burnout and doesn't know how to get off the merry-go-round.

Melanie laments, "I've worked my entire life! I never played. If I wasn't cleaning the house, I was doing other chores for my mom while she worked. It's not fair! It's time for me—I hate my life and don't want any more school. School won't get me anywhere, anyway. I have friends with master's degrees and they work at Starbucks. Education is no guarantee."

Yikes, how do I argue with that? She's right: A degree is not a promise for a suitable career, but it sure the heck is a better idea than not earning at least an associate degree to learn basic discipline and various subjects to carry her into the future. When I questioned Melanie about what she'd do without school, she stared blankly and didn't say a word for what felt like an eternity. I stayed quiet. Finally she whispered, "I don't believe school will realize my dream. I've had nothing but letdowns my whole life."

Food As A Drug

It's true Melanie had many letdowns and had to grow up early in life. I understand. I had to wake up and grow up by twelve, which catapulted me into a major eating disorder for years because I had poor coping skills. Melanie was headed in the same direction. She admitted she was eating nothing but junk food and hitting the take-outs and drive-thru because she was too tired to cook.

As we narrowed in on her fears, she began to gleam with some hope. It's true Melanie wasn't crazy for math and was about to flunk the course. It's also true Melanie took a certification test to become an IT tech and didn't pass. She has had many letdowns in this school of life. But I reminded her that's what builds a backbone and endurance as we power through life. She is lacking "course-confidence,"; she says, as we identify her dreams.

Melanie has no desire to be an IT person, none. And she'd make a mighty fine one at that. But it's not her dream. She wants to become a psychologist. She's strong and determined and has lived life from a non-entitlement place. Melanie is not a quitter; she's a fighter.

She admits if she didn't have the *stupid math class*, her confidence would be through the roof. And the thought of having to retake the class is so terrifying she'd rather quit. And so she's stress-eating large amounts of food and packing on the weight to add to her low self-esteem and lack of confidence, not to mention her swings of highs and lows.

Food, mood, and money are surely getting in Melanie's way. Melanie noticed when she eats certain foods she feels drunk with excitement or so angry she could punch someone. She's craving sweets day and night and finds when she eats them she feels excited and that when she eats starchy foods such as pasta and French fries she calms down. She's swinging from high to low and spending a fortune chasing down her moods. Melanie is not only eating out of control, but at the same times she has wakened her food addiction.

When I was in the doctoral program doing my research, interviewees and patients described the experience of food addiction in the way we described all other addictions. Words such as 'sober,' 'intoxicated,' and 'substance' described, while we compared the two worlds: active addiction versus spiritual recovery from the trigger foods.

I was on a quest to see if a correlation existed between recovery and spiritual awakenings and found this was the case. I find the same with money and spirituality as well, but that's for another chapter on the spiritual side of releasing your obsession with money so that you can *heal from the inside out.*

While I was researching food addiction, those who were in recovery from drug addiction described food as a drug—even pinpointing certain foods. On many days those in the interview process of which I took part were so hung over from a binge, we couldn't perform simple tasks such as answering the phone, returning calls, making appointments, or showing up for engagements—and all the while, we hid our addictions. Isolation protected us. Melanie is also isolating with her food binges.

Like Melanie, all of us reacted to certain foods as if they were drugs, creating mood alterations powerful enough to hold us in a pattern of binge eating, despite our best efforts to try to break the behavior. These foods for us *are* drugs; through chemical reactions, they eventually cause a production of brain substances that have a drug-like effect on the body.

We know these brain chemicals as neurotransmitters. A neurotransmitter is a chemical substance that carries impulses from one nerve cell to another. They act as messages within the brain that help control the body.

If we make a beeline for crackers, pasta, bread, pretzels, or any other simple carbohydrate when experiencing anxiety, tension, or irritable moods, we are most likely looking for serotonin—a nerve chemical (neurotransmitter) that turns on when these foods are metabolized. We are self-medicating, and temporarily, we will feel calm.

Our bodies naturally make serotonin, but some of us don't produce enough. Antidepressant medications such as

Celexa, Cymbalta, Prozac, and Paxil, to name a few, are used to increase the serotonin. Serotonin plays a huge role in mood and appetite.

Cravings for starches and sweets can turn on and off depending on the level of serotonin, which regulates mood, sleep cycles, memory, and pain tolerance. Relatively high levels of serotonin have a calming effect that leads to a clearer mind and stable mood. Low levels of serotonin sink the mood, and clarity is lost—hence, a binge to knock us out of our pain and agitation.

Dopamine and norepinephrine are other neurotransmitters that also play key roles regarding food and mood. For instance, low levels of these neurotransmitters are, like low levels of serotonin, associated with an increase in depression. Increasing dopamine and norepinephrine improves mood, alertness, mental clarity, and the ability to cope with stress. Foods higher in protein will raise the dopamine and norepinephrine levels.

Though all these hormones may have similar effects, helping with mental clarity, reducing depression and anxiety, and stabilizing mood, excessive serotonin can cause sleep disturbances, insomnia, irritability, and mental confusion. For the food addict too, much in the way of simple carbohydrates will drastically increase the level of serotonin, leading to these negative effects. Eating adequate amounts of protein is critical for the food addict then to bring down the high serotonin and normalize moods.

It isn't uncommon for food addicts to fill up on pancakes laced with syrup (for instance) to increase their serotonin levels and then go for a sizzling steak to pull the serotonin down, hence vacillating between highs and lows—*uppers and downers.* And this is exactly what Melanie was doing to produce her ups and downs.

Chocolate, which contains phenylethylamine (PEA), a substance that stimulates the release of dopamine, also helps regulate the mood and explains chocolate cravings. Chocolate, in fact, often serves as an anodyne—a self-medication—to relieve distress or pain that we can't even put our finger on. We ignore our dark emotions and feed ourselves instead, as a balm, which eventually leads to furthering our addictions. Maybe the cravings and increased consumption are a last-ditch effort to regulate moods.

So here you have it: food, mood, and money all rolled into one. Binge eating is expensive as is trekking to restaurants, fast food drive-throughs, and take-outs. All are costly, creating more debt and more worry about money and how to bring in more of it.

Melanie claims she has no time to cook and certainly no time to go food shopping. I ask her to add up how much she spends per week on fast foods, take-outs, and quick stops at the gas station for candy. The sum blows her mind. She is spending a whopping $125 and more every single week. This adds up to $500 a month, if not more. She's baffled. Melanie barely makes that much money with her two jobs, leaving her always broke and wanting to work more to resolve that problem. But this isn't the ideal resolution as working more is creating overwhelm and burnout, leading to the idea of quitting school while an education would provide an opportunity for a better life in the future.

Melanie held onto what life was like pre-college, pre-pandemic—a time when she was used to doing what she wanted, but with two jobs and school her schedule has become a burden. Now she believes she has no time to shop and cook and feels buying takeout is easier. Also, her classes are on Zoom so she's stuck in the house for hours on end, with no socialization. By the time school ends for the day, she's starving, lonely, anxious, and depressed, so she then buys multiple items from McDonalds to make up for the foods she didn't have. Says she's too lazy to get up at seven to cook.

Melanie is aware of her problem that she's stress eating, admitting she has self-awareness and knows what she's doing but can't stop. She feels good gorging on foods and not thinking about all that overwhelms her. That is, she feels good for the moment. She wants immediate relief, even though she knows it won't last long term. When I couple how distraught she was breaking up with her boyfriend of three years, not passing the IT certification exam, the pandemic and lockdown, along with two jobs and school, that she's burning out makes sense.

Furthermore, to keep awake, she's drinking gallons of coffee and Red Bull, trying to push through, yet everything in her life is falling apart. Her grades have plummeted; she's not getting along with co-workers, not to mention her mom, and she has lost all of her friends. Melanie is in dire straits—yet she has this dream to become financially independent and never have to worry again. We need to hone in on this dream and build her SMART.

Melanie bounces from sad to overwhelm. Not so long ago when she went through the breakup with her boyfriend, and all her girlfriends had disappeared because she was never available to hang out with them, she dropped twenty pounds. She felt depressed, leading to no appetite. But when she became stressed, she bounced the other way, eating everything in sight, gaining twenty pounds.

She says she's gobbling up fast food as if it's her last supper. McDonalds is making her jones for more of the bad stuff like sugar, salt, and fat. Obsessed, eyes glistening, she admits she loves wearing sweats and hitting Mickey-D's despite the expense.

I understand where Melanie is coming from because I went through something similar. In my college days, I went to work bartending in downtown Chicago until five in the morning. I left there totally wiped out. Nightly, I stopped at the sub-shop, snagging a super sub, chips, a few cookies, and a malted milkshake. I slept a couple of hours, grabbed the train into the city, and sat disheveled in school by eight, only to return home to catch a few more hours of sleep, and then went back to work again. Like Melanie, I wondered how these school kids could afford not to work, but they had different parents who didn't make them find jobs.

After working through the reality of how miserable Melanie was during her middle school and high school years, when she didn't have money, or an out from her situation, she found her first job. She was lonely and hungry for attention, which the job filled. The money gave her a high. It meant she could buy what she wanted—so she thought.

But this all came to a halt when the coronavirus hit and Zoom classes became the new norm. She felt a prisoner in her bedroom, once again alone. She'd stay locked in for hours with little to eat, "rotting in her room," so that by the time she came out, she was starving, wolfing down enormous amounts of food to satisfy her yearning for something. In time, her hair began falling out in clumps.

Money, too, brings on a rush of feeling—a surge of the neurotransmitter dopamine. What do I mean? Well, when you purchase something, often you have this chemical reaction that triggers an intense, giddy euphoria. Your brain is rewarding you with a high, a desire for more. We were under a spell of wanting this item (e.g., jewelry, a pair of shoes, and of course food such as takeout foods or dinner in a fancy restaurant). This chemical response allows us to feel something. The brain lights up and brings on a bodily emotion.

These days, Melanie is doing well. Her weight has reset; she stayed in school. We worked her SMART with plans to restore her balance by having her cut back on work and shop for non-processed foods. She's back in her yoga class and hanging out with friends.

Now she has a healthy balance, goes to Whole Foods and eats natural foods such as yogurt, fruits, and salads... and loads of water. Melanie says she craves eating avocado, arugula, and turkey slices for breakfast. Her hair loss has ceased, and money is no longer an issue because she's saving more and spending less.

Melanie learned quickly that saving her pennies went a long way. You'll see for yourself in Chapter 14 how easy putting aside money for that rainy day can be.

Personal Inventory Questions

1. It's true: "It's never ever too late to be who you might have been," as George Eliot states. Who you might have been is still right there within you, ready to show him/herself. Ask yourself, who was I supposed to be? Perhaps you are, right now, doing exactly what you were meant to do. Great! Are you your authentic self?
2. Well-intentioned parents encouraging us to become more, often to fulfill their own dream of who they might have been, can put a stop to personal wishes. This is fine if their dream is your dream, but often it's not. Are you fulfilling your parents' dreams?
3. Though Melanie attended the tech school, this path was not quite what she had in mind as to how she wanted her future to go. Melanie didn't want to be an information technology (IT) specialist working with computers, telephones, and fax machines. The job felt cold and distant, more of what she had grown up with. Melanie joined the ranks of many who start early in a career that's

not a good fit for them. What was your first job? Did it turn into your career?

4. Burnout is physical and mental exhaustion—and with it comes a sense of dread about work, and frequent feelings of cynicism, anger, and often irritability. Burnout is an extended period of stress that feels as though it cannot be mitigated. Have you ever experienced burnout? If so, how did you work through the symptoms?
5. Food, mood, and money were surely getting in Melanie's way. Melanie noticed when she ate certain foods, she felt drunk with excitement or so angry she could have punched someone. She craved sweets day and night and found when she ate them she felt excited, and that when she ate starchy foods such as pasta and French fries, they calmed her down. Do you notice highs and lows from specific foods? How does it affect your life?
6. If we make a beeline for crackers, pasta, bread, pretzels, or any other simple carbohydrate when experiencing anxiety, tension, or irritable moods, we are most likely looking for serotonin—a nerve chemical (neurotransmitter) that turns on when these foods metabolize. We are self-medicating, and temporarily, we will feel calm. Are you turning to food as if to a drug—self-medicating? Which foods cause you the greatest highs or lows or a combination of the two?
7. Melanie claimed she had no time to cook and certainly no time to go food shopping. I asked her to add up how much she spent per week on fast foods, take-out, and quick stops at the gas station for candy. How much do you spend on processed foods? Have you ever sat down to see just how much money is going out to buy foods that leave you wanting for more?

8. To stay awake, Melanie was drinking gallons of coffee and Red Bull to push through her tasks, yet everything she tried to do was falling short. Are you going for stimulants such as caffeine, nicotine, or chocolate for energy? Do you find the lift is long lasting or the feeling only plummets shortly after, making you want more, or leaving you in heaps of anxiety?
9. Melanie plugged in SMART to work through her dilemmas. What would your SMART (Specific, Measurable, Attainable, Relevant, and Time-based) look like after reading Melanie's story? Has it changed from when you worked through the personal inventory questions in the last chapter? What changed? What stayed the same?
10. Money too causes a lift in feeling—a surge of the neurotransmitter dopamine. What do I mean? Well, when you purchase something often you get this chemical reaction that triggers an intense, giddy euphoria. Your brain is rewarding you with a high, and a desire for more. What spending ignites your neurotransmitter dopamine?

Chapter 14

Saving Pennies Goes A Long Way

The pessimist sees difficulty in every opportunity.
The optimist sees the opportunity in every difficulty.
~Winston Churchill

Are you the pessimist or the optimist—the choice is yours. Which do you want to be? We all have opportunity even in times of difficulty. When you rise above and plunge forward, you may well find a pot of gold at the end of the rainbow. Take Butch, who is disabled and can't work because he has trouble standing and sitting for long periods of time. He had a terrible accident at one time and lives in pain. He could have seen through the eyes of a pessimist, difficulty in every opportunity, but no, he saw opportunity in every difficulty.

One night on the way home from one of his motorcycle rides, a car coming around the corner blindsided him, making a very wide turn. At this spot, while a rail protected car drivers from cascading over the edge into the ravine, it didn't protect Butch. The night was rainy, the roads were slippery, and Butch lost control of his bike, breaking through the rails, falling far below, where he lay for hours before being discovered. The result of the accident was that Butch broke his back and lost his leg. Still, he never complained through the arduous process of physical therapy and learning to walk with a prosthetic leg.

Now here's the best part. Butch learned from his great-grandmother that you could create money out of anything. She told him to use his imagination along with vision and a great result could appear in his life. She also told him to save most and spend little. Once upon a time, Butch had worked at a fabulous job selling parts at a high-end auto shop. He'd made a substantial income and loved his job. On the weekends he rode his motorcycle along the seashore for hours on end.

He couldn't go back to his job, and with no severance pay, a mortgage, a motorcycle payment—though the motorcycle had become scrap metal—and with little savings, Butch had to do something. Rather than becoming depressed as many of us would have, he lived on the skirts of optimism. He saw bright when others saw dark. He laughed when others might cry. He dreamed—and dreamed big, always.

Butch's faith in God was unshaken as he rebuilt his life from the ground up. The sales from Butch's Bargain Basement, his newly grown business, though for many years were minimal at the start, each dollar he put into his savings thrilled him. In time, Butch paid off his home and was able to afford a fancy van with all the fixings to accommodate his physical limitations.

Butch has a knack for finding goods in the oddest places. He goes online searching for deals and closeouts. He frequents the dollar stores and other bargain stores for deals. He's no stranger to used bookstores and garage sales. Butch has his antennae shooting straight up for opportunity. And everyone in town knows it. Butch has set up a makeshift store in the back of his home, where he displays all of his finds. His advertisement is all word of mouth.

So if you 're looking for a used, but good shape anything, you may find it at Butch's Bargain Basement as he calls his shop. He has a flashy little sign he crafted out of wood, chiseling out the letters with colors of all sorts to fill the space—a snazzy sign swaying above his makeshift basement. I wondered why "basement" when he lives in sunny South Florida with no basement in sight. "I always wanted a basement, but it wasn't a reality, so I created it in my mind. Hence, Butch's Bargain Basement."

Now Butch no longer rides his bike but he's grateful for the days when he rode for hours on end, feeling the cool breeze in his face, tooling around the ocean edge for miles and miles. He's not bitter; he's living in gratitude because he learned the best lesson, that of living in the moment, that tomorrow is promised to no one. He believes everything happens for a reason and that seasons come and go. Now, he's finding pleasure in helping others discover their treasures in his so-called basement.

As a young child, Butch always saved his pennies because his grandma reminded him often that pennies saved go a long way. She emigrated from South America with the clothes on her back, period. She took the first job she could find, which was cleaning houses. She cleaned the most magnificent homes, finding pride in her work. One home was so impressed with her work they invited her to move in as their full-time housekeeper.

Abuela (Grandma) didn't have any expenses and now didn't have rent to pay, so every penny she earned, she saved. Soon, she met the love of her life and had children and grandchildren, always reminding them they can build wealth by saving as she did. She earned enough to buy her own home and cleaned for so many that she hired a team of cleaners and built an amazing business. But she never forgot her roots and what she did to get where she ended up.

Butch not only picked up his grandma's positive attitude, but her business sense as well. He wants for nothing and feels proud of all he has. He didn't inherit his money; he earned it.

And his grandma still cleans a few homes, though she doesn't have to, but she loves the families and the homes she's maintained for many years.

Comparing To The Joneses

How easily we become caught up in defining who we are in relation to those around us. Butch doesn't look like a wealthy man. He lives in a simple fashion. He owns his home and vehicle, living debt free, but he doesn't present himself as a rich man or even slightly wealthy. Though he's not wearing the fancy clothes or driving the newest vehicle, he's quite comfortable financially. As of the last time we spoke, he had over a million dollars tucked away.

I remember walking my pup in an affluent side of town, admiring all the fancy homes overlooking the water. Many had high-end cars parked in their driveways and boats tied to the docks. One home in particular really struck my fancy as it was on the point, with nothing but water views. *Oh, how wealthy they must be*, I thought. Right now, the house is in foreclosure; the grounds are unkempt, and the boat is half sinking. What happened?

A neighbor informed me they were living well beyond their means and their lifestyle caught up with them. Of course, we never wish that on anyone, but sometimes we want to be like the other guy because they look so rich—and they are not. They're living big when they don't have the means.

But then in that same neighborhood, I know Roy, who also has pride in quite the mansion, with a boat attached to a lengthy dock, pristine grounds, and nice cars parked in the driveway. Yes, Roy looks rich, and he is. But he started off without money, grew up in an impoverished neighborhood, often displaying holes in his pants and with the soles of his shoes flapping and having no money for lunch. He ventured out early in life delivering papers in the neighborhood on his bike.

Roy loved the outdoors, lost himself in the joy of riding his bike, free of school, not enmeshed in the anger that awaits some at home, because his home was filled with love. He was happy, proud to have a job at thirteen, and feeling the wind beneath his wings, with no obstacles standing in his way.

Roy had a giant jar he put all his money in, and when it filled, he'd take it to the bank where he opened a savings account. He lived on the measly amounts of money his mom could scrape up as she encouraged him to keep saving and dream big. He did.

In time, Roy grew a bank account with enough money so that he could put some in the stock market as his single mom pushed him to do. His investments compounded and tripled and grew beyond his wildest imagination. He studied hard and saved money, the two jobs his mom instilled in him. The jar kept filling, and he'd diligently bring it to the bank and then put the money into investments. Meanwhile, Roy's grades in school were very good. He earned a scholarship that paid for his degree in finance. He loved numbers.

Nowadays, Roy lives in his fancy house with all the amenities. He still saves. He also gives to charities. He has two fine sons, who together have a neighborhood lawn service where they earn a good deal of money. All the money goes into a jar and then off to their savings—just like dad. Roy didn't spoil his sons. They know what they have to do—fulfill two jobs: one being school, and the other being saving their money. These boys don't pursue a life of luxury or play. They are learning to earn and make it on their own.

Roy saw firsthand too many spoiled kids in his community wearing top name brands and driving fancy cars turning to drugs, alcohol, and partying. He didn't want his own kids to get by without earning. He also saw many lose their money because they weren't cautious; they let down their guard. Roy has the mindset that earning money is easy, but holding onto it is another task.

The Psychology of Money by M. Housel, makes the same point, noting that keeping money requires humility, and the fear that what you've made can be taken away from you just as fast. Housel also shows that even if 'wealthy' is not a word you'd use for yourself, the lessons apply to everyone, at all income levels. He referenced two multimillionaires who both lost their money because they let down their guard, spending and taking risks.

"The pessimist sees difficulty at every opportunity. The optimist sees the opportunity in every difficulty," Winston Churchill said. Clearly, looking at both Butch and Roy they saw opportunity even in the dark times. We also can't let down our guard by spending and taking risks, a caution that comes as part of the success equation —we must save for those hard times, as surely they will come.

Housel says financial freedom requires frugality and an acceptance that at least some of what you've made is because of luck, so past success can't be relied upon to repeat indefinitely. I'd like to add to that thought: Perhaps some of the money made is in part frugality and luck, but I'd dare to go a step further and add the need for prayer to the mix. Prayer is powerful. Oxford Dictionaries defines prayer as a solemn request for help, or expression of thanks addressed to God or another object of worship.

At this point, we turn the corner to the next and final part of this book where we hone in on gratitude and the power of prayer, along with recovering from past bad money behavior, not to mention *healing from the inside out.* This is what you'll see when we slide into Part III: **Turn The Corner.**

Personal Inventory Questions

1. "The pessimist sees difficulty in every opportunity. The optimist sees the opportunity in every difficulty," according to Winston Churchill. Are you the pessimist or the optimist?—the choice is yours. Which do you want to be? We all have opportunity even in times of difficulty. Or do you find in certain situations you tend in one way, while other times not? Dig deep; examine when you lean negative and when positive.
2. Take Butch who is disabled and can't work, as he has trouble standing or sitting for long periods of time. He had a terrible accident years ago and lives in pain. He could have seen difficulty in every opportunity through the eyes of a pessimist, but no, he saw opportunity, in every difficulty. Are you like Butch? Would you be upbeat during such trying times?
3. Perhaps you have been through some difficult times, as most of us have. Given your personal situation, how did you power through it? Did it knock the wind out of you, changing the direction of your life? How did your attitude fare?
4. Butch learned from his great-grandmother that you could create money out of anything. She told him to use his imagination along with vision, and success could appear in his life. Who was your money influencer? We tapped into this discussion in earlier personal inventory questions, but now, at this point, perhaps your answer changed.
5. And on this note of money influencers, consider who was a positive influence, and who contributed negatively to your negative behavior. Usually, we have one on each end. My mom was not good with money, nor was her mother, yet my father was amazing, as was his father, both living simply yet building wealth. Examine both

sides and plug in your behaviors to see who made you who you are today, money-wise that is.

6. Butch's grandmother emigrated from South America with no money, job, or permanent home. She cleaned houses to make her way. My grandfather emigrated from Italy and learned to lay brick, not to mention bootlegging. Pick one of your grandparents and study their behavior and your thoughts about that person as they shaped your life.
7. How easily we become caught up in defining who we are in relation to those around us. Butch doesn't look like a wealthy man. He lives in a simple way, yet he's a millionaire. Think about someone you thought was wealthy, and then taking a deeper look, you might have seen they were in debt. How did that impact your understanding of wealth?
8. And how about Roy, who prides himself on quite the mansion, with a boat attached to a lengthy dock, pristine grounds, and nice cars parked in the driveway. He saved when he was a small child, building wealth young. He lives large, but he earned it. Would you like to be a Roy? Do you believe saving pennies can go a long way?
9. *The Psychology of Money* by M. Housel makes the point that keeping money requires humility, and fear that what you've made can be taken away from you. Do you live in humility? Think about your personal stories of those who had wealth and lost it? Could they have done something different?
10. Housel also shows that even if "wealthy" is not a word you'd use for yourself, the lessons applies to everyone, at all income levels. What is the lesson for you? And do you apply the word wealthy to yourself? How would you describe yourself?

Part III

Turn The Corner

Chapter 15

Power of Prayer, Recovery, And Healing From The Inside Out

Seeing is not believing.
Believing is seeing!
You see things, not as they are, but as you are.
~Eric Butterworth

"Seeing is not believing" is a powerful statement. And "Believing is seeing" is even more so. And understanding that to see things not as they are, but as *you* are opens the floodgates of awareness. Couple this awareness with the power behind prayer, recovery, and healing from the inside out, and a whole lot of good can pop up in your life!

You might wonder how prayer, recovery, and healing from the inside out has anything to do with releasing the obsession with money, but it does on so many levels. Personally, I think luck and coincidences are only a small percentage of the marvelous happenings in our lives. Perhaps divine intervention plays a bigger role.

Perhaps we have many lessons about miracles to learn. What you discover and what happens for you is up to you and your intentions. For many, when they encounter a dark season in life, prayer comes to mind as an instinct. The prayer may not be one from religious instruction; in fact, for most people what comes forth in times of trouble is not a rote litany of memorized prayers.

Prayer is a conversation with the higher source that works for you, which can lead to recovery of the heart, mind, and soul, bringing you a healing from the inside out. When finances are out of whack and worry is your only known feeling, bending the knee, connecting with your Divine wellspring brings peace and tranquility, and most of all, hope that everything is going to be all right.

The other day I was reading *Mother Teresa's Reaching Out in Love: Stories Told by Mother Teresa,* a compilation of stories about her holy life. One story really resonated with me in which she expressed how surprised she was to see the increasing number of drug addicts among young boys and girls from rich *and* poor families and how she went on a mission to find out why this was so.

In Mother's findings, she learned often these children come home with no one in the family there to receive them. She says, "Our children depend on us for everything—their health, their nutrition, their security, their coming to know and love God. For all this they come to us with trust, hope, and expectation."

After reflecting on her words, I remembered coming home to an empty home night after night when I was twelve, and where it led me. My thought about Mother Theresa's words was *And then they grow up and they come to me with addiction(s) and a host of psychological challenges, one of which is a spiritual quest for healing from the inside out.* I had those challenges as well from my early, empty start. My blessing was in my formative years when I had a Catholic upbringing, attending church and parochial school.

And of course we have no spiritual healing without recovery—at least from my view. And prayer is the glue sealing the hope and help from the higher source. Prayer is personal, with no rules—a spiritual communication between the person and their God or higher power of choice. I believe the relationship is a two-way street of talking and listening for guidance. I always thought of God as a father figure and a best friend rolled into one.

Dropped To Our Knees

Often, when we drop to our knees with no way out and nobody to turn to, that higher source becomes our go-to. It's at our lowest of lows—and also at our highest of highs when we can give thanks and gratitude for all the blessings in our life. The experience is a humble moment that costs no money. It's a gift flowing from what we understand as the Divine.

When twisted in knots filled with fear, the body goes into overload, hurting emotionally, physically, and spiritually, leading to going nowhere fast. At this time of pain, we put our pride to the side, seeking hope, admitting our need. This is a time of humility. All religions and spiritual practices are based in prayer.

One thing I noticed working in my profession with addictions and eating disorders, money obsessions are often part of the equation. And another thing, I noticed is often the addictions sprout from lack of love, which begins in the home. Not that I'm talking about abusive homes because that might be so, but I'm also referring to permissive, negligent homes, homes without prayer, among other situations, such as homes of the over-privileged and the underprivileged.

Life dishes up good and bad, happy and sad at any given moment. Tomorrows remain a mystery until they are upon us. Often, during our darkest days, that's when we turn to God, our higher source for guidance and relief. This is when we're bent into a pretzel, and we see no way out, and fear is gripping so tightly we can't breathe. We've all been there a time or two, in our lives, wondering how we'll ever come out of it.

I recall Jayden, a recovering alcoholic, who lost his job—and then his son, whom he had custody of with alimony, moved out, ending the alimony along with government support. Bobby was eighteen, and the rule was if you quit school and you were eighteen, the government aid stops, along with alimony. Bobby quit school after turning eighteen. In addition, Jayden's two renters in his divided home both moved out. Life couldn't have seemed any dimmer.

Jayden, in total despair, couldn't bear what he was feeling, which was desolate and defeated. He had worked tirelessly to keep himself afloat, with a good run of success. He'd scraped together enough money to pay his mortgage, feed his family, and meet all the expenses that come with life, and he'd had money left over. Jayden wasn't a saver of money; he lived in the moment—being carefree and whimsical.

On this dark day, his troubles caught up with him. Scared, he drove to the liquor store in a storm of fear, purchased a bottle of Jack Daniels, drinking himself into a stupor. He continued day after day, drinking by night, passed out by day. Soon, the mortgage was past due, food was scarce, and he'd maxed out his credit cards. Oh, yes, he was charged with a DUI, and soon after, his car was repossessed. Dark days indeed!

At this low point, Jayden reached out for help. He was in trouble with the law, his money was depleted, and he had no job in sight. His son was out there on the loose, and Jayden was drunk, in the grasp of losing everything. With nothing going his way, he made his way to Alcoholics Anonymous, a Twelve-Step program, and rekindled his love for God. He was broke, desperate, and frightened.

Often at our worst times, that's when we turn to our higher source, rekindling our spiritual self, opening the door for prayer and recovery. On the last night Jayden was drinking, he blacked out and was awakened by a banging on his car window. Screaming and yelling pursued him. The sound seemed so far off that he thought he might be dreaming.

Jayden heard a crash and felt glass hitting his face. A hand reached into the car, unlocking the door and shoving him to the side. Moments later, he felt someone tapping his face, "Wake up, wake up… Are you trying to kill yourself!!"

Jayden had passed out on the railroad tracks, moments away from being crushed by a train. He remembered nothing. He had blanked out the entire day. Rocked to his core, when he was awake and clear minded for the first time in months, he felt filled with gratitude to be alive. He wept like a baby, sobbing, begging for God's forgiveness and help. This was a turning point for Jayden. *He had another chance at life.*

Jayden had much experience with drinking and driving, along with the consequences from years of making his way out of such disasters in his younger days. He had never gone through a spiritual recovery but maintained a white-knuckle sobriety with the chance of a relapse always lurking in the background. And then he did relapse—and in a big way, drinking himself into oblivion night after night.

But this time he was not so lucky. Death would have been right there had they had not found him only minutes before he would have been crushed by the train. His car didn't fare so well. At this point he realized his life too would be crushed if he didn't get a grasp on his drinking, and he did. He was clean and sober for ten years until all the mishaps piled up. Jayden is an attorney, so he is no fool to the consequences of his actions. He also knows all the steps to recovery, which he then implemented.

Loss of money can drive us to our knees and rekindle our addictions or poor choices of the past. Jayden worked tirelessly to get out of debt in his younger years. And here he was again in debt. Back then, he had a credit card he struggled to get to go down, but with every payment it never was paid off. He was upset, feeling he had no way out, no reason to keep paying if he could never actually pay it off. He lost any miniscule amount of motivation he could muster up to pay it off because "the needle wouldn't move." He developed a what's-the-point mentality.

But Jayden climbed out of his debt by working diligently and paying down what he owed. He realized that keeping his balance on his credit card prevented him from making a dent, and the balance only rose.

And now here Jayden was in this situation again—greeted by debt and fear, and worse, a rekindled problem with alcohol. But this time differed from all those years before. This time, Jayden could use his expertise as an attorney, making his way out. Also, he found power in prayer, asking for deliverance from his burden of alcoholism. He had another chance, but this time built with a support team comprising the Twelve-Step group, the God of his understanding, and psychotherapy.

Jayden never missed his AA meetings, often attending several in one day. He found prayer again and recovery. In time, he paid off his debts and found a job, and life slowly returned to normal. He found new renters. His son, Bobby, had his own awakening returning home and contributing money to help with debts, also attending a GED program to complete his high school requirements. Both father and son awakened and began anew.

Life has a way of slamming us down when we least expect it. Tomorrow is promised to no one, and today is a gift. Jayden found giving service healing. At his meetings he heard so many stories of hardship that he used his ability in the legal realm to help others.

Jayden started his own practice working sometimes *pro bono* (professional work undertaken voluntarily and without payment) and at other times at a very low rate. Twelve-Steppers from all walks of life showed up. Jayden put Bobby to work, teaching him many tasks required in his law practice, prompting Bobby's desire to go into the legal field too. These were all works of service that contributed to Jayden's healing from the inside out. Recovery took hold and life became much more meaningful.

And Then There's Janika

Yes, out of the dark comes light. Janika's situation differed from Jayden's, as she was addicted to Xanax, running the streets to get her fix. She suffered from severe anxiety and was prescribed an anti-anxiety medicine when she was quite young. For years, the pills worked as intended, and she never abused the medication until dark days fell upon her.

Janika came from an empty home. She was a latchkey kid, allowed to roam the streets and live life any way she wanted. Being home alone terrified her and sent her anxiety raging. She brought males home to keep her company when her dad worked—which was almost always. She had no mother.

Janika took more and more medication, not able to make it to her prescription renewal. Often, she found herself in the

ER to bridge her fix until her next refill. Each month she promised herself she'd take only the prescribed three a day, which always turned to six and seven, forcing her to find the rest out on the streets or at the emergency room. She was frightened. She'd been on medication since she was a young child. For years, she'd managed, but when her dad passed away well in his nineties, Janika felt terrified.

She didn't want to be alone. She'd never been alone. She had lived alone with her dad since she was born and had never moved out so that they had been enmeshed and tangled in each other's lives. Though her dad worked long hours in his very profitable business, he was rarely home. When he passed away, her father left a rather large inheritance for Janika to live comfortably for the rest of her life.

But with this overpowering drug addiction, Janika spent the money, hitting the streets to buy more Xanax to hold her over. And because being home alone terrified her, she hung out at the casino, spending large amounts of money. Though she had a handsome sum of money to carry her through until her elder years and beyond, she was slowly chipping away at what was to be her safety net for her remaining years. Janika didn't work. She was too anxious and couldn't stay focused.

Janika was a hot mess, which brought her to me for psychotherapy. She had gone through the revolving door of several treatment centers with little success until she fell to her knees when the police swarmed her complex, looking for the drug dealers and purchasers. She hid behind a tree, heart beating so loudly she thought they'd hear her. She froze. She shook in fear for hours on end, believing for the first time she was in trouble, really in trouble.

"I'm in duck sauce this time," she'd said to me. And she was. She repeated, "I'm going to change, I promise." But the promise fell on her own deaf ears until she truly was in duck sauce with no way out. The fear was the greatest she'd ever felt in her life—right up there with the passing of her dad, as she said.

To her relief, the police didn't go after her but arrested a rather large drug-dealing ring. While in hiding, she prayed and prayed—admitting that until that night in hiding, she wasn't really a praying kind of person. She was so afraid that all she could think of was the Blessed Mary she'd learned about from her family as a small child. She was so hungry for her non-existing mom that she blended Mom and Mary all those hours she hid, listening to the swoosh of helicopters flying overhead with the spotlight just missing her.

Janika promised in her prayers that if she made it out of this without being caught, she'd seek help for her addictions, both gambling and Xanax. And she did. This time, she was ready. Her overwhelming anxiety was more than she could bear. She didn't want to be in her own skin. Nothing was working for her, and she could find no relief. The magnitude of the anxiety was mentally, physically, and emotionally draining her.

Today, however, Janika is doing well. She no longer goes to the casino and is off the Xanax, which was replaced with a non-addictive anti-anxiety medication. She also bought a baby grand piano and plays sweet music again the way she did as a child. It calms her. She took up meditation and yoga by the beach, often saying, "I love relaxing by the beautiful moon—I feel the mommy I never knew and the Blessed Mary and my beloved dad." I believe she does.

And Then There Was Me!

As you've read throughout any of my works, I too had addictions and today live in recovery. My first addiction was to food, which crippled me for a good chunk of my youth. And to compensate for the food, I smoked cigarettes, thinking that would help me curb my appetite—but it only created an addiction to nicotine. I knew early in life I could easily turn to drugs, but for the grace of God, I knew better than to go there.

I recognized after years of trial and error, schooling, and working with Weight Watchers of Greater Miami for thirteen years interacting with the clientele, that some of us had an eating disorder, which needed to be addressed. I had binge eating disorder, bulimia through *over*-exercising, and food addiction. These gripped me with worry and fears. And I was broke.

I learned after three decades of struggling with my food to build a ritual of healthy habits that worked for me. A ritual of going to bed at the same time and rising at the same time was one habit I developed. Included in my health regime now, too, is walking, swimming, or biking daily; eating actual foods and avoiding sugar, flour, and wheat; and staying away from alcohol and all illegal substances. And most important, I live within my means, rather than keeping up with the Joneses, looking rich or "well-to-do."

Eating healthfully, engaging in moderate exercise, and drinking water as my main drink cleared my pimpled face and released my weight, while propelling myself away from sugar, flour, and wheat cleared my addictive craving for junk foods. Today, my weight is stable, up and down within a two-to three-pound range. And I'm debt free!!

Nowadays, I swing between 138 and 142—which was exactly where I started a full-blown eating disorder. I was hungry at twelve because my body was growing, and hormones were raging. I felt my body change and panicked. I thought I was going to become heavy. I didn't know bodies change when we change from being a girl to being a woman, meaning bigger hips, breasts, and curves where I didn't know curves belonged.

When my weight got to 142, I freaked—and then let the eating disorders begin. I was going on thirteen. From there, I suffered the range of a healthy weight to a hundred pounds heavier and then back down again. I seesawed up and down. Perhaps if I'd been content at the 142 all those years ago, I could have spared myself decades of an eating disorder, self-loathing, and body image distortion. Perhaps.

At one time I smoked two packs of menthol cigarettes a day—hoping to ward off a higher weight. I chose junk foods over alcohol—most of the time—not for health but for a calorie bargaining chip as alcohol, I thought, had more calories and led to more eating.

Drugs. Thank goodness I didn't go down that rabbit hole, but surely I could have, especially choosing cocaine as a weight controller—but my fear of my parents *killing* me kept me from that. And of course, for me, pot was a no-no because it would make me eat, or so I thought. Also, I needed to always be in control—at least where substances were concerned.

Today, no cigarettes, no alcohol, moderate exercise, proper food, spiritual nourishment including wonderful books, journaling, and writing are some ingredients I employ to live my best life. Also, I've found laughter, smiling, and pure fun to be important. Blessed with the gift of life, cherishing and respecting it might give us the best opportunity to age gracefully, ward off illnesses—and if we get sick, maybe we can pass through such quickly.

The power of prayer was what got me through. I prayed for recovery. I prayed for peace in my thoughts and actions. I soon healed from the inside out. I understood that my outer appearance wasn't what was most valuable, but what I harbored within. What Eric Butterworth says is true: "Seeing is not believing. Believing is seeing! You see things, not as they are, but as you are."

We all have dark seasons in our lives. And swapping one addiction for another is not uncommon—plus, inevitably at some point, money factors in. But we can always have hope and can always find help. Open your eyes and open your heart, and most important, believe. Jayden, his son Bobby, Janika, and I all demonstrate situations in which prayer, recovery, and healing from the inside out took hold. And money always seems to be the backdrop. If money is what you yearn for, remember the almighty dollar is not always so almighty as you shall see in Chapter 16.

Personal Inventory Questions

1. "Seeing is not believing. Believing is seeing! You see things, not as they are, but as you are," says Eric Butterworth. At this point in the book, who are you? What do you see?
2. Personally, I think luck and coincidences are only a small percentage of what drives the happenings in our lives. Perhaps divine intervention plays a bigger role. Perhaps we have lessons to learn. What you learn is up to you and your intentions. For many of us, when we go through a dark season in life, prayer comes to mind as a natural instinct. Do you turn to prayer?
3. What does prayer look like for you? Are you one to recite prayers you learned as a small child, or simply have conversations with the God of your understanding?
4. Mother Teresa speaks to how "Our children depend on us for everything—their health, their nutrition, their security, their coming to know and love God. For all this they come to us with trust, hope and expectation." Who did you turn to in the spiritual realm?
5. When twisted in knots filled with fear, the body goes into overload, hurting emotionally, physically, and spiritually, leading to going nowhere fast. At this time of

need, we put our pride to the side, seeking hope, admitting our pain. Can you recall a time you felt twisted in knots? At what point did you recognize you needed help?

6. On the last night Jayden was drinking, he blacked out, wakened by banging on his car window. Screaming and yelling pursued him. The sounds seemed so far off that he thought he might be dreaming, but he wasn't. Jared was moments from being crushed by a train. This was his bottom. What was your bottom? And where did it lead you?
7. Jayden started his own practice working sometimes *pro bono* and at other times at a very low rate. He found substantial reward giving service. What service do you give?
8. Janika took more and more of her prescribed Xanax medication, not able to make it to her prescription renewal. Often, she found herself in the ER to bridge her fix until her next refill. Becoming addicted to medication is not uncommon, particularly when someone is going through hard times, whether financial, emotional, or spiritual. Have you ever been caught up in abusing your medications? If so, what led to that? What was the catalyst for your obsession?
9. I too had my hardships with addiction, reaching lows of epic proportion but managed—at the pace of a snail—to climb out of the abyss. What about you? Which person, Jayden, Janika, or possibly I, resonated with you? Why?
10. For sure we can find a power in prayer, with recovery at its heels leading to healing from the inside out. What does healing from the inside out look like to you?

Chapter 16

God And The Almighty Dollar

Surrender.
Let silence have you.
And if you find you are still swimming
on the surface of the ocean,
Let go and sink into the depths of love.
~Kar Kirpa Sahib

Well, here we are hugging up against God and the almighty dollar. Some see the dollar as their God, while others give away money because they feel building wealth is wrong. Some see the dollar as sin, a bad thing. Are God and the dollar in competition? Can we be wealthy and godly? Is it possible money has replaced God for many?

God and the almighty dollar! Have we, the people, put them in opposition to one another? Maybe the time has come to: "Surrender. Let silence have you. And if you find you are still swimming on the surface of the ocean, let go and sink into the depths of love." Love. Love is the ticket. And God is love. The almighty dollar is not going to love you. Never.

In several places in the Bible, Jesus asks people to leave their possessions, loved ones, and all their monetary worth to follow him. That would be hard to do, and many did not—though many did. Could you?

Ecclesiastes 5:10 says: "He who loves money is never satisfied by money, and he who loves wealth is never satisfied by income. This too is futile. Whoever loves money never has enough; whoever loves wealth is never satisfied with their income. This too is meaningless." Those who love money will never have enough.

In other words, don't put everything on money as the answer for all. And don't put the money in one place—"If the clouds be full of rain, they empty themselves upon the earth: and if the tree fall toward the south, or toward the north, in the place where the tree falleth, there it shall be." ~ Ecclesiastes 11:3

Don't hold the money so tightly as if it will not replenish. The clouds, when full of rain, will disperse plentiful showers upon each of the parts of the earth without distinction, by which it is refreshed and made fruitful. Perhaps we should be like the full clouds showering and sharing our good fortunes. Rain will come and rain will go. And wherever the tree falls, there it shall be.

Seeds are sure to sprout, but you never know where disaster or prosperity will strike. Many unanticipated things will occur in life. Life is unpredictable; things are not always going to go the way you would like them to go.

Living A Simple Life

We need to find a balance. Spending more time making money than making time with God is never a good idea. Fr. Peter Rookey, whom I've mentioned probably in every book I've ever written, was a simple yet famous healing priest from Chicago, who under the guidance of God performed many miracles. I first met Father in 1999, shortly after my mom suffered a massive stroke, leaving her paralyzed. He prayed with and over her many times.

Though my mother never walked again and remained confined to her bed for the remaining years of her life, she became kinder and softer and his prayers forever changed all of us who gathered around him.

Father Rookey was a holy, humble man. He ate one meal at the end of each day, never knowing from where it came. He owned two outfits, one for mass and one for daily wear. He lived poor—he was a Servite Friar in the Roman Catholic Church. He passed away in his sleep just short of his 98th birthday on September 10th, 2014, the day after my 57th birthday. Though he is physically gone, his words live on in me.

Father Rookey taught me faith and perseverance. I was in great awe of him—especially as a food addict focused on food—watching someone who didn't put food first, nor money, nor material things. This was something I hoped to master back in my early recovery days, given my food addiction and finances.

The room he slept in where he was housed with other Sevites was sparse, with one twin bed, a writing table, a lamp, and one small closet for his two outfits, shoes, and other scant possessions. He rose early in the morning, did 100 pushups, and stood on his head for fifteen minutes every day—well into his late eighties, early nineties. He prayed and healed and said mass—always giving of self.

He put God first, not the almighty dollar. He made God his job—rather than the world or being a busybody. He understood money can manipulate and control others, and yet it also can be used for good to feed the hungry and clothe the poor.

Father Rookey knew how to sit in silence, making the space to listen to God for instruction and guidance. He wasn't watching television or spending time with other electronics. No, he was present in prayer. When he talked, he poured out his heart—but before and after, he sat quietly to refill himself with God's fuel.

Father Rookey understood we are not of the earth—which I'd really heard for the first time at a reading at my mom's viewing. I realized all the possessions, all the things we gain—all of it—stays right here on earth.

Clinging To Stuff

Knowing we can't take stuff with us when we transition to the abyss, I'm amazed how many cling to their stuff. Are we layered with the seven deadly sins? According to Roman Catholic theology, the seven deadly sins are the seven behaviors or feelings that inspire further sin. Some typically ordered them as pride, greed, lust, envy, gluttony, wrath, and sloth. Often obsessing over money leads to several if not all the seven deadly sins.

Too often, money serves as a high. I know many who buy a bunch of clothes and then return them in the next day or two. What's driving them is not the clothes but the purchase. An adrenalin addiction, a drive to experience the adrenalin high of getting and spending, lies behind the urge to acquire stuff instead of a seeking a high on God, or whatever Source you align with.

A need to buy stuff in order to feel something is a sure sign the person has a hole inside. To make the dollar the Almighty is a road to misery. Stuff doesn't fill you. What are you really looking for?

I had a lengthy conversation with a patient I'll call Rana, who's struggling in two areas with gripping obsessions. Her first issue is dieting. She has a strong aversion to rules with her food. I get it. So we eventually transitioned from discussing diet to considering a healthy lifestyle that fit her way of life.

The second obsession we looked at regarded money, or lack of it. Rana wants a house with the white picket fence, but she isn't willing to live poor so she can live rich. She's not willing to stop her obsessive spending. She admits the almighty dollar is what she hungers for as a replacement for the sugary chocolate substance she once yearned after.

Rana blurted out, "I feel that going on a diet and saving money both scream deprivation." Rana fears if she lives poor, she'll be poor. She believes the idea of "act as if…" goes against the concept of living poor to live rich… that she'll end up poor.

We unpacked her irrational thinking. Living poor to become rich is not acting as if she *is* poor but allowing the focus to go on the savings to buy the lovely house. If she keeps spending thousands of dollars (yes, you read that right!) on trinkets and *whatevers* so she can act as if she's rich, that will take her straight to poor.

We reminisced about the days when processed food made her feel good, so good she packed on seventy pounds. She feared changing that behavior resembled deprivation. When we focused on the recovery, using the lovely foods to bring her to a whole, healthy place, she morphed into a different person.

I reminded her the action is the same with her spending sprees. Spending is a high but leads to poor. Rana grew up with Dad spending and spending, because he could—at least when he made substantial money. Now he's retired, the money has dwindled, and he can't make it on his retirement fund. He had to sell his home, drastically changing his lifestyle.

We talked about the lesson here. Dad made money "the Almighty." As long as he bought stuff, he felt puffed out and rich. But look what happened. With inflation, no saving habits, and continuous spending, he ran out of funds. This was a splashy, fancy kind of guy living on a vast estate, traveling to Europe at a whim.

All good, but not looking forward, thinking money would miraculously continue to pour forth was a grave error.

Rana grew up never wanting for anything. Dad loved her through money. He bought whatever her heart longed for. This transaction produced a total high for them both until he lost his home, and she went through two losses of homes, moving from the fancy side of town to the less than appealing.

Rana strives to recreate with her child the life memory of having whatever she wanted. No, was never a word she heard. I was curious how long the high lasted. She responded with a giggle, "Oh for about five minutes." Rana and Mom, and now Rana's daughter, are three generations of the same behavior. A way of life…

I reminded Rana that if food is on course, then saving is on course, then the mind is correct, thus opening the door to release the obsession with money.

We need money for survival, but not to the point we depend on money while edging out God. To think I have money, and that's all I need, can lead to the seven deadly sins referenced earlier.

I completely understand that Rana harbors lots of fear about owning her own home, since her home vanished when she was a kid, not once but twice. This was devastating for a child used to being given everything she wanted. To think that kind of having could be no longer was terrifying. Rana thought money would continuously flow, and that with it she needed nothing else.

Rana learned while young that money was the savior to all. And now, living in less luxury than the house she grew up in, admits she's like an addict with the credit cards and spending. She can't control herself, purchasing before she thinks about it. When her financial coach suggested she might want to put her cards in a safe deposit box to slow down the spending, she reacted the way a drug addict might.

When the cards were securely in safekeeping, she paced back and forth, chewing her fingernails down to the nubs, eyes wide, spinning, jonsing for the next fix. Yet when we examine how she had felt about spending, she recalls it was not giving her the joy she wanted. The high was brief, followed by a deep drop into sorrow.

Rana recognized that putting money on a pedestal was creating more hysteria for her. The sporadic, wild spending blocked the vacations and the owning of a home that she so desperately wanted. The spending was a false happy, the worship of a false God, a belief in false idols. The cards in her purse gave her a false sense of security.

The goofy spending made Rana *feel* rich when, in reality, it created debt. She spent $25 on decadent chocolates that barely lasted two days but made her feel wealthy for a moment. I suggest the feeling can be one of exhilaration, knowing you can buy something and choosing not to. You can replace the high of spending with the high of saving.

Instead of *acting as if* by spending out of control, we talked about imagining her wealth into reality, as you will see in Chapter 17.

Personal Inventory Questions

1. Maybe the time has come to: *Surrender. Let silence have you. And if you find you are still swimming on the surface of the ocean, let go and sink into the depths of love.* So many love money and believe it will bring them happiness. Do you believe that?
2. Well, here we are in a contest between God and the almighty dollar. Some see the dollars as their God. Where do you put God, or the source of your understanding? Where do you put money? Are they in competition?

3. Several events depicted in the Bible show Jesus asking people to leave their possessions, loved ones, and all their monetary worth to follow him. Doing so would have been tough, and many didn't follow—though many did. Could you have?
4. Ecclesiastes 5:10 tells us he who loves money is never satisfied by money, and he who loves wealth is never satisfied by wealth. How much do you love money?
5. Father Rookey was a holy, humble man. He ate only one meal at the end of each day, never knowing where it came from. Can you imagine not knowing where your one meal would come from? Or that you'd only take one meal a day?
6. Often, obsessing over money leads to several if not all the seven deadly sins. Some typically order them as: pride, greed, lust, envy, gluttony, wrath, and sloth. Do you, as most of us, harbor any of these sins? Which ones do you align with?
7. Rana wants a house with the white picket fence, but she isn't willing to live poor so she can live rich. She's not willing to stop her obsessive spending. Do you struggle with wants versus what you need only to give up later to reach for the wants?
8. Rana blurted out, "I feel going on a diet and saving money scream deprivation." Rana is not alone in her comparison between dieting and saving. She saw both as deprivation. Do you?
9. Rana and Mom, and now Rana's daughter, are three generations of the same behavior. Each wanting what they want when they want it without thinking about how they pay for these wants. To them it's a way of life. Is it? Do our generational connections become our way of life?

10. When suggested by her financial coach she might want to put her cards in a safe deposit box to slow down the spending, Rana reacted like a drug addict. How would you behave?

Chapter 17

Imagine Money Into Reality

With a closed mind and heart,
The light cannot enter.
~Shelby Taylor Weaver

What would imagining money into reality be like? Is that possible? Well, yes, it is possible to imagine money into reality, but how you begin the process is important. Shelby Taylor Weaver writes, "With a closed mind and heart, the light cannot enter."

Open your mind and heart and let the light in. With a closed mind and heart, how can you imagine the possibilities? The important first step in imagination is to make sure you're going by your imagination, not that of another.

Mark Nepo, author of *The Book of Awakening, Having the Life You Want by Being Present to the Life You Have*, says, "We are born with only one obligation—to be completely who we are. Yet how much of our time is spent comparing ourselves to others, dead and alive! This is encouraged as necessary in the pursuit of excellence. Yet a flower in its excellence does not yearn to be a fish, and a fish in its unmanaged elegance does not long to be a tiger. But, we humans find ourselves always falling into the dream of another life"

Stop doing that! Yes, imagine money into reality—though not another's idea of money but yours. Often we secretly aspire to be like someone else, particularly in whatever they have. Have what you have, not what another has. If we're always chasing what others have, it interrupts our own opportunity to be our authentic self. Nepo hits it spot on eloquently, "We experience the tension of comparing, as if there is only one ounce of being to feed all our hungers. But the Universe reveals its abundance most clearly when we can be who we are."

This is the point I hoped to drive home throughout this book. You can imagine what you want into reality, but don't make it another's dream, make it your dream. And how you do that is by staying mindful.

Stay in the reality of where you are and move from that point. Don't imagine a home on the ocean when you don't have a job or you're knee-deep in debt, expecting to obtain the enticing ocean property without putting forth the work. That's magical thinking. And from the previous chapters touching on magical thinking, you should understand that's not the way to bring forth money into reality.

Being Mindful

Today my goal is to stay present. Have you ever tried this? The mind always wants to think about what needs to be done next or what we already did. Stop for a moment and connect to your now. What do you see? What do you feel?

Focusing on the here and now is difficult for most. What makes me fixed on staying present is the surrounding chaos. Many of my loved ones, especially in the wake of Covid, are experiencing tough situations, which encourages me to sit still in gratitude for what I have and am thankful for.

Recently, I took a morning walk along the Intracoastal Waterway and Atlantic Ocean. The view was spectacular. I saw the sun peek out over the purple/orange backdrop on the ocean shoreline. A new day was about to begin. My legs were strong and my energy abounded. My fur-child Southern

Grace moved with me as if we were one. Her tail swished side to side, showing her joy at being with me out on a walk. She lives in the now.

Did you ever notice that your fur and feather babies live in the now? They're not thinking about yesterday or tomorrow, just this moment. What would that be like for you?

Suppose a person learns they have an illness. Let's say they have a rare disease and soon they will no longer be able to see. I would imagine for the time left they would look at everything with attention, knowing soon they would be overcome by a sea of darkness. Do we need to learn of an impending illness before we connect to the moment?

I wonder why not see today as if it were our last view of the world? Or live each day as if it were our last. What would we do differently? Who would we want to spend time with? What would we say that we've not said?

To rein ourselves in to the moment, we can practice mindfulness. The dictionary defines mindfulness as calm awareness of one's body functions, feelings, content of consciousness, or consciousness itself.

I am totally conscious of my fingers dancing over the keys, putting words together. I am told mindfulness is the path to liberation and enlightenment. It is the intense purpose of staying in the now. I get this. For years I obsessed overpaying off all monies owed to the tune of hundreds of thousands of dollars. My goal was to become debt free.

During this quest, I found remaining in the present difficult because I was living for the future of no debt. I had a special birthday that year: 9-9-09. What made that day special beyond the cool numbers? I had decided two years prior to pay off all my debts, including my student loan with Miss Sallie on September 9, 2009. I kept my nose to the grindstone for two years and hadn't wavered one iota to purchase anything that wasn't of absolute necessity. I learned to live with less and appreciate the gifts around me daily.

I accomplished my goal and on Wednesday, 9-9-09, I wrote my last check to Sallie Mae and enthusiastically dropped it in the mailbox on my way to work. I thought I would hear a chorus of angels burst into song. I did not. But what I did experience was a keen awareness of peace and liberation. I no longer was a slave to owing a student loan.

I then moved on to freedom from my home mortgage and on Friday 11-11-11, I freed myself once again, this time from Mr. Sun Trust. Once more I enthusiastically dropped the last check in the mailbox, but this time I knew the choir of angels wouldn't burst into song, but I would—and I did.

I was free, completely debt free. All credit card debt, car debt, student loan debt, and house debt were gone. I felt as light as a feather in the wind—free at last from the burdens of debt.

So, today I am present. I refuse to think about what needs to be done next or what I already did. I am present with each breath in and out. I am present to the sounds of birds singing and the whispers of the wind as it winds through the palm trees out my window. I am here and now.

What makes me fixed on staying present is the surrounding chaos. Loved ones are at personal crossroads–forced to face difficult situations—which encourages me to sit still in gratitude for what I have and am thankful for.

Before I could emerge from debt, I imagined what being debt free would be like. It seemed to me like a taste of freedom. It seemed like a relief. It seemed to me like the answer to all of my worries, fears, and insecurities. And it was.

Nothing feels as good as being debt free. So what do you do to imagine money into reality? You imagine the steps that will lead you to the money.

Steps to Imagine Money Into Reality

1. **Identify Your Money Dream:** What do you want to imagine? Is it owning your own home, or is it being debt free, or is it to travel? Be specific in the dream. My dream was clearly to eliminate the monkey of debt that was tightly wrapped around my neck.
2. **Identify What Money Can Do For You:** Money can protect you and help you take care of what you're afraid might cause pain in the future. I didn't want the pain of living my retired years in poverty. I wanted to avoid the pain of being in that constant fear of where the next dollar would come from.
3. **Identify Your Feel Good:** What is the money going to bring you that will provide you with happiness and satisfaction? Maybe that diamond ring you always wanted or the red Corvette you've dreamed of owning. That's fine. Maybe that ocean-front property, with a plan in place.
4. **Identify Your Money And Others:** Perhaps you want to leave money to your loved ones, or you want to know you can take care of those in need. This is good. Leaving money is a noble thing to do, especially if you've lived well by teaching your kids how to respect money and give to others less fortunate.

When I climbed out of debt, I imagined what it would be like. I imagined being free of the worry as to how I'd pay my basic bills. I imagined what letting the money grow in case I should need it would be like. And the more it grew, the less I wanted to spend, the less obsessed I became. This was an eye opener for me.

I always thought the more money you have, the more you spend, but it turns out for me the opposite was true. And I suspect the opposite may be true for you, too. It's sort of like dieting. When a person is told they can't eat cake, they might jones for cake. But when they feel good with all the other luscious foods available, they no longer want the cake.

When you have the money, you no longer jones to buy what you thought you might want. The real goal is to understand you and money.

Money IS Personal

Our feelings and beliefs about money are highly personal, but the frustrations of us all may be the same. Over the years I have been privileged to go into the minds and hearts of many only to learn the fears of pretty much everyone are the same, whether the fears concern weight, aging, eating disorders, or money. And often one fear crosses over to the other.

When the question comes to money, the continuous fretting sounds something like this:

- *I've been poor and I'll always be poor.*
- *Life is not fair. I'm not lucky when it comes to money.*
- *I wish I never had to worry about money.*
- *If I had money, all my worries would disappear.*
- *I don't have control over how much money I can make, let alone save.*
- *Making financial decisions terrifies me.*
- *I'm not good with money. I'll always be poor.*
- *I'm sick of thinking about money. This fretting is crippling my mind.*
- *I feel as though I'll never have money.*

Just Let Go

Sometimes, the way to riches is to let go. To stop the obsession with money or amassing material objects may be the means to have a direct line to a money flow. Think of money as a plant. First you need good soil, rich with minerals to support your seed. Next, water with a ray of sunshine and voila, watch the plant push its way through the dirt and burst forth into something big.

Put your money in a jar. Start with pennies if funds are low. You need good intention, rich with belief to support your dream. Next, sprinkle *want* dust, with rays of positivity, and watch your money burst forth, spilling out of its container so that you need another container for the overflow. Now, go back to the instructions. Put money in the jar and repeat the process. Soon, you have a further overflow, making the need for yet another jar.

Remember piggy banks as a kid so you could save for that rainy day. Be that kid now. Save and reap the rewards.

Money has a way of coming and going in our lives—a natural cycle of ebb and flow. Some say if you can earn it once, you can earn it again, while others say you may have luck once not to have it again. I'm a believer of the former. If you can do it once, you can do it again, as you'll see in Chapter 18, Rich To Poor, To Rich Again.

Personal Inventory Questions

1. What would imagining money into reality be like? Is that possible?
2. Shelby Taylor Weaver writes, "With a closed mind and heart, the light cannot enter." Is your mind closed? What about your heart?
3. Mark Nepo, author of *The Book of Awakening, Having the Life You Want by Being Present to the Life You Have,* says,

"We are born with only one obligation—to be completely who we are." Are you living completely who you are?

4. If we are always chasing what others have, it interrupts our own opportunity to be our authentic selves. Whose life are you chasing?
5. Today, your goal is to stay present. Have you ever tried this? The mind always wants to think about what needs to be done next or what we already did. Stop for a moment and connect to your now. What do you see? What do you feel?
6. Before I could get out of debt, I imagined what being debt free would be like. Do you imagine what being debt free would be like? What would that look like to you? Explore the idea and let your imagination make it your reality.
7. When you have the money, you no longer jones to buy what you thought you might want. What do you think you'd buy? Why? The goal is to understand you and money.
8. Over the years I have been privileged to go into the minds and hearts of many, only to learn so many of the fears of people are the same, whether regarding weight, aging, eating disorders, or money. What are your continuous fears?
9. Now that you've listed your continuous fears, how can you change the dialogue and turn your thoughts into positive affirmations rather than fears. Instead of "I will always be poor," how about thinking "I am rich"? List reasons you're rich.
10. Money has a way of coming and going in our lives—a natural cycle of ebb and flow. Some say if you can earn it once, you can earn it again, while others say once may be luck, not to happen again. What do you say?

Chapter 18

Rich To Poor To Rich Again

The truth you believe and cling to makes you unavailable to hear anything new.
~Pema Chodron

When I was a little girl at the age of eight attending St. Anthony Elementary School, we often had movie day. I have no memory of the movies but one, *Gone with the Wind.* It's based on the runaway bestselling 1936 novel, *Gone with the Wind* by Margaret Mitchell. In a nutshell, this famous and controversial American novel pulls us into the lives and experiences of a host of colorful characters during (and after) the Civil War in Georgia with money as the key focus of the major character, Scarlett.

"The truth you believe and cling to makes you unavailable to hear anything new," are the wise words of Pema Chodron. My truth, which I believed and clung to, was that if things are tough to deal with, deal with them tomorrow, which made me unavailable to hear anything new, such as deal with it today. Now where did I get that idea!

The movie version of *Gone with the Wind*, which I watched fifty-plus years ago, through very young eyes, stayed with me, etched in my mind, especially the parts where protagonist Scarlett O'Hara, a headstrong young woman who throughout the story struggles to save the plantation while ignoring her feelings and living in the moment—declares she will deal with her emotions tomorrow. Her quest is to live rich and never worry about money again.

Scarlett, the beautiful, spoiled daughter of a well-to-do Georgia plantation owner, used every means at her disposal to claw her way out of the poverty she found herself in during and after the Civil War. Her famous declaration was, "I'll think about it tomorrow." And often, when times are disturbing, I do the same thing. And maybe you do too.

Keep in mind this is a controversial novel/film because it ignores the horrors of slavery, not to mention presents many scenes painting painful stereotypes of people of color. My mention of the book here only regards wealth to poverty, hunger, and the struggles to save the plantation.

The experience of fearing losing everything and the striving for money to make all the worries go away is something many have undergone. This story that engaged my eight-year-old self was my first conception of having and losing money, and it marked me from a young age. And this *is* a book on releasing the obsession with money. Scarlett was obsessed, beyond most of our comprehension, willing to do the unthinkable to restore the riches she had been accustomed to at a young age.

Flash back to when I had this idea I wanted to write a novel loosely based on my Great, Great Grandma Abbie, who was born in 1849. Her life, I imagined, was fascinating in that she experienced many losses, including of loved ones who died during the Civil War. That was a time of hardship so crushing it changed the course of many lives, and Abbie's too. Unlike Scarlett, Abbie was from the North, seeing the war through a different lens but a war that presented hardship nonetheless.

I have to be honest. I hated history classes growing up, as they seemed so boring. But once I began researching the years through which Grandma Abbie lived, I came across tons of history I had no clue about. So my quest to hunt down that timeframe so I could better understand the era she lived in began. In my pursuit, I saw that her poverty was glaring, followed by wealth—and back and forth—and that experience sparked my interest because at the same time I'm writing my novel, I'm writing this book on money obsessions and the two books have collided.

There are no coincidences. I grew up in a wealthy home, but as I've noted I lived poor; hence, "poor little rich girl" was my nickname with classmates in high school and carried on in my young adult life with friends. And then, I really was poor, but I was okay because I lived that way, anyway. Unlike Scarlett, I didn't live a plush life and then a poor life, but rather had a long streak of poor before I became comfortable financially.

As I researched for my Abbie novel, I wanted to feel those years from the perspective of both the North and the South to grasp the thought process. My intention was not to praise *Gone with the Wind,* the second most-read book to the Bible, but to understand how I, a young Catholic girl, watched this movie which planted the fear of poverty in me and how I went into denial. And along *my* journey I realized how the poverty and death and life changes stripped many on both the North and South sides of the war.

One decision I made was to read Mitchell's bestselling novel, the classic *Gone with the Wind*, and *Team of Rivals: The Political Genius of Abraham Lincoln,* by Doris Kearns Goodwin, simultaneously, so that I could grasp the timeframe from the Southern view along with the Northern view. Why both sides? Well, I live in Florida, the South, and I was born and raised in Illinois and Wisconsin, the North. I wanted to grasp and understand both the North and the South.

And following this quest, I plunged into the money aspect and the impact it had on both sides, along with the spiritual and/or religious aspect. Like me, Scarlett came from a Catholic background. In fact, her mother, Ellen, was a staunch Catholic, weaving her faith into every aspect of her life, while Scarlett couldn't tap into the spiritual concepts, but Lincoln (who'd had a harsh and impoverished childhood) could.

And then you had Lincoln's wife, Mary, spending obsessively, borrowing when family debt was mounting, and Scarlett, who starts as a spoiled rich girl, going to poor and hungry back to living rich again, spending obsessively, because she could.

Though I'm not delving into detail regarding either account, as that's not the goal of this book—but money and poverty and hardships, and how to power through them is. And spirituality and/or religion is weaved throughout all of my writings—so we can *heal from the inside out.* Scarlett wasn't healed from the inside out. She didn't live life in prayer, where Lincoln talked about God and thought about God in his quiet decision moments. (Lincoln's stepmother had brought a Bible with her to the backwoods where they lived.)

I'm in awe of the era, as I hadn't really paid attention to what went on during those times, such the great unrest in the country and division. And here I am all these years later, and I'm still feeling what Scarlett went through growing up in great luxury to descend into poverty, to know hunger and hard work, to think like a man and become business minded, which is not something women did back in that day.

So for years when times were tough I'd say, "I'll think about it tomorrow," a posture that branded the little eight-year-old, wide-eyed kid watching such a movie. Of course my tomorrows weren't as dangerous a situation as portrayed in the movie and I wasn't as broke, though I was broke.

Alone And Poor

I was alone, poor, and had to make money doing things I didn't want to do and accepting it as my lot in life if I was to climb out of the poverty. Often I worked two and three jobs only to be knocked back down financially, spiritually, and physically. But I'm grateful I had these experiences because they caused me to morph into who I am today. I'm strong and vibrant and a very good saver.

Like Scarlett, I never wanted to know about hunger again. I never wanted to be broke and wonder how I'd pay my taxes. I never wanted to depend on another, but to be strong and independent. And like Lincoln, I aspired to live my best life, to listen to others mindfully, and to always weave the God of my understanding into all my works and decisions.

Living rich to poor and back to rich was Scarlett's story. Lincoln was poor and in debt from Mary's spending, and I started from wealth but lived poor to comfortable. Scarlett lived big, then suffered during her days when she lived in poverty. Lincoln was frugal, but his wife, Mary, spent obsessively. When I, myself, was broke, it wasn't by choice. When I lived frugally, however, I did so by design, and that decision made a big difference for me, leading to living financially comfortably and secure.

Live Poor To Live Rich

I've said so before, but my mantra is worth repeating: Live poor to live rich. Again, I'm not talking about the person who is uber rich but the modestly wealthy sort. And how, you might ask, does one live poor to live rich and release obsessions with money?

And what wealthy means is personal. Rather than one man's junk is another's treasure—one man's poor is another man's rich. So you can live poor by choice to build wealth.

When you live a simple lifestyle and work more, you can save more and move from debt to wealth.

I lived poor, so that I could live rich. When I earned a good living, I behaved as if I were making the same small amount I was accustomed to. With the extra money, I began the snowball payment plan Dave Ramsey advocates in *The Total Money Makeover: A Proven Plan for Financial Fitness.* With slow and steady precision I nibbled away at my debt as you'll see.

But first I want to talk about John. John was the father of a patient, Gigi, whom I saw many, many years ago. John was homeless. His teenage daughter came to see me distraught, knowing her father was *out there* suffering and alone.

Gigi cried through many sessions cleaning out the tissue box, blowing her nose and dabbing her eyes. My heart hurt. I felt so bad she was carrying this burden when she should have been having fun with her teenage friends. She hid from everyone the *secret*, as she called it, that her dad lived in his car while she lived in a pleasant apartment with her mom and sister. One day I had the bright idea to invite her dad to one of her sessions.

I braced myself for what I thought would be a smelly, tough hour of psychotherapy. To my surprise, when I opened the door to gather my patient and her homeless dad, a handsome, lean, muscular man, was with her in the waiting room. Clearly, this couldn't be the dad she'd sobbed over for months on end!

But he was. John, smelling of sweet wood and mint, sauntered into my office and let us in on *his* secret. John had two pensions, had retired early, sold everything he owned, bought two cars—one a souped-up old van designed like an RV to live in and one to drive. He cleverly moved the van around to avoid being given tickets.

John wasn't poor. He worked out at a high-end gym daily where he lifted weights and showered. He had several bank accounts and a PO box. *John was living just fine.* In fact, that day, he told his daughter Gigi he had a rather large IRA and savings account, not to mention a checking account filled with money.

John had tired of living the fast-paced life and owning a home, weighed down by all the responsibilities that came with these. One day, he'd had enough. He was deeply depressed and suffered from a heart condition. He left it all.

John's doctor had told him he'd better make some quick changes, or he wouldn't be alive in a few years. That the stress of the lifestyle he was living would eventually take him down. John was a drinker, smoker, and only ate processed foods. Something clicked. He decided he was going to step out of society and live a different life. And he did. He's living poor, so he can live rich.

Often, John flies off to Italy for a few months to hike and live with the Italians. His father and mother were from Northern Italy and he always wanted to learn about their culture and speak the language. He did just that, learned about Italy and speaks the language beautifully. He writes a travel blog, earning a small income, and lives his life exactly the way he wants. Gigi, though, was furious. She felt betrayed.

I reminded her about how worried she was about her dad, and now she can put that to rest and live her life. Her father always paid his child support, though he didn't have a good relationship with his former wife. He didn't want her to know about his new life because he feared she'd take him for every penny he had. This explained to Gigi why her dad always brought her and her sister little treats—sometimes quite expensive ones, while other times candy or foods.

John is living his life the way he wants to. He is no doubt quite wealthy but living as if he's not. It's a choice. Living frugally is a choice. "The truth you believe and cling to makes you unavailable to hear anything new." (Pema Chodron). Gigi clung to the belief that her dad was poor, down and out, living in the streets. She was furious with her mom, hating her for what she did to her dad.

Gigi held to this belief and was unavailable to hear anything new. Gigi's mom had told her repeatedly that her father wasn't poor and lived the life of Riley. That he didn't want for anything and traveled the world doing as he pleased, while *she* was actually living paycheck to paycheck. Now Gigi's eyes are open. She realized we have choices; how they choose to live their life is up to the individual.

"The truth you believe and cling to makes you unavailable to hear anything new," are the wise words of Pema Chodron. Pema Chodron has a story too. She left her life as mother and wife to become an American Tibetan Buddhist. She is an ordained nun, former archarya of Shambhala Buddhism and disciple of Chogyam Trungpa Rinpoche. She wasn't always living this life.

Pema Chodron was born Diedre Blomfield-Brownn in 1936, in New York city. She attended Miss Porter's School in Connecticut and graduated from the University of California at Berkeley. She taught as an elementary school teacher for many years in both New Mexico and California. She has two children and three grandchildren.

She left the life of mother and grandmother to walk the life of a guru with wisdom and honesty, writing many popular books. She is committed to assisting organizations that serve at-risk communities, particularly those organizations which promote healing and growth through mindfulness practices. She lives life making a difference for others.

Minimalist Anyone?

I recall a woman, Millie, who became obsessed with becoming a minimalist. At the time the concept was quite popular, and still may be today. Though we can find a myriad of books, podcasts, YouTube videos, and anything in between on the concept of minimalism, the concept is a rather simple one.

A minimalist is one who lives with less than, in terms of material possessions. Now of course some take this to extremes, like the minimalist who lives with less than one hundred items in their possession. Oye! This type of minimalist doesn't own a car, a home, or even a television. They don't have a career and live in exotic places. This is not the type of minimalist I'm referring to.

Millie bought a cottage out in the wilderness up in the Midwestern region of the United States. She wanted to have the feel of what living with less would be like. She reminded me of Dr. Dyer, who also lived as a minimalist. Dr. Wayne Dyer was an internationally renowned author and speaker in the fields of self-development and spiritual growth. He was a person I followed, and who impressed me with his philosophies and spiritual awakenings from when I was nineteen years old until his passing in September 2015. In his case, he gave away all of his belongings to live without such extras, moved to Hawaii, and lived out his life.

Millie was afraid to go to extremes, so she dipped her toe in the water first by purchasing a second home, a small one-bedroom cottage in the woods surrounded by wild animals and trees. Her adventure took her to long weeks out in the wilderness, living simply.

Though Millie didn't give up all her possessions, she learned to live without television, the Internet, or any fancy lifestyle she was accustomed to. She plugged in her dream of something to look forward to. What is your something? Check out Chapter 19 to find your something.

Personal Inventory Questions

1. "The truth you believe and cling to makes you unavailable to hear anything new," says Pema Chodron. What do you cling to that makes you unavailable to hear anything new?
2. When I was a little girl at the age of eight attending St. Anthony Elementary, we often had movie day. I have no memory of the movies except for one, *Gone with the Wind.* What movie did you watch as a young child that affected you? How does it continue to affect you?
3. Scarlett O'Hara throughout *Gone with the Wind* struggles to save the plantation, ignoring her feelings and living in the moment—saying she will deal with her emotions 'tomorrow.' Do you deal with your emotions tomorrow?
4. The experience of fearing losing everything and the striving for money to make all the worries go away is something many have. Do you yearn for money? If so, where does this yearning stem from?
5. Abraham Lincoln's wife, Mary, spent money obsessively, borrowing, with debt mounting, while Scarlett starts as a spoiled rich girl then becomes poor and hungry, to return to living rich again, spending obsessively, because she could. Do you fit in either of these stories' spending tendencies? What is the root cause of your spending?
6. I was alone and poor and had to make money doing things I didn't want to do, accepting it as my lot in life if I was to climb out of the poverty. Often, I worked two and three jobs only to be knocked back down financially, spiritually, and physically. What are your early money memories? Are you the same today as you were back then?

7. How, you might ask, does one live poor to live rich and release obsessions with money? I've said it before but it's worth repeating, live poor to live rich. What does living poor to live rich mean to you?
8. Gigi cried through many sessions, cleaning out the tissue box, blowing her nose and dabbing her eyes as she recounted her dad living out in the streets, homeless. As the reality turned out, he wasn't living so roughly after all. How did Gigi's story sit with you? Why?
9. Pema Chodron had a story too. She left her life as mother, grandmother, and wife to become an American Tibetan Buddhist. Can you imagine walking away from your life, as you know it, to join a ministry of some sort? Could you?
10. Millie became obsessed with becoming a minimalist, giving up her passions to live a simpler life. The idea sounded awesome, but the reality sounded dismal. What are your thoughts about living as a minimalist? Could you let go of your stuff?

Chapter 19

Something To Look Forward To

Bring into play the almighty power within you,
So that on the stage of life you can fulfill your high destined role.
~Paramahansa Yogananda

For sure, life will have difficulties, challenging times, no matter what you do, say, or think. That's life. But you don't have to sit on your backside and give up, accepting this as your lot in life. No, you can push through and grab hold of something that's waiting for you. We've learned through life's hardships that behind every bad lies a good, after every storm a calm comes in, and with every tear we'll find laughter. As we power through life, we can grab hold of the realness of all of this.

To look forward to more—so much more—the first step is to stop trying to prove yourself to others—one, because it will get you nowhere, and two, because the others probably don't care. You will always find Debbie Downers in your life—the naysayers. That's inevitable, but you don't have to be a part of that team. You can stand tall and go for your dreams one step at a time, one day at a time. Look for the pot of gold at the end of the rainbow, for surely it is there.

How you might ask? Well, as you read through this book, the message was, and is, that it's up to you. Nobody is going to do it for you. Nobody. If you've been gifted money, you have a good chance it will be gone with the wind. Earn your own money, build your castle of dreams, in whatever shade is right for you. One man's junk is another's treasure. What is your treasure? No one else can determine who you shall be or how much money is the right amount for you.

We come into this world alone and we leave alone. Life is a solo journey. Besides realizing that you are unique in this world, you also must accept that you are always alone. Yes, you may have people around you, and you may love freely—all good—but no one, I mean no one can ever feel what you're feeling or know what you are knowing in the depth of your thoughts, regardless of whether you are around one person or thousands of people. You live in your private inner world, making thoughts and decisions a gazillion times throughout the day.

The Concept Of Aloneness

Consider the example of Guido, a forty-year-old property owner and manager combined, making a very handsome living. He has the world by the tail, buying whatever he wants. And he earns every penny, working smartly and efficiently. Anyone observing Guido's life would believe he didn't have a care in the world. His wife, Marla, is a total knockout, always making heads turn. She is kind and quick to smile, not to mention put everyone at ease.

Guido came to me for therapy some years ago, totally distraught, wringing his hands, grimacing as he blurted out, "My marriage is a sham, and I can't do this anymore."

"What can't you do?" I asked.

"I can't put on this charade anymore. I have dreams and plans and an entire world to explore, and with Marla I have nothing to look forward to."

Whoa, what is going on here, I wondered.

Guido's confrontation with his aloneness surfaced almost out of nowhere, as he was inching closer to forty. He reported how he had been sitting in his reading room one evening staring at his wife, who was preoccupied with one of their four children oblivious to the swirling whirlwind of thoughts in his head. Right then and there he had the feeling that this woman he'd been married to for the past thirteen years didn't really know him. That she was a stranger to him.

Guido questioned why he was still married. The understanding became crystal clear to him for the very first time that Marla would never, ever know the private inner workings of his mind. This thought shook Guido to the core, with him thinking if this was all there was to the marriage, how could he go on for another thirty years—or 'until death do us part.' He was at such a loss with these feelings that he turned to therapy for guidance.

In our early sessions, he'd jump up, pacing back and forth like a caged animal, begging for solutions to what he thought was a devastating problem. He was thinking about divorce, running away, or maybe taking on a mistress. He couldn't fathom spending another minute staring at his wife, knowing she didn't understand him, and that he didn't know what thoughts went through her head.

In time, as we covered what was really going on with Guido, we uncovered his fears of not being understood. He had this idea that his significant other, his soulmate, his forever person should know his every thought, his every whim. As we progressed in therapy, we unraveled the reality that every human being has his or her own inner thoughts, the inner world for him or her alone. That feeling everything of another was impossible.

Sure we can know somebody well, really well, but not so thoroughly that we know every single thought and feeling—that would be impossible. We are human beings, not mind readers. Since his wife could never know for certain what he was thinking nor could he know her every thought, I suggested he might stop putting the pressure on himself, and on her, to accomplish the impossible.

At this point, a glimmer in his eyes showed he'd had that aha moment. He no longer had to burden himself with trying to know her totally, and vice versa. This was the first time he could let this go, giving himself permission to be a separate entity, that it was okay he had his own inner world, and Marla hers.

Guido is not alone in these thoughts. So often couples are stuck on this idea that they have nothing to look forward to, that they are caught in a situation with a long-time marriage of emptiness. And in Guido's case, he became hyper-focused, almost obsessed with how much money he had, and if he divorced how would he be able to keep his money. He was concerned that all he had worked for would go to child support and alimony.

Mania Can Be Confusing

Yes, Guido had quite a story in his head, and perhaps you might, too. I once worked with a patient, Ely, who suffered from bipolar disorder, swinging mostly high, but when low he was really low. He had been married to Dee for nearly thirty years when he wasn't sure anymore. Their four daughters had grown and flown, leaving Ely and Dee empty nesters and for the first time alone, without a kid between them.

Ely was in a manic state when he showed up at my office for our usual session, eyes lit like those of a tiger after his prey, exclaiming, "I'm done with Dee. I can't stay married anymore to a woman who doesn't have a thought, plan, or ability to converse deeply with me."

Now this wasn't clear to me, as I'd worked with Ely on and off for years, but this time was different. He was ready to leave, for real. And he did. He divorced Dee and off he went to make his fortune. So he thought. He was on a quest to find someone who "got" him, someone he could read, and she him, in every whimsical thought.

He wanted to travel, see the world and love someone deeply with the feelings returned. He dated one woman after another, racing through each affair, trying to find that something which was missing in Dee. At one point, he went off all of his medications because he decided he didn't need a mood stabilizer. He was just fine. So he said. Ely blew through his savings, nearly losing his business, and sunk so low that he nearly died in the garage in his car, hoping to end it all.

To his great good fortune, Dee happened to be stopping by his home after he rented a house a few doors down from their home of thirty-plus years. She franticly yanked him out of the car, calling 911, and saved his life. Ely then saw his Dee in a new light, realizing the love they shared was the real deal, and that he didn't need to know her every thought and that she didn't have to share his love of politics, read the paper, or stay tuned in on what was happening in the world.

Ely had much to look forward to. Life was precious, and now his eyes and heart were open to unlimited possibilities, with and without Dee. The two had a splashy second wedding, with all four daughters, their husbands and Ely's little grandchildren all attending. This moment was the start of something spectacular for them. They bought a second home for Ely to go to and write the memoir he had always wanted to write. He found his bliss without expecting Dee to join him in his every whim. And you can too!

We Are Solo Agents

We are solo agents coming into this world alone and exiting alone. Each individual has an existence within to work through and understand. Guido and Ely are not responsible for knowing every little thing about their wives, inside and out. That insight was a great relief for Guido. He for the first time grasped the understanding that we are solo entities, accountable to our own selves. That Marla couldn't understand every inner working of his mind was a normal state. How could she, as he had his own inner world? And Ely realized he had a fast mind, living in an eddy of ideas, and that Dee was calm in her style, and he couldn't change her, nor should he try.

My intention with this point is not to scare you, but to free you. This is your journey to move through. This is your story. You are paving the way for others to follow, but it is you who's living your life. And you have so much life in front of you to become what you want to be, even if you believe you are closing in on your own last chapter.

As long as you have breath in you, you have something to look forward to. Joy is personal. Awe is yours and yours alone. And with your life comes the realization that you are not someone else. Stop comparing yourself to others; *there is only one you*, and you take that you with you wherever you go. Guido is Guido, and Marla is Marla. And Ely is Ely, and Dee is Dee. They can coexist in this beautiful world, but one is not responsible for the other to be happy. Happiness is up to the individual.

You are you. You do not have to be understood by your beloved, or anyone. We move through life with our own inner worlds and may share a world with another. As I write this piece, I'm sitting at my getaway home alone with my pooch and parrot, putting my thoughts on paper. I don't expect my husband to understand my swirly mind, nor do I expect to completely understand his.

My husband is a forever musician who practices for hours daily when not working at his restaurant. He has his love of music and dreams of his own. And that's good. He likes his music—and sometimes loud. I'm quiet and love to write. He's a movie buff; I'm glued to books. I love the beach, and he doesn't like sand in his shoes. Yes, we are different people, yet so much alike.

I like to think of us as one coin. He's on one side, perhaps the tail, and I the head—yet we are one coin—one beautiful coin. We don't have to be the same person, but we can share some of the same dreams, and some dreams that are not the same. That's the beauty of being a unique being.

Too often, we try to conform to what society and families want us to be. But in reality, you only have to be you. Be yourself. Dream big. And know you always have something to look forward to. Caterpillars are blooming into butterflies and we have beautiful sunsets and memories to share—all to look forward to. But inside, your thoughts and beliefs and wonders and experiences are yours alone to explore and understand.

"Bring to play the almighty power within you, so that on the stage of life you can fulfill your high-destined role," Paramahansa Yogananda tells us. Your high-destined role is yours to fulfill, not your mother's, father's, sister's, brother's, daughter's, son's, husband's, wife's, society's, or that of anyone I missed. To look forward is to stop looking backward. Stop regretting and wishing for something else. Do something about it. Create your magic now.

As I was writing this piece, I was only hours away from a minor crisis I was having at my getaway house. The air-conditioning stopped working. I live in sunny, hot and humid Florida. I had scooted away for nine days, alone. I was working remotely for four days as the pool was being resurfaced. It's a mighty old pool my grandmother built in the latter part of the 1970s.

At the same time we were having a storm to beat the band, with no stop in sight, which meant I could lose power any moment, with no cool air. I had cleared the time to work from here, thinking I'd have a cool home. And the rebuilding of the pool? Nope, not going to happen, as long as we had storms with thunder and lightning. Life is unpredictable. We never know what tomorrow will bring. Despite the best-laid plans, something can go wrong, and often does.

When the AC went off, I pouted for a bit, especially when Tim, the air conditioning fellow, said maybe he could come out in a few days. What! This is Florida; we live in air conditioning all year round. After I got past my hysteria, I cranked open all the windows that probably hadn't been open since 1970, I kid you not. They were sticky and crackling, but I managed, and a decent cross-breeze started coming from off the ocean.

I felt self-empowered. I realized again that I am alone, just as you're alone, and things don't always work out the way we want them to, so we adjust. I filled my big mug with chunks of ice, instant decaffeinated coffee, and water, topped with unsweetened almond milk. I was good. Oliver, my Eclectus parrot, was as happy as could be as he was chatting with the egrets, otherwise known as heron, and the seagulls were singing with them, all in concert.

The herons are long-legged, long-necked, freshwater and coastal birds in the family Ardeidae, with other recognized species. Then, one heron enjoyed inching his way to the window, chatting along. And Gracie was pleased too as she pushed her face into the screened window, sucking in fresh air. Life is good. It's as good as we make it.

And my nine days turned into thirteen, as Tim, the air conditioner guy, pointed out a loose wire near the unit attached to the wall, warning me this looked like a serious problem. And it was and is. The electrician came out along with Duke Energy and confirmed this was a fire waiting to happen. I continued to feel self-empowered as I put one fire out after another (no pun intended). But the point is, I'm a solo unit and felt good that I put so many situations in order as a unique individual.

Bird Houses And Duck Houses—Who Knew!

My brother-in-law, Emil, is long retired from his work as a conservationist, but never stopped working in his own way for what he wanted. He loves to work his land and even found a gift in making duck houses and birdhouses for people all around the nearby communities. He doesn't need the money, but it's flowing in for these darn houses that bring others such joy—which brings him joy.

What is your joy that fulfills you, one you can share with others? You have much to look forward to even if you only choose to sit in a rocking chair watching the logs burn in the fireplace. Or you might just watch your cuddly pup snuggling against one of your grandchildren. You have so much to look forward to as long as you have breath. And the almighty dollar isn't what's going to give you something to look forward to.

I remember Lesley was waiting for her great-aunt to pass away, as she was quite wealthy, with plans to pass her riches down to the great nieces and nephews. Lesley would tell me in session that she just couldn't wait for that money so that she could finally live her life the way she wanted to. I questioned how her life would change. Lesley believed she would be happy and free with the money.

Well, aunty died and left an enormous fortune to Lesley, her brother, and a few other great nieces and nephews. Her brother spent his load on drinking and drugging and passed away at thirty-five. The few other great nieces and nephew put the money aside for their children and lived comfortable lives. Lesley at first spent her money on jewelry, a fancy car, and a luxurious home. But to her surprise, she wasn't happy—she was miserable.

We ferreted out what she really wanted. She wanted to live out in the country up North where the weather was cooler. She wanted to climb mountains and hike. She wanted to have a barn filled with farm animals, collect fresh eggs every morning, and pick wild berries in the evening. She wanted to ride horses out into the sunset and just exhale. And she did exactly that. After the passing of her brother, she realized money was not the road to happy, but to responsibility.

So I leave you with your own power to be you. And to dream big and know you always have something to look forward to. Life is precious—more precious than obsessing over money. Moving on to Chapter 20, I have one final thought…

Personal Inventory Questions

1. You can look forward to more—so much more. The first step is to stop trying to prove yourself to others: one, because it will get you nowhere, and two, because the others probably don't care. Who are you trying to prove something to? You can stand tall and go for your dreams one step at a time, one day at a time. Why do you need that other person to support your dream? Explore why you look to others to fulfill your wants.
2. Earn your own money, build your castle of dreams, in whatever shade is right for you. One man's junk is another's treasure. What is your treasure? By now, reading this book, you know you better than when you started—tap into your authentic self and dig out your treasure.

3. No one can ever feel what you're feeling or know what you know in the depths of your thoughts, regardless of whether you're around one person or thousands of people. You live in your own inner world, making thoughts and decisions a gazillion times throughout the day. What thoughts swirl in your mind that nobody really knows? Who are you in your inner world, and who are you in your outer world?
4. Guido was struggling with his marriage to his long-time wife, Marla. One day out of the blue, he had this feeling that his wife of thirteen years didn't really know him. That she was a stranger to him. Do you feel your life partner is a stranger? What about your family, siblings, or cousins?
5. Guido had this idea that his significant other, his soulmate, his forever person should know his every thought, his every whim. This is impossible. We can never know the inner workings of another person. And it's okay. Is this a new concept for you? Did you think you knew your significant other, or that you should?
6. Ely blew through his savings, nearly losing his business, which caused him to sink so low he nearly died in the garage breathing his car's exhaust with the hope of ending it all. How low have you sunk as it revolves around money? What would you do differently in hindsight?
7. "Bring to play the almighty power within you, so that on the stage of life you can fulfill your high-destined role," Paramahansa Yogananda advised. Wouldn't that be something, to fulfill your high-destined role? How can you bring into play the almighty power within you?
8. As I was writing this piece, I was only hours past a minor crisis at my getaway house. The air-conditioning had stopped working, and as you read, many sagas continued

throughout my stay that could cause anyone to curl up in a corner, and surrender, giving up. But when you face a situation head on, you will often feel good because meeting a challenge feels self-empowering. What have you done to self-empower your uniqueness?

9. My brother-in-law, Emil, has a gift for making duck houses and birdhouses for people all around the nearby communities. He doesn't need the money, but it's flowing in, for these darn houses bring others joy—which brings him joy. What is your joy that fulfills you, which you can share with others?
10. Lesley inherited a great deal of money from her aunty. For years, she had banked on receiving this money, believing it would make her happy. And at first it did. She spent her money on jewelry, a fancy car and a luxurious home. But to her surprise she wasn't happy, she was miserable. Why didn't the money Lesley longed for make her happy after all? What did you glean from Lesley's story?

Chapter 20

Final Thoughts

Every time you don't follow your inner guidance,
you feel a loss of energy, loss of power,
a sense of spiritual deadness.
Shakti Gawain

It's a balmy, rainy day on the west coast of Florida where I'm spending the next thirteen days alone to reflect on my life with all its twists and turns. I knew as a small child that no one could box me in—I was a free spirit. I loved to run, hang from trees, and play kick the can with the neighbors. I never was a girly-girl following the crowd.

I danced to my own beat, listening to my inner guidance, the very one we all hear whispering our course of direction in this life. Ignoring what it says will lead to *a loss of energy and power and lead to a sense of spiritual deadness.* When I was a little kid, I was always daydreaming about creating stories of make-believe, playing with animals and out in nature. I wanted to live freely.

My dad was one to give me bear hugs and rub his whiskers into my face, holding me tight. I loved his love but not being held so tight. It wasn't comfortable. And it left my face burning red. But later, when I turned five, the affection stopped, and I missed it. The lesson I learned is that sometimes even if we're uncomfortable we need to stay the course. Behind every cloud, the sun awaits.

When I was in my early twenties, I moved to downtown Chicago from the suburbs to avoid the long commute. I'd already been bartending and made substantial money in a quaint family-owned Italian restaurant called Seneses Winery. We were a close-knit group for many years, sharing stories of hardship, college trials and errors, love, and even death. To leave my happy nest of friends and once again start over from scratch was a big decision.

I tired of the long commute to DePaul University, so leaving my safe nest became a reality. I moved without a job in place. I thought getting a job with my skill sets would be easy-peasy, and tons of nightclubs stretched for blocks on end on Rush Street in Chicago. I was wrong. I applied everywhere. The biggest problem was most clubs wanted me in a skimpy outfit showing lots of cleavage and derriere, and that was a double no for me.

I went months without a job, and money ran out, leaving me broke, again. I was desperate, so I went to apply for food stamps and some kind of assistance. Terrified, I was at one of the lowest points in life. The irony was my wealthy dad lived in Chicago too, but he set the tone, without saying it, ever—that we were to find our own way through school and all our endeavors—since I was a kid.

The fellow taking my information looked at me kindly with chocolate, deep-set eyes. He had black hair, a mustache, and beard. His face was kind. Softly, he told me I didn't have a chance. He offered to continue to fill out the paperwork but assured me I'd be denied. I was baffled. I had needed all my being to apply for help—something I didn't want to do with every ounce of me—but I had pushed forward out of desperation.

I had one jar of peanut butter in the fridge, a head of lettuce with salad fixings, and a few cans of tuna, tea and skim milk. That was it. I had no money in the bank and my rent was now past due. How in the world could they deny me? I felt small, tiny, sitting in that chair, looking up at this stranger for help with pleading eyes.

He gently shook his head, stayed quiet for a moment, tapping his pencil to his lips before he said, "I'm sorry but how can you get approved? You have more education than I. You live in a studio apartment on Orchard Street. You have a car and you have a checking account." *What? But there's no money in my checking account,* I thought. So, I was turned away. I walked off, crushed.

This was the best thing that ever happened to me. I got down from my high horse and applied as a server at a pizza joint to make my ends meet. Bartenders do NOT want to be servers; waitressing is beneath us, a step down. But I got over my arrogance and went to work for Prosciuttos, a pizza joint off Michigan Avenue, which is where I met my best guy friend, Michael, who drove horse carriages throughout the city.

Eventually, I found a lovely bartending position at a quaint club. The name escapes me, but the managers' faces do not. They were not sweet and kind, like my beautiful Seneses family at the Italian restaurant. They were harsh and pushed every bit of energy out of their employees. I walked out of there each night with loads of money, sore feet, and a banging headache from listening to music so loud I shook from the trauma it brought to my heart and body.

I was an excellent bartender, fast and furious, making the establishment money along with myself. I was at liberty to wear my personal designated uniform of black pants, white tux shirt, and a thin black tie. NO showing of body parts. I was a mean machine climbing out of debt when I had been penniless only a few short months before. Life, or the universe (God for me), has a way of working things out in the time that events are meant to unveil.

The lesson was to work, no matter what, and trust the rest will turn out as it should. And it did. And it will for you too. Work smart toward your dreams, save money, and give money. Love and love freely. Be true to yourself and to those around you, and miracles will flow your way. The lesson was to never give up—that quitters never win, and winners never quit.

"The lesson is every time you don't follow your inner guidance, you feel a loss of energy, loss of power, a sense of spiritual deadness," writes Shakti Gawain. Find your authentic you and follow your inner guidance—it's there ready to guide you to your spiritual awakening.

Richard Carlson in his, *Don't Sweat the Small Stuff…and It's All Small stuff: Simple Ways to Keep the Little Things from Taking Over Your Life*, reminds us, "When you look at life and its many challenges as a test, or a series of tests, you see each issue you face as an opportunity to grow, a chance to roll with the punches. Whether you're being bombarded with problems, responsibilities, or even insurmountable hurdles, when these are looked at as a test, you always have a chance to succeed, in the sense of rising above that which is challenging you."

He says if, instead, you see each new issue you face as a serious battle that must be won in order to survive, you're probably in for a very rocky journey. Often we believe the only time we're going to be happy is when everything works out just right.

I've tried to make it obvious in story after story in this book, *Releasing Your Obsession With Money: Heal from the Inside Out,* the happy endings came from working through the trials and tribulations. Life is full of lessons and one is that money isn't always what brings happiness. You and your inner workings are what brings happiness.

Now go take on your life without obsessing over money. Work smart and save, and you'll be better off than you think. Obstacles will come and obstacles will go—that's life. But you have the choice of how to work through each challenge and rise above, coming out stronger than you were before.

Thank you for spending time with me and my thoughts throughout these pages. I hope my words lit your excitement to become your best self for you. I look forward to sharing my next book with you on how to release your obsession with your darn phone, and anything techy. God bless you… and your journey through this life and all that awaits beyond…

Acknowledgements

This book represents a personal inquiry into a confusing aspect of my own experience. As I began to make sense out of unexpected changes in my life, patients with the same needs emerged. This ultimately led to my writing about my discoveries, to share with others in similar situations.

No book is written without the contributions of many people. My wish is to recognize every spoken and unspoken inspired word, but I don't have enough pages, so regrettably I can only mention a few.

I wouldn't have written about these things if not for my husband, Joe, who encourages me to follow my dreams, no matter how small or how large they may be. Also, I thank my sons, Kris and Benjamin, who have always been a source of help with technical, legal, and administrative tasks beyond my comprehension. And I must mention with gratitude my beloved parents, Benjamin and Joan, who shine down from heaven, prompting me to continue to move forward in my efforts to help those with similar challenges to the ones I faced.

No book can sing without a great editor, which goes without saying. My editor, G. Miki Hayden, is a godsend. This is our fifth book together, and we have become quite a team. She miraculously breathes life into this mission of mine to help others make peace with the obsessions within many of us. G. Miki's suggested edits helped me move out of the way of the work at hand, shaping and rounding it into a true journey.

Last, a huge shout-out to ALL my patients over the past twenty-five years, who taught and continue to teach me. Thank you from my heart!

Bibliography

American Psychiatric Association. (2013). *Diagnostic and Statistical Manual of Mental Disorders (5th ed.).* Arlington, VA: American Psychiatric Association Publishing.

Blank, D. (2017). *Be The Gateway: A Practical guide to Sharing Your Creative Work and Engaging an Audience.* Madison, New Jersey: WeGrowMedia.

Carlson, R. (1961). *Don't Sweat the Small Stuff...and It's All Small Stuff: Simple Ways to Keep the Little Things from Taking Over Your Life.* New York, NY: Hyperion

Carlson, R. (1998). *Don't Worry, Make Money: Spiritual and Practical Ways to Create Abundance and More Fun in Your Life.* New York, NY: Hyperion.

Collier, R. (1976). *Riches Within Your Reach: The Law of the Higher Potential.* Ramsey, New Jersey: Robert Collier Book Corporation.

Galbraith, J. K. (1972). *The Great Crash 1929.* Boston, MA: Houghton Mifflin.

Hicks, E. & J. (2006). *The Law of Attraction: The Basics of the Teaching of Abraham.* Carlsbad, California: Hay House, Inc.

Hill, N. (1960). *Think & Grow Rich.* New York, NY: Ballantine Books.

Hill, S. (2019). *Dangerous Prayers: 50 Powerful Prayers That Changed the World.* Nashville, Tennessee: Thomas Nelson.

Housel, M. (2020). *The Psychology of Money: Timeless Lessons on Wealth, Greed, and Happiness*. Hampshire, UK: Harriman House.

Katie, B. (2003). *Loving What Is: Four Questions That Can Change Your Life*. New York, NY. Harmony Books.

Kearns Goodwin, D. (2012). *Team of Rivals: The Political Genius of Abraham Lincoln.* New York, NY. Simon & Schuster.

Le Joly, E. & Chaliha, J. (2002). *Mother Theresa's Reaching Out in Love: Stories Told by Mother Teresa.* New York, NY. Barnes & Noble, Inc.—The Continuum Publishing Company.

Mitchell, M. (2014). *Gone with the Wind.* London, England: Pan Books.

Nepo, M. (2000). *The Book of Awakening: Having the Life You Want by Being Present to the Life You Have.* San Francisco, CA: Conari Press, and imprint of Red Wheel/Weiser LLC

Ortigara Crego, L. (2017). *Release Your Obsession With Food: Heal from the Inside_Out.*
Hollywood, FL: Madeira Publishing.

Ortigara Crego, L. (2018). *Release Your Obsession With Diet Chatter: Heal from the Inside Out.* Hollywood, FL: Madeira Publishing.

Ortigara Crego, L. (2019). *Release Your Obsession With Cheat DAZE: Heal from the Inside Out.* Hollywood, FL: Madeira Publishing.

Ortigara Crego, L. (2020). *Release Your Obsession With AGING: Heal from the Inside Out.* Hollywood, FL: Madeira Publishing.

Parson, H. (1994). *Father Peter Rookey: Man of Miracles.* Australia: Divine Mercy Publications.

Pressfield, S. (2012). *The War of Art: Break Through the Blocks and Win Your Inner Creative Battles.* New York, NY: Black Irish Entertainment, LLC.

Ramsey, D. (2003). *The Total Money Makeover: A Proven Plan for Financial Fitness.* Nashville, Tennessee: Thomas Nelson, Inc.

Siegel, B. (1993). *How to Live Between Office Visits: A Guide to Life, Love, and Health.* New York, NY: Harper Collins Publisher.

Stanley, T. & Danko, W. (1996). *The Millionaire Next Door: The Surprising Secrets of America's Wealthy.* Marietta, GA: Longstreet Press, Inc.

Weiss, B. (1988). *Many Lives, Many Masters: The True Story of a Prominent Psychiatrist, His Young Patient, and the Past-Life Therapy That Changed Both Their Lives.* New York, NY: Touchstone, An Imprint of Simon & Schuster, Inc.

About the Author

Dr. Ortigara Crego, a clinical psychotherapist, addiction psychologist, and visiting professor in private practice, has worked in the field of eating disorders for well over two-and-a-half decades. She earned a doctorate in addiction psychology and a master's degree in social work with the emphasis on mental health, and is certified as an eating disorder specialist, Master's certified addiction professional, and national board-certified clinical hypnotherapist.

Dr. Ortigara Crego worked in the weight-loss industry for well over two decades. She speaks and blogs on recovery from compulsive/obsessive behaviors using spiritual and mind approaches to healing. She is the author of *Release Your Obsession with Food: Heal from the Inside Out*, a groundbreaking book on recovering from compulsive eating and spiritual deficits; *Release Your Obsession with Diet Chatter: Heal from the Inside Out*, a much needed book on quieting the drunken mental monkeys once and for all; *Release Your Obsession from Cheat DAZE: Heal from the Inside Out*, a further exploration of cheat days and living without obsessions on weekends, vacations, travel abroad, and cruising; *Release Your Obsession With AGING: Heal from the Inside Out,* learning to age gracefully while fully embracing life. She contributed several chapters to SAGE Publications' Volume 1 and Volume 2 of the *Encyclopedia of Obesity* and runs a blog at Weightcontroltherapy.com.

Dr. Ortigara Crego's professional affiliations include the National Association of Social Workers, the National Board for Certified Clinical Hypnotherapists, the International Association of Eating Disorder Professionals, and the American Psychological Association.

Stay In Touch!

Please contact me at drlisaort@weightcontroltherapy.com. I would love to hear from you and learn from your experiences. Stop by my website: http://weightcontroltherapy.com to see what I'm up to and where I'm speaking next, along with what books I have planned, such as the next in the Release Your Obsession series, *Release Your Obsession with That Darn Phone: Heal from the Inside Out.*

You can also find me on Facebook: http://www.facebook.com/Drlisaortigaracrego and on Twitter http://www.twitter.com/Drlisort and on Instagram http://www.Instagram.com/Drlisaort where we can engage in lively discussions on topics of health, including mental, physical, and spiritual wellbeing.

Made in the USA
Monee, IL
08 November 2026

67971949R00177